# CONFLICT RESOLUTION
# AND
# ETHNICITY

# CONFLICT RESOLUTION
# AND
# ETHNICITY

## Mohamed Rabie

Westport, Connecticut
London

**Library of Congress Cataloging-in-Publication Data**

Rabīʿ, Muhammad.
  Conflict resolution and ethnicity / Mohamed Rabie.
     p.  cm.
  Includes bibliographical references and index.
  ISBN 0–275–94598–7 (alk. paper)
     1. Ethnic relations.   2. Culture conflict.   3. Conflict
  management.   I. Title.
  GN496.R32   1994
  305.8—dc20       94–6381

British Library Cataloguing in Publication Data is available.

Library of Congress Catalog Card Number: 94–6381
ISBN: 0–275–94598–7

First published in 1994

Praeger Publishers, 88 Post Road West, Westport, CT 06881
An imprint of Greenwood Publishing Group, Inc.

Printed in the United States of America

The paper used in this book complies with the
Permanent Paper Standard issued by the National
Information Standards Organization (Z39.48–1984).

10 9 8 7 6 5 4 3 2 1

# CONTENTS

Preface                                    vii

1   Conflict and Peace                       1

2   Roots of Conflict                        21

3   Conflict Management                      45

4   The Peace Process                        67

5   Political Dialogue                       85

6   Negotiation                             111

7   Mediation                               131

8   Ethnicity and Conflict                  155

9   The Shared Homeland Model               173

10  Conflict and Change                     197

Selected Bibliography                       221

Index                                       225

To my friends,
Peter Glotz and Falicitas Walch

# PREFACE

Conflict is one thing that no human being or functioning organization can escape. We all experience conflict and deal with it routinely as we interact to build families, make friends, earn a living, define ourselves, enhance our social status, and carry out our duties toward others. Conflict may destroy existing relationships and may create opportunities for the establishment of new ones, making it both painful and promising.

To explain how and why conflict arises, what role it plays in shaping our lives and international relations, and how to manage it in a manner that minimizes the pain and maximizes the promise is a complex and most difficult task. But without trying, our suffering will increase and certain opportunities created by conflict will be lost. This book is about conflict and its management. My treatment of the subject is both descriptive and prescriptive.

My interest in this subject was born only recently, despite the fact that my entire life was colored and very much influenced by conflict. In 1985, I became involved with an endeavor to negotiate a joint Israeli-Palestinian declaration of principles, a task that took four years to complete. And in 1988, I conceived the idea and helped construct the process that led to the U.S.-PLO dialogue. My participation in and contribution to several other Arab-Israeli dialogue groups and forums were also instrumental in sharpening my ideas and helping me focus on conflicts rooted in ethnic rivalry and clashing national identities.

This book may reflect a perspective not shared by some experts and professionals of conflict resolution. I believe that I have a unique perspective shaped by a unique experience. I am a product of two different, largely antagonistic cultures, a practitioner of conflict resolution motivated by a strong desire to serve the cause of peace, and a keen observer of societal processes of socio-political transformation. Sharing my experience and perspective with others is a duty I cannot and do not wish to evade. I hope this book will contribute to both our understanding of conflict and our ability to construct political processes and envision new ideas to resolve it.

## ACKNOWLEDGMENTS

I am grateful for the generous grant provided by Germany's prestigious Alexander Von Humboldt Stiftung Foundation, which enabled me to spend seven months in Germany, to travel to other European countries where ethnic conflict adn the search for a resolution are critical, and to interact with European colleagues in the field. My gratitude also goes to John Murray, former director of George Mason's conflict resolution clinic and professor of political science at the American University in Cairo, Egypt, for the time he devoted to reading the working manuscript and making valuable suggestions. My assistant Soraya Deifallah deserves many thanks for her patience, dedication, and willingness to accommodate my writing habits, which drive me to perpetual revisions until the manuscript is wrested from me.

*Chapter One*

# CONFLICT AND PEACE

People, being products of different cultures, historical experiences and environmental settings, identify with different groups and tend to have varied values and perceptions. Because different peoples face different sets of social, economic and environmental challenges, they nurture different socio-political goals and expectations. To fulfill these goals and expectations, people form associations, develop loyalties, and engage in cooperative as well as competitive relationships with other individuals, groups, and socio-political and economic organizations. The processes through which such relationships develop and interact are usually slow, complicated, and largely unintentional.

People form associations to protect, enhance, or promote interests and ideas. The process through which such goals are defined and sought causes the initiation and intensification of other forms of human, organizational, and systemic interaction, which in turn force all involved parties to continuously cooperate and compete with each other, almost always instantly and unintentionally. In fact, all individuals and organizations are actors in one process or more that functions within cooperative and competitive frameworks simultaneously.

Cooperative interaction is the component of a social process that seeks to enhance the position of all concerned parties as one unit or group. Competitive interaction is the other component of the social process through which each party within the same group seeks to enhance its position vis-à-vis its other partners. This in turn causes the internal dynamics of all social and societal processes to change, leading to the weakening of certain associations and the strengthening of others, the disintegration of certain organizations and the forming of new ones.

Thus, both cooperative and competitive interaction represents a process of change and transformation to modify or replace power relationships, causing conflict to arise and prevail.

Due to these complicated processes of forming group identities, developing loyalties, and establishing socioeconomic associations, people are divided into thousands of ethnic, national, socio-economic, socio-political, and religious groups. While some ethnic and national groups were able to form their own states, most others were unable to do so; and while some socioeconomic groups were able to achieve objectives, most were not. Consequently, many ethnic and religious groups are forced to live as minorities within nation-states governed by groups other than their own. These states were more oriented toward pursuing objectives reflective of the values and socio-political interests of the majorities.

Diverse human interests and needs, largely incompatible religious and social beliefs, and competing individual and group goals cause conflict to arise and prevail. Moreover, different loyalties, cultural values, ideologies and geopolitical considerations provide a fertile ground for the planting and nurturing of conflict within and between states. Disparities in wealth, natural resources, technology, and power among social classes and ethnic groups within and between states have also been a cause of increased grievances and conflict.

Socio-economic groups within states are formed around issues that reflect people's ability to gain socio-political status and economic wealth. Groups that demonstrate an ability to succeed are characterized as rich and influential; others lacking such an ability are mostly poor and powerless. Due to this, socio-economic, psychological, and cultural gaps develop between the two groups, straining their relationships and causing them to become less cooperative. Meanwhile, the rich and influential develop socio-political mechanisms to protect their gains and nurture attitudes to justify their position, which often include a tendency to belittle, if not dehumanize, the poor and powerless. The poor and powerless develop socio-cultural mechanisms to protect their own identity and nurture attitudes to blame their misfortune on the rich and influential. The ability of the first group to maintain and even enhance its position serves in almost all cases to further undermine the ability of the latter, causing its relative position to deteriorate. Left unattended, the relationship between the two groups would become conflictual, and "structural violence" would become an integral part of everyday life in society.

Structural violence is a concept first introduced by peace researcher Johan Galtung in 1964. He argued that social structures could be violent, causing individuals and groups to endure unnecessary suffering. The implication is that certain social structures place constraints on individuals and groups, preventing them from developing their potential and thus achieving their legitimate goals. They do this in a manner that often denies people the opportunity to realize that such a possibility even exists.[1] Since "structural violence" implies that force is used continuously in society to defend perceived interests (which is not always the case), it is more appropriate to replace "structural violence" with "structural injustice."

Cultural values, religious beliefs, and socio-political loyalties and systems tend to be stable over time; nevertheless, they are not static in nature or function. They live in a state of continuous change under the influence of a multifaceted interaction between national and international forces that represent and reflect group and state interests as dictated by the complexity of the fast-changing regional and global economic, political, and security environments. Interaction between human aspirations and economic realities, between ethnic and national loyalties, and between the political and economic processes at the national and international levels have continued to shape and reshape group consciousness and state and interstate relations.

Conflict, therefore, is a normal product of diversity in beliefs and values, differences in attitudes and perceptions, and competing socioeconomic and political interests among individuals, social classes, ethnic groups and states. Ideology, culture, and historical experience in particular make people different from each other, and at times cause them to feel that they are the negation of the other. Because conflict is about values, beliefs, interests, and perceptions, it occurs at every level of human and state interaction. John Burton says that conflict is "related to human relationships at all societal levels, and those are affected by the total environment, by the future planning, by levels of education and human needs and satisfaction."[2]

For example, the individual experiences conflicts within himself when he tries to achieve personal objectives and engage in processes to reconcile desired goals with obligations, particularly to the society at large. Economic concerns competing for clients and markets to serve and for resources and opportunities to exploit are also in conflict with each other. States claiming the same piece of land or natural resource are also in conflict in trying to maximize national benefits at the expense of each other. Group loyalties and class interests generate other conflicts that are caused not only by facts but also perceptions. Therefore, the way a particular conflict is perceived and resolved must take into consideration the past and future relationships between the conflicting parties.[3] Conflict, simply defined, is a relationship perceived by one or more concerned parties as unfair, unworkable, or both. The feeling it engenders reflects both a state of mind and a state of economic and political affairs characterized by disagreement, intense competition, and mutual hostility. Conflict in society occurs when power, interests, or values are distributed in a manner that makes certain groups feel constrained and discriminated against.

Peace is also a product of individual, group, and state interaction at the many levels of social, political, and economic life. It is the other side of conflict, the side that represents harmony and reflects a mutually satisfying relationship. But since human as well as organizational interaction is a continuous process of gradual change and transformation, neither conflict nor peace exists without the other, making them two societal and mental states in flux. Even in situations where conflict is severe, each conflicting party exhibits a large degree of harmony and maintains an intragroup relationship characterized by cooperation and cohesion, often only temporarily while conflict persists. Internal unity and solidarity is always needed to gain legitimacy and enhance power to wage or sustain conflict. Conflict and peace are two interchangeable, but always coexisting, processes that can be enhanced or weakened, accelerated or de-escalated, maintained or abandoned, but never eliminated.

Both conflict and peace must be viewed as states of mind and states of socio-economic and political affairs that characterize individual, group, state, and institutional relationships at certain points in time. Since time never stops, conflict and peace must also be viewed as social processes, or agents of social change and transformation that serve human needs and fulfill individual, group, and state aspirations at different phases of their development cycles. In performing their tasks, conflict and peace produce social ends, some positive and others negative. Peace achieved through coercion and domination is neither good nor lasting but could be workable in serving limited goals in the short run. Peace that comes at the end of human life is usually complete but very much feared by almost every human being. Conflict that leads to stimulating dialogue and inducing honest and fair competition is an agent of positive social and economic change.

Quincy Wright, writing in the 1950s, warned us against identifying inconsistencies of opinion with conflict. He argued that the coexistence of inconsistencies of opinion in society may be an essential condition of human progress: "It is through the contact and competition of differing opinions and methods, and the eventual synthesis of thesis and antithesis that history is created."[4] Because of this, definitions of conflict and peace have become important issues, particularly to those engaged in conflict resolution and the promotion of universal peace.

Despite the fact that conflict is an integral part of life and cannot be eliminated, the word "conflict" commonly refers to situations that suffer from severe, unhealthy competitive processes associated with violence. Similarly, the word "peace" refers to situations in which cooperative processes are strong and conflict is generally free from violence and does not threaten prevailing cooperative relationships. Because of that, peace has always been perceived by most people as good, while conflict is bad. But examined from a wider socio-economic perspective, neither peace nor conflict is all good or bad. In fact, peace without conflict is stagnation, and conflict without peace is chaos, making peace and conflict two preconditions for continued human progress and organizational regeneration.

Conflict characterizes a state of relationship that is more competitive than cooperative and generally viewed by one or more parties as unhealthy or unacceptable. Peace, in contrast, characterizes a state of relationship that is more cooperative than competitive and generally viewed as healthy and mutually beneficial. Conflict resolution is an approach to dealing with severe and harmful competitive processes with a view to changing them or lessening their intensity and impact on conflicting parties. It is an intervention by a third party to reform existing relationships by effecting institutional and attitudinal change. Fostering peace and peaceful coexistence largely means dealing with issues and initiating social processes to strengthen cooperative relationships and promote new ones to expand and deepen cooperation.

## CONFLICT

As mentioned earlier, conflict is neither good nor bad and does not always lead to unquestionable consequences. Conflict that contributes to dishonorable competition, to accentuating differences between social and political groups, or to widespread violence that inflicts pain on others is bad and always leads to undesirable consequences. It is this type of conflict that people fear and have over the centuries devoted a substantial share of their time, talent, and resources to contain and resolve. In contrast, conflict that induces people to work harder and be more efficient is good, particularly when competition induced by it provides mutual acknowledgment and respect of rights and interests.

Within families, business concerns, professional associations, and community organizations, conflict is the norm rather than the exception. And because of its disruptive nature and consequences, it tends to force societies, institutions, and social and economic systems to continuously evaluate their performance and re-examine their prospects. Meanwhile, creative thinking and new ideas and modes of social and business organization are continuous sources of conflict and the means to conflict resolution. They usually serve as instruments to uncover hidden deficiencies, redefine existing problems, and identify future challenges. At the same time, they also identify untapped individual resources and redefine communal potentials, creating new relationships and helping resolve conflict. In performing both tasks, creative thinking, new ideas, and innovative modes of organization disrupt the status quo, enhancing the positions and interests of some while undermining those of others.

A positive response to such disruptive forces and agents of change usually leads to making the system and its many organizing components more productive and efficient. A dynamic system that recognizes and incorporates creativity is more likely to be more responsive to human needs, societal interests, and global change. In contrast, failure to respond to the urging of such forces is more likely to lead to political polarization and economic stagnation in general and, possibly, to a gradual disintegration of the system of rules and relationships that tie people, their groups, institutions, and states together.

Conflict and its many manifestations disrupt established systems, orders, and intergroup relationships, causing them to lose balance and become instable. Conflict resolution works to modify existing systems and change relationships, restoring stability and balance. Nevertheless, certain conflict-resolution measures tend to treat conflict as a negative development and, consequently, deal with it through actions to suppress change and preserve the status quo. Since conflict is a process that never stops, however, it may be possible to suppress its causes and postpone its manifestations, but only for a short time. As Quincy Wright has said, "Even total defeat in war may not remove the causes of conflict, and after a time, the defeated may revive and renew the conflict."[5]

Conflict, therefore, is primarily the result of change that signals the deterioration or increasing irrelevancy of existing societal systems and intergroup relationships. In certain cases, it may signal the disfunctioning of one or more of the major societal systems, such as the political system. It may also signal the general corruption of the prevailing value system or the obsolescence of the traditional wisdom and its basic assumptions that form the foundations of the overall socio-cultural system, leading to widespread popular discontent. "In many instances," says James Laue, "the origins of conflict are in nonfulfillment or blockage of fundamental human needs."[6]

Conflict has many faces and is usually carried out by political, economic, legal, or social means as well as by force and war. These means express themselves through either coercion or persuasion: "The former usually involves violence and has the character of physical conflict; the latter need not involve violence, though violence may be utilized as a method of persuasion."[7] Such methods are often used by police to extract confessions from suspected criminals and prisoners of war. Economic sanctions to limit people's access to employment, food, and medical supplies and legal procedures to constrain their movement are means of persuasion, using structural rather than physical violence to carry out conflict.

Societies, small and large, traditional and modern, have developed techniques to manage the disruptive forces and restore balance to the affected systems and organizations. Some tools and methods are formal and well structured; others are informal and loosely structured. "Informal methods of conflict resolution," says Edward Sherman, "have long existed in civilized societies."[8] Although Sherman did not identify the so-called "civilized societies," he meant the Western democratic ones.

An examination of the ways traditional societies deal with conflict reveals that they are generally better equipped than the West to deal with social and interest-related conflicts but less able to resolve value-related and power struggle conflicts. But because societies have different cultures and historical experiences, conflict-resolution techniques that many nations have developed over time are not the same and may not work outside their own cultural contexts.

Societies that have developed flexible and extensive rules to deal with conflict are more likely to maintain political stability and social peace, while undergoing social change and responding to national and global challenges. They are societies that view conflict as a natural component of social life and as a normal consequence of human and institutional interaction. In this context, conflict becomes a reflection of diversity, not enmity, and conflict-resolution techniques become tools and rules to regulate diversity while preserving unity. These techniques are tools to reduce tension, moderate conflicting views, and seek new ways and frameworks for forming new consensuses and promoting cooperation among the many diverse views and groups.

Societies that have failed to develop viable conflict-resolution techniques, and those that have maintained that the traditional political and belief systems remain valid regardless of time, are more likely to experience open conflict. Because no society can live in isolation, facing today's global challenges and constantly changing group perceptions and needs can fast transform minor conflicts into social chaos, economic dislocation, and political disintegration. Societies that are ethnically heterogeneous and more inclined to resist change and those dominated by regimes that view creativity and diversity with suspicion and fear are much more susceptible to violent conflict.

Conflict-resolution techniques that such societies are more likely to apply are measures to preserve unity, maintain continuity, suppress dissent, and eliminate diversity. They resort to such measures because they view political dissent as a destructive force and consider ethnic diversity as a threat to national unity. In a global environment of profound social and political change, growing interdependence and an emphasis on democracy and human rights, preserving unity at the expense of diversity is a recipe for either suppression and stagnation, or social upheavals and violent confrontation.

Regardless of how effective or ineffective societies have been in developing their own conflict-resolution techniques, no society has managed to totally resolve conflict, eliminate its causes, control its forces, or predict its outcome and thus prepare for its many consequences. As a result, all societies continue to experience conflict, struggle with it, and change under its influence, going into different and sometimes opposing directions.

While some societies and regimes, like the former Czechoslovakia, have responded to political conflict by embracing democracy, others, like the Algerian regime, have become more authoritarian. Yet others, like Yugoslavia and Somalia, have failed to deal with their socio-political problems and consequently have fallen into civil war. The failure in Yugoslavia, for example, has led to political disintegration, economic dislocation, the loss of tens of thousands of lives, and the near-total destruction of the country's social infrastructure and ethnic and religious group relations. Conservative estimates of the victims of Yugoslavia's civil war, reported George Zarycky, put the death toll at 200,000: "Few of these are soldiers of organized armies who died on the noble fields of battle. This war was about rag-tag militias, looters, weekend Serb mercenaries and raiders, thugs killing civilians, 'ethnic cleansing,' mass rape as military doctrine, depopulation, the wholesale destruction of towns and villages."[9]

Conflicts are usually divided into two major categories, interest-related and value-related. Conflicts over trade issues, state security considerations, regional influence, and even over territory and natural resources are generally considered to be interest-related. Conflicts caused by competition between similar economic and professional groups, and disputes between labor and management, are also categorized as interest-related. Other conflicts within and between states caused by matters related to political ideologies, religious beliefs, cultural rights, national sovereignty, and the socio-political status of minorities are considered value-related. Nonetheless, most international and all ethnic conflicts are both interest-related and value-related at the same time.

Conflicts that emanate from clashing values and hostile perceptions are usually hard to define and harder to resolve peacefully. In contrast, conflicts that emanate from competing interests are easier to define and often resolved without resorting to violence. However, most ethnic and state conflicts are caused by a mixture of competing interests, hostile relationships, and clashing values, making them complex in nature and generally hard to resolve using a single set of conflict-resolution rules.

"Conflicts over interests," reported Hugh Miall, "were easier to resolve peacefully than conflicts over values and relationships. The international dispute settlement system is in fact reasonably well equipped to handle disputes of the first type. There is more difficulty when fundamental differences of values are concerned, perhaps because values are non-negotiable."[10] This conclusion was a result of a study that investigated several conflicts, some of which were resolved peacefully and satisfactorily.

Conflicts emanating from competing economic and political interests are easy to define and manage, if not resolve, particularly when occurring within societies and among states that exhibit cultural diversity and political tolerance. Tolerance, however, is not an absolute value but a relative one that changes over time, reflecting changing social attitudes and group ideologies. In fact, peoples and societies claiming tolerance tend almost always to take different positions toward different issues, particularly cultural and ethnic issues.

For example, German intolerance toward non-Germans in general during the rise of Hitler was almost totally transformed after 1945. In 1965, the German minister in charge of labor went to the train station to personally greet the two millionth foreign worker that arrived in Germany. At the time, the economic immigrants entering Germany in search of better economic opportunities were welcomed and called *Gastarbeiter*, meaning guest workers. By 1992, however, German tolerance was generally replaced by hostility, not only toward economic immigrants but also toward political refugees. Demonstrations, riots, and acts of violence were repeatedly committed by forces of the political right and ultranationalists against foreigners seeking political asylum. Even international students seeking German education were not spared. A popular movement supporting the basic demands, though not the tactics, of the rightist groups emerged in the 1990s to challenge established laws that dealt with refugees. Before the end of 1992, the German government, faced with increased violence and deepened economic recession, announced plans to deport tens of thousands of Gypsies back to Romania, despite full knowledge that Gypsies were facing discrimination and possible persecution in their Romanian homeland.

"The deportation is all the more troublesome in light of the 500,000 Gypsy deaths in Nazi Germany. Sure, modern Germany did not kill them, nor did it kill millions of Jews. Nazi Germany did. But Germany has rightly accepted responsibility for the Jewish deaths and made reparations. It has not done so in the case of the Gypsies," wrote Mark Stoneman.[11] On the contrary, the German government increased aid to Romania, in part to induce its government to accept the deported Gypsies. For many Gypsies, deportation back to Romania means persecution for the second time in one lifespan. But for the German authorities, deportation of Gypsies is a measure to appease certain domestic political groups, reduce social tension at home, ease potential economic pressure, and reduce pressure caused by immigration.[12]

In the United States today, Jews are more tolerated and accepted by the American Christian majority than are Muslims. Judaism is viewed by almost all Christian Americans as an integral part of their cultural heritage and value system. Islam, in contrast, is generally viewed as a threat to that value system, culture, and way of life. And while it is acceptable, even at times desirable, for American intellectuals to be associated with many controversial causes, it is highly undesirable for any American intellectual to be associated with a Muslim or an Arab cause, even when that cause is promoting democracy and Western values in Arab and Muslim countries.

Arabs and Muslims, on the other hand, have more tolerance for race than any Western society; they tend generally to be color blind. Muslims, however, have less tolerance for religious diversity, and almost no tolerance for religions that function outside the contexts of Islam, Christianity, and Judaism. Arabs, moreover, have less tolerance for political and ideological dissent and tend to place little value on political dialogue and cultural interaction with alien groups.

While some societies like the American one are more socially and politically tolerant, they are less racially and culturally tolerant. No society or culture therefore has a monopoly on tolerance, nor can any society or culture be called tolerant or intolerant without much reservation and qualification.

In societies where tolerance generally prevails and cultural diversity is accepted, most conflicts tend to be interest-oriented. Labor-management disputes in the Western industrialized states, for example, involve easily identifiable issues and clearly defined goals. While most issues are contradictory, they are not irreconcilable. And while goals tend to be different, they are seldom incompatible because conflicting parties normally share an interest in building long-term cooperative relationships that are mutually rewarding. Relationships, in turn, are generally governed by laws, state and professional regulations, previously negotiated agreements, and signed contracts. Consequently, new disputes are usually settled through well-established procedures and institutions and in accordance with governmental laws and regulations. As a result, the conflict-resolution processes in such societies and regarding such issues usually follow known patterns and produce largely predictable outcomes.

According to Hugh Miall's study, international conflicts related to territorial and resource disputes appeared to be more amenable to peaceful resolution. In contrast, "civil conflicts were more often resolved through violence than purely international ones."[13] Civil conflicts usually are associated with ideological rivalry, power struggles to control government, ethnic collision and enmity, and political secession. Miall's study thus confirms that interest-related conflicts are easier to define and resolve than value-related ones.

Civil conflicts caused by ethno-national, religious, racial, and cultural differences are today more dangerous, more frequent, and, once started, costly, hard to control, and harder to resolve. They are more costly and difficult to resolve because few rules and principles of conflict resolution have been developed to deal with them. Differences in cultural backgrounds, value systems, and world views make the development of a universal theory to understand and deal with human value-related conflicts nearly impossible. Michael Banks says, "We live in a world in which conflict is rarely understood and often mismanaged."[14]

Nevertheless, "unless conflicts within ethnically divided societies are dealt with meaningfully for all concerned, this could lead to conflicts between states," endangering regional and maybe world peace as well.[15] Because of that, ethno-national conflict presents a challenge "to man's creative capacity of seeking new political ways and developing instruments of law to diffuse this conflict and safeguard the peace."[16] Chapter 9 of this book provides a new model to deal with this type of conflict, taking into consideration the socio-cultural and political dimensions rooted in the past as well as the economic dimension that extends far into the future.

Conflicts and the processes to settle them are social instruments to modify or reshape old relationships among adversaries. In so doing, the rules and procedures of settling disputes usually work to replace the old, largely discredited relationships with new ones more conducive to cooperation. But when known rules of conflict resolution within a society become outdated or fail to settle conflict peacefully, most disputes tend to escalate into individual, group, and class hostility, leading to confrontation and widespread violence.

Laws, rules, and techniques to regulate or resolve conflict cease to be useful when they fail to incorporate in their assumptions the many national and international changes that affect people's identities, positions, relationships, and perceptions of others' expectations. In times of profound and sudden socio-political change, old assumptions become increasingly irrelevant, and established procedures and rules begin to lose their validity and credibility. Such changes occur as a result of dramatic shifts in ideology, profound economic transformations affecting class structure, or drastic political upheavals and military defeats. They are socio-political convulsions that undermine the legitimacy of the old socio-economic system while weakening central authority. Examples of such changes can be seen today in the former communist countries of Asia and Europe, particularly in Georgia and Azerbaijan. They also characterize situations in several other parts of the world such as Iran in 1979, Algeria in 1992, Cambodia in the 1970s, and Somalia in 1991.

Political structures, legal instruments, and social and economic relationships are both causes of conflict and tools of conflict resolution. Structures and relationships that enable one segment of a society to dominate all others are instruments of discrimination and causes of conflict. They create monopolies and facilitate the concentration of power and wealth in the hands of certain groups whose members usually display little or no interest in promoting equality or justice. Under certain conditions, they may even become tools of political repression, economic exploitation, and social and cultural persecution of the other, leading to the institutionalization and perpetuation of structural injustice.

Failure to change group or ethnic relations that are unfair and unjust by peaceful means and through political dialogue and socio-economic restructuring usually leads to violence. Violence, however, could be the tool used by the oppressed to press their demands, or the measure employed by the oppressor to silence and further repress the oppressed. In most cases leading to violence, the legal tools and social patterns of conflict resolution often lose their legitimacy before the outbreak of hostilities. This usually happens because new perceptions develop and prevail on at least one side of the conflict that the old rules were either lenient and permissive or unfair and repressive.

Therefore, conflict reflects a relationship between two or more parties characterized by tension, mistrust, suspicion, and often hostility. Because of its nature and socio-political impact, conflict forces all parties concerned to view their relationship as unfair or unstable and thus unworkable, particularly in the long run. Conflict, moreover, reflects attitudes on both sides characterized by contradiction, antagonism, and sometimes mutual exclusivity. Such attitudes may be based on undisputable facts, strongly held ideological beliefs and cultural values, questionable but deeply rooted perceptions, or simply, competing group interests. Thus, "struggles over identity, values, power and scarce resources are at the heart of all conflicts."[17] Conflict resolution is an art and a social process to transform by peaceful means hostile relationships into new ones more conducive to dialogue and socio-economic cooperation.

## PEACE

The high cost of violent conflicts and war, both in human and material terms, has invoked much interest in peace studies and activities. These studies and activities are meant to underline the cost of conflict, identify its social, economic, environmental, and political causes, and define the prerequisites for peace. Peace activists in particular tend also to campaign against war and oppose most, if not all, state activities that promote or prepare for war. They further seek to articulate a new concept of a peaceful world to guide and encourage all peoples to make such a concept a reality. Johan Galtung says that "the values that can be derived from general concepts of peace should be our basic guide to the future, not data from a highly unpeaceful world. Only by escaping that prism of the past can the peace researcher make meaningful contribution to an ever transcending world."[18]

The popularity of peace studies and peace activities has led to the creation of "peace camps" in most countries of the world, particularly in the West. Such camps usually consist of individuals and organizations that oppose war, express concern for victims of violence, and promote tolerance and political dialogue between antagonists aimed at resolving conflict and achieving peace. They tend also to advocate active involvement in peacemaking and in educational programs and activities to change people's and states' attitudes toward each other. Such activities and programs have the double task of seeking to create new national and international environments more hostile to the idea of war and, at the same time, more hospitable to the idea of universal peace.

Peace has always been perceived as the opposite of war and the negation of violence. Peace, therefore, is a situation generally characterized by the absence of war and violence in which human interactions are conducted in an orderly manner and disputes arising from such interactions are settled peacefully. Individuals, groups and nations are free to pursue their legitimate goals without coercion. Peace, therefore, is both a state of mind that reflects attitudes against violence and toward dialogue, and states of socio-economic and political affairs that are more conducive to peaceful coexistence, justice, and cooperation. However, all situations have a life of their own, and states of mind and political and economic affairs continue to evolve and change, causing power and wealth in society to be continually redistributed. Therefore, peace must also be viewed as a process to facilitate societal transformation without violence and undue injustice.

Narrowly defined, "peace is the absence of war,"[19] a definition used primarily by military strategists and students of *Realpolitik*. Broadly defined, "peace is the least application of violence and coercion to the individual human being and to the freedom of access of the individual to cherished values."[20] Peace has also been defined in terms that do not limit its domain to the absence of war, but extend it to mean universal harmony and liberty as well.

President John F. Kennedy seemed to have some other definition of peace in mind when he spoke at the American University in 1963. He said: "I am not referring to the absolute, infinite concept of universal peace and good will. Let us focus instead on a more practical, more attainable peace, based not on a sudden revolution in human nature but on a gradual evolution in human institutions."[21] President Kennedy, with his mind on U.S.-Soviet relations, particularly in the wake of the Cuban missile crisis, added that "peace is a process, a way of solving problems."[22]

The varied peace definitions have given rise to the concepts of "positive peace" and what might be called "passive or negative peace."[23] James H. Laue, for example, defines peace not only as a cherished goal sought by all individuals and states, but also as "a process of continuous and constructive management of differences toward the goal of more mutually satisfying relations, the prevention of escalation of violence, and the achievement of those conditions that exemplify the universal well-being of human beings and their groups from the family to the culture and the state."[24] It is a definition of positive peace that moves from the elimination of violence to dealing with the causes of conflict and proceeds to achieving universal happiness.

Positive definitions of peace transform conflict resolution into a continuous peacemaking and peacekeeping process to deal with social conflict and create the socio-economic and political conditions that guarantee social justice. Thus, to the proponents of positive peace, the elimination of hunger and poverty and the establishment of justice are the true conditions of real peace and the most effective social measures to reduce the threat of war and undermine the causes of serious conflict. For such a peace to become a reality, they advocate, among other things, the creation of international superstructures to deal with regional and interstate conflict and limit the powers of the nation-state. In addition, they call for the establishment of a new international economic order that guarantees a more balanced distribution of global resources among nations, and effects the restructuring of trade relations between the industrialized and the developing countries on more equitable terms.[25]

However, proponents of passive peace argue that the order of priorities should be reversed. They maintain that the tendency to commit mass violence, which characterizes many intergroup and international relations, is in itself a primary obstacle to the establishment of justice and the fulfillment of human goals. Thus, as Robert Pickus says, "establishing the minimum conditions for the non-violent resolution and prosecution of political conflict becomes the first objective."[26]

In countries where democracy does not exist and where the control of authoritarian states over peoples' lives and fortunes is real, the nonviolent resolution and prosecution of political conflict is an impossibility because violence is the major tool of the oppressor rather than the oppressed. Democratization as the first order of concern, which the proponents of a limited definition of peace further advocate, cannot be effected without freedom and liberty, two conditions for access to cherished values. Therefore, a realistic definition of peace ought to take both arguments into consideration. This is particularly important since the proponents of positive peace tend to view it more as a process and less as a stationary state of political affairs, while the others see it generally in opposite terms.

In fact, human experience seems to indicate that the absence of war and violence cannot be maintained without social justice, and social justice cannot be achieved under conditions of war and violence. Consequently, an operational definition of realistic peace would probably describe it as the absence of violence under conditions and relationships that provide for the nonviolent resolution of political conflict and the freedom to pursue legitimate individual and group goals without threat or coercion. Peace, to be real and human, must be understood and employed as a continuous process to lessen social tension, resolve political conflict, and create conditions to pursue freedom and justice through a gradual evolution of human perceptions and socio-political institutions.

Thus, a strategy for universal peace must deal not only with war but also with the very forces and conditions that cause the eruption of war and induce the spread of violence in the first place. It must also strive to change a people's perceptions of the other in order to humanize the adversary, acknowledge his grievances, and legitimize his basic concerns. Above all, it must lay the foundation for transforming existing group relationships and state and civil society institutions, with a view to creating new more dynamic ones committed to promoting compatible visions and values with developing shared interests.

## INTERNATIONAL CONFLICT

Conflict and peace are complex issues of great concern to all peoples and states without exception. They are issues that touch the lives of all individuals and groups, influencing their thinking, state plans, and international relations in general. International conflict, being interest-related as well as value-related, has made the concepts of international conflict and world peace very much interrelated and interlinked.

Even when the international conflict is centered around one easily defined issue, such as border disputes, the complexity of interstate relations tends to make international conflicts hard to define and harder to resolve. State relationships, being multifaceted and complex in nature, tend to transform the simplest of state conflicts into multidimensional ones.

In addition, social tools and legal instruments to deal with international conflict have generally lagged behind those developed to deal with national conflicts, specifically interest-related conflicts. Some experts argue that the current world system is not conducive to conflict resolution and peacemaking. Louis Kriesberg, for example, said that the world system "has no effective international law and no government or a coalition of governments possess enough power and credibility to arbitrate conflicts and impose settlements."[27] Others, however, argue that the world system does have a "large, complex and very effective international legal system," though it may not apply well to issues of international control.[28] The truth may lie in between because the United Nations, despite having outlawed the use of force to settle international disputes, cannot prevent war or even anticipate international conflict.

The successes achieved by mediators, arbitrators, facilitators, psychologists, and city planners in dealing with social, business and community disputes have largely eluded professionals, diplomats, and organizations dealing with international conflict in general and value-related conflicts in particular. In fact, most Western models dealing with international conflict limit themselves to negotiations and are to a large extent modified versions of those meant to deal with national, mainly interest-related conflicts. But because of the complexity and strategic nature of international conflicts, most of the known models of conflict resolution and control have remained inadequate, relying mainly on assumptions that have little relevance to most international situations.

In addition to their apparent shortcomings, international conflict-resolution models have failed to capture the seriousness of the most prevalent international conflicts of our time, the ethno-national and religious conflicts. This is primarily due to their complex nature and sudden rise, particularly after the end of the Cold War, the collapse of communism, and the disintegration of the Soviet empire. They are value-oriented conflicts caused by incompatible beliefs, unfulfilled expectations, deeply held though largely irrelevant historical memories, and a general loss of popular direction in a troubled world.

This type of conflict will command most of our attention as we proceed to build a model for mediation and negotiation and develop a strategy for peace. Our model, however, will not stop at the level of explaining international conflict and prescribing a way to deal with it but will articulate a framework to facilitate the establishment and maintenance of international peace, international here meaning regional rather than global.

Looking at the world political map, we will notice that there is hardly any state that does not suffer from serious conflict or face deep political, social, environmental, and/or economic problems giving rise to conflict. At the same time, none of these states knows with confidence how to deal with its problems, which seem to be growing more complicated.

As problems intensify, the longing for peace and stability intensifies as well, making conflict and peace two integral parts of daily life—the first a part of our real life, the second a part of our dreams. While the first works to reduce the quality of life, the second works to inspire hope and give the fight for a better life meaning. But despite all developments in the fields of conflict resolution and peacemaking, both conflict and peace have remained beyond our capacity to fully understand, much less employ to narrow the gap between the reality and the dream. This gap can never be narrowed in a meaningful way without hard work, perseverance, imagination, and above all, a belief in the dream itself.

Efforts to resolve conflict cannot be separated from those meant to establish and foster peace. Whoever works for peace works also to undermine the causes of conflict, particularly in situations of structural injustice. Whoever works to resolve conflict works also for the containment of violence, and subsequently for the enhancement of the prospects of peace. Thus, a commitment for peace cannot be honored without a similar commitment to eliminate structural injustice, and a strategy to resolve conflict cannot succeed without a similar strategy to establish peace and replace the damaging competitive relationships with others more conducive to cooperation.

Discussions of conflict and peace center on two major viewpoints, one of the realists, the other of the idealists. The first viewpoint appears to be driven by a desire to understand the world as it is, and to construct models and theories to manage world affairs and predict future developments based on past experience and current circumstances and premises. It is a viewpoint that accepts the world as given and devotes most attention not to changing it, but to preserving the status quo and manipulating the active socio-political and economic forces to attain and maintain advantage. This is done largely by building models and theories that give legitimacy to existing relationships and influence group and state behavior to conform to prescribed models.

The idealist viewpoint, however, tends to reject the existing world as corrupt and oppressive and seek the construction of creative models for a new, more efficient and equitable world that reflects its ideals. These are models built to predict the harm that would be caused by continued patterns of production, consumption, and environmental damage. Such models are used to implore people and states to modify their behavior to avoid catastrophes and move toward a more equitable distribution of resources.

The increasing complexity of life in general has made both viewpoints, taken separately, less realistic and less helpful. A realistic and efficient theory of conflict resolution would have to rely on and be guided by a realistic theory of future change. Because such a theory does not exist today, efforts must be made to enhance our understanding of the forces most likely to shape the future as a way to contribute to the eventual development of a general theory of social change and international relations. Otherwise, all our work will be incomplete, our experience limited, our expectations beyond our means and most goals beyond our reach.

Richard Rubenstein wrote recently that "major episodes of unanticipated social conflict during the past three decades have called attention to the failure of existing social theories to develop an adequate conception of the human individual in society."[29] He further argued that there is a need for a new theory to help us understand the world in which we live and explain to us change that is taking place.

Michael Banks says that "we need a vision of the world as a whole and the way in which it all fits together."[30] Kenneth Boulding wrote that "the record of peace research in the last generation is one of very partial success. It has created a discipline [but] it has made very little dent on the conventional wisdom of the policy makers anywhere in the world."[31] This makes the issues confronting specialists of conflict and analysis, conflict-resolution practitioners, and peace researchers important and complex. The rest of this book will deal with such issues in the hope that a modest contribution will be made to plug a little hole in the knowledge gap that exists today.

Our approach in the remainder of this book is one that combines both the viewpoints of the realist and idealist and sees their validity. We strongly believe that no rational person can function and survive outside reality; we also strongly feel that no human being should be asked to abandon the ideals of having a better, safer future. Thus, we approach conflict and conflict resolution realistically, and deal with peace and peacemaking futuristically.

## NOTES

1. See introduction of John Burton and Frank Dukes, eds., *Conflict: Readings in Management and Resolution* (New York: St. Martin's Press, 1990); and A.J.R. Groom, "Paradigms in Conflict," in John Burton and Frank Dukes, eds., *Conflict: Readings in Management and Resolution* (New York: St. Martin's Press, 1990), pp. 90–92.

2. Burton and Dukes, Introduction to *Conflict*, p. 2.

3. Dudley Weeks, *The Eight Essential Steps to Conflict Resolution* (Los Angeles: Jeremy P. Tarcher, 1992), p. 10.

4. Quincy Wright, "The Nature of Conflict," in John Burton and Frank Dukes, eds., *Conflict: Readings in Management and Resolution* (New York: St. Martin's Press, 1990), p. 18.

5. Ibid., p. 28.

6. James H. Laue, "Combinations of the Emerging Field of Conflict Resolution," in W. Scott Thompson et al., eds., *Approaches to Peace* (Washington, D.C.: United States Institute of Peace, 1991), p. 301.

7. Quincy Wright, "Nature of Conflict," p. 25.

8. Edward F. Sherman, "Applications of Dispute Resolution in the Israeli-Palestinian Conflict," in Elizabeth Warnock Fernea and Mary Evelyn Hocking, eds., *The Struggle for Peace* (Austin: University of Texas Press, 1992), p. 99.

9. George Zarycky, "Unparalleled International Cowardice," *The Washington Post*, July 25, 1993.

10. Hugh Miall, *Peaceful Settlement of Post-1945 Conflicts: A Comparative Study* (Washington, D.C.: USIP Conference on Conflict Resolution in the Third World, October 1990), p. 14.

11. Mark R. Stoneman, "The New Germany," *The International Herald Tribune,* October 7, 1992.

12. Flora Lewis, "Gypsies Without a Voice and a Status," *The International Herald Tribune,* October 2, 1992.

13. Hugh Miall, *Peaceful Settlement,* p. 8.

14. Michael Banks, "Four Concepts of Peace," in Dennis J. D. Sandole and Ingrid Sandole-Staroste, eds., *Conflict Management and Problem Solving: Interpersonal to International Applications* (New York: New York University Press, 1987), p. 260.

15. See Dennis J. D. Sandole, *Conflict Resolution in the Post-Cold War Era: Dealing with Ethnic Violence in the New Europe* (Fairfax, Va.: Institute for Conflict Analysis and Resolution, George Mason University, October 1992), pp. 10–16.

16. *Rights of Nationalities and Protection of Minorities* (International Institute for Nationality Rights and Regionalism, Munich, Germany, 1984), p. 7.

17. James H. Laue, "Contributions of the Emerging Field," p. 302.

18. Galtung was quoted by A.J.R. Groom, "Paradigms in Conflict," in John Burton and Frank Dukes, eds., *Conflict: Readings in Management and Resolution* (New York: St. Martin's Press, 1990), p. 92. See also Johan Galtung, "Violence, Peace and Peace Research," *Journal of Peace Research,* 6, 3 (1969):167–91.

19. Robert Pickus, "New Approaches," in W. Scott Thompson et al., eds., *Approaches to Peace* (Washington, D.C.: United States Institute of Peace, 1991), p. 232.

20. Myers S. McDougal, "Law and Peace," in W. Scott Thompson et al., eds., *Approaches to Peace* (Washington, D.C.: United States Institute of Peace, 1991), p. 139.

21. Cyrus Vance, *Hard Choices* (New York: Simon and Schuster, 1983), p. 20.

22. Ibid., p. 20.

23. See Michael Banks, "Four Concepts," pp. 259–60. See also Dennis Danole, "Conflict Resolution in the Post-Cold War Era," pp. 14–15.

24. James H. Laue, "Contributions of the Emerging Field," p. 301.

25. See Edward Azar, "Protracted International Conflicts: Ten Propositions," in John Burton and Frank Dukes, eds., *Conflict: Readings in Management and Resolution* (New York: St. Martin's Press, 1990), p. 15; and Bertrand Schneider, "A New Approach to the World Problematique," in Suheil Bushrui, Iraj Ayman, and Ervin Laszlo, eds., *Transition to a Global Society* (Oxford: Oneworld Publications Ltd., 1993), pp. 86–97.

26. Robert Pickus, "New Approaches," p. 232.

27. Louis Kriesberg, *International Conflict Resolution* (New Haven, Conn.: Yale University Press, 1992), p. 17.

28. John Murry, written comments on a draft of unpublished manuscript, 1993.

29. Richard Rubenstein, "Unanticipated Conflict and the Crisis of Social Theory" in John Burton and Frank Dukes, eds., *Conflict: Readings in Management and Resolution* (New York: St. Martin's Press, 1990), p. 316.

30. Michael Banks, "Four Concepts," p. 60.

31. Kenneth E. Boulding, "Future Directions in Conflict and Peace," in John Burton and Frank Dukes, eds., *Conflict: Readings in Management and Resolution* (New York: St. Martin's Press, 1990), p. 41.

*Chapter Two*

# ROOTS OF CONFLICT

Conflict, as previously stated, is a part of our life, a basic component of our group identity, and an agent of change that influences every relationship. Because of that, the roots of conflict cannot be found in one set of issues or attributed to one event or development. Causes of conflict, be it personal, communal, or international, as well as the means to deal with it, must be sought in the totality of the human environment, the physical, social, economic, political, and technological. Most conflicts also require that all dimensions of the local, national, and international environment be taken into consideration.

Since conflict is an integral part of life and a basic component of every relationship, efforts should not be directed toward eliminating it, because such efforts will fail. Rather, we should focus on managing conflict with a view to minimizing its negative impact and maximizing its positive role. Morton Deutsch wrote, "Conflict can neither be eliminated nor even suppressed for long. Conflict is the root of personal and social change. The social and scientific issue is not how to eliminate or prevent conflict, but rather how to live lively controversy instead of deadly quarrels."[1]

Therefore, our focus should be on ideas, values, images, belief systems, socio-political structures, and societal processes that make people engage in conflict and encourage them to seek solutions to end conflict. The aim should therefore be to introduce new ideas, institute new values, and build new socio-political structures both nationally and internationally to make human and institutional interaction more cooperative and less competitive and conflictual.

Edward Azar wrote, "One of the most devastating predicaments in the world today is the simultaneous occurrence of conflict and underdevelopment. Groups which seek to satisfy their security and identity needs through conflict are in effect seeking change in the structure of their society."[2] This means that conflictual behavior is a product of certain unsatisfactory structures and that new satisfactory structures would be needed to change conflictual behavior.

Conflict-resolution processes should emphasize reforming existing relationships through attitudinal, institutional, and structural change as well as change in the laws that govern societal processes. While it is important to know how people normally behave, it is more important to know under which circumstances their behavior changes, particularly from being cooperative to competitive to conflictual. Knowing that would help us know which circumstances, structures, and societal processes could alter or modify human and institutional behavior to make it more cooperative and less conflictual.[3]

The societal processes that we have in mind are the political process, the economic process, the socio-cultural process, and the mass media, or the informational and communications process. These processes will be discussed and their national and international roles examined in the last chapter of this book. They are processes that interact in a dynamic reinforcing manner, cooperating and competing to influence individual attitudes, social values, socio-economic and political structures, and to reshape communal and interstate relationships across cultures and political boundaries.

Conflict characterizes human life and group and state relationships at all levels. While conflict within families, among business concerns, and between professional associations and socio-political organizations is largely of interest only to those involved in it, international conflict is of interest to the world community at large. Even when interstate conflict is strictly bilateral, such as disputes regarding sovereignty over largely unimportant territory, a conflict's outcome tends to set a precedent that affects other disputes of a similar nature. If the powerful state or group imposes its will on the weaker one, the sovereignty of smaller states and the rights of smaller minorities are threatened.

Conflict is generally divided into two major categories, interest-related and value-related. Interest-related conflicts tend generally to characterize state relationships and socio-economic interaction between social, economic, and political organizations, not ethnic groups. Value-related conflicts, on the other hand, tend to characterize relations between cultural groups, particularly ethnic, national, and religious communities. As Dudley Weeks states, "A value is something we consider to be of significant importance. A value can involve a belief, a principle, or even a pattern of behavior we have come to perceive as extremely worthwhile."[4]

Conflict, moreover, may be characterized as national or international, domestic or interstate. Regardless of such characterizations, no national or domestic conflict could develop and persist without direct or indirect outside intervention, and no interstate or international conflict could develop and continue without domestic support. Many international conflicts were and still are a function of purely domestic considerations, while other domestic conflicts were and still are instigated and supported by foreign international forces. This simply means that domestic considerations and problems such as ethnic rivalries, religious intolerance, and economic need do play a major role in causing international conflict. At the same time, international ideological rivalries, cultural or political quests for global dominance, and economic security interests pursued by great and regional powers are also a major cause of national conflict. Thus, it would not be unreasonable to attribute most international conflicts to domestic considerations, or blame the majority of national conflicts on international developments and interventions.

National conflicts that have international implications and those that are totally or partially provoked by global developments will command more attention in this study. They are conflicts of importance to national and international relations and are destined to change the structures and functions of the modern nation-state and its national, regional, and international role. In a highly interdependent world, such conflicts are also destined to have a profound impact on prospects for human and group rights, regional stability, universal peace, and global prosperity. International conflicts that center around border disputes will receive little attention because they tend to be well-defined and are largely amenable to established rules of international law and procedures of international conflict resolution, particularly arbitration and adjudication.

The current map of international conflict clearly indicates that most conflicts are ethnic- and value-related rather than interest-related and border disputes among neighboring states. Because of this, it has been difficult to clearly define such conflicts and devise workable political mechanisms to contain them once they erupt into violent confrontation, let alone resolve them in a satisfactory manner. As Quincy Wright has stated, "Coalitions are usually formed to face an outside common enemy and thus they tend to displace their internal hatred and differences upon the external enemy. When the enemy disappears, animosity reappears among the former allies."[5] The civil war in Afghanistan is an example of group conflict turned inside after the group has defeated the external enemy.

At times, it has also been difficult to persuade the major parties to a conflict to sit together to discuss common problems. Rationality seldom prevails and often is crushed under an outburst of mass emotions. This is partially because rationality cannot be separated from its larger cultural and psychological contexts, making each party's frame of reference and view of the causes of conflict different from those of others.

Value-related conflicts are disputes over loyalties, individual beliefs, group identities, ethnic relations, cultural perceptions, and values. They are issues that do not lend themselves easily to political compromise and thus tend to be non-negotiable. They are also difficult to define outside their own cultural contexts, which makes them hard to communicate to others whose cultures are different. Despite an accelerated movement toward the development of universal values, unique historical experiences and socio-cultural formations have continued to influence people's worldviews, driving them in different, at times opposing, directions. Culture thus plays an important or decisive role in provoking conflict, sustaining it for generations, and helping resolve it.

Conflicts that are interest-related and reflect disputes over borders between sovereign states are easier to define and manage. When rationality prevails on both sides, and a political will develops to end it, the conflict becomes easier to resolve as well. The Israeli-Egyptian dispute over Sharm El-Sheikh, which Israel occupied in 1967, was resolved through adjudication, and the small resort town of Taba was returned to Egypt after the World Court ruled in favor of Egypt, ending an Israeli occupation that lasted about two decades. Nevertheless, most border disputes between sovereign states have increasingly been transformed into value-related conflicts, due to the rise of ethnicity and the re-emergence of nationalism. Examples of countries where ethnicity has become a complicating factor are the former Yugoslavia, Georgia, Sri Lanka, India, Sudan, and Ethiopia. As Louis Kriesberg states, "Political boundaries imposed by states cause many international conflicts as ethnic groups seek new borders to correspond to their identities often violating borders claimed by other ethnic groups."[6]

In addition, the mechanisms to manage most interest-related conflicts and the frameworks to deal with their implications were developed and proven largely workable. Arbitration, adjudication, mediation, and negotiation were successfully used to resolve several border disputes and interest-related conflicts. Settlements that proved workable and durable acknowledged the reality of interests of all those involved while fashioning new arrangements to redefine state or group relationships to meet perceived needs, serving as examples to facilitate the resolution of similar conflicts.[7]

Many conflicts that are value-related are also interest-related. Every conflict, in fact, tends to involve more than one issue and more than one party, regardless of its nature. As A.J.R. Groom stated, "What appears on the surface to be interests frequently are a manifestation of some basic fear and values that have not been admitted, perceived or defined."[8] Adversaries engaged in one conflict are more likely to be parties to other, less important conflicts. This in turn tends to affect their attitudes and relative positions and consequently the outcome of each conflict to which they are a party. Conflicts are also subject to the influence of domestic

economic pressures, socio-cultural patterns, and international developments, which keep changing the balances of power among the players
and thus the ability of concerned regimes to influence events in their
favor and control their own fate. Meanwhile, perceptions of the importance of time has also been changing, making all conflicts either more or
less complicated, and the need to resolve them more or less urgent.

Conflicts may be controlled, contained, or partially settled, but seldom
totally resolved. A conflict is considered resolved when the outcome of
the settlement to be negotiated and ratified is perceived by all conflicting
parties as acceptable and binding and meets the standards of fairness
and justice.[9] A resolution, says A.J.R. Groom, is "a situation in which
relationships between parties are legitimized and self-sustaining without
the intervention of third parties and without the imposition of behavioral
patterns."[10] However, the multiplicity of parties and issues involved in
almost all conflicts means that no party will be fully satisfied, and no
party will be totally denied. Even in cases involving the use of violence
to settle conflict by force, "defeat" as Louis Kriesberg said, "is never
total and victory never permanent."[11] Consequently, compromise solutions tend to characterize the outcome of most settlements, particularly
political settlements of interest-related conflicts. Settlements, however,
are more likely to fall short of addressing all issues involved in any
conflict regardless of its nature. Subsequently, they tend to leave most
conflicts alive, though at much lower levels, or in states of depression
and stagnation that do not pose serious threats to the newly established
orders. This in turn necessitates that relationships be reviewed regularly
to encourage cooperation, reduce competition, and prevent conflict from
re-emerging.

## STATE STRUCTURE AND CONFLICT

The modern state tends to control territories on which more than one
ethnic, religious or cultural group lives. At the same time, almost all
states, rich and poor, democratic and non-democratic, tend to be governed by one ethnic or cultural group, or a political and economic elite
that neither represents all peoples nor treats them fairly and equally. No
government represents all of its citizens or seeks the welfare of all of its
individual constituents with the same degree of commitment.

Nevertheless, governments claim absolute sovereignty, demand group
loyalty, and impose individual sacrifices on all people under their control. While governments, regardless of their behavior, often escape the
punishment of the people for mistakes committed, most people cannot
escape the punishment of government. As a result, the power and legitimacy of governments in every society are almost always under attack,
particularly from the social groups and ethnic minorities that see them-

selves as victims of the established order. In turn, governments and the ethnic groups and/or political and economic elites they represent are always fighting back to protect their own interests and suppress or appease the opposition. In the process, they make conflict and conflict resolution a living experience that affects the lives and perceptions of all people.

People grouped together tend to develop identities of their own and assign individual and group tasks to be accomplished. Interacting groups, meanwhile, tend to develop conflicting views of themselves as superior to or victims of the other, causing social distance to increase, stereotyping to develop, and conflict to arise.[12] Conflict thus is an outgrowth of group diversity and cultural differences, often heightened by the failure of those in power to act on the needs of their constituencies as they perceive them.[13]

People living within individual states normally belong to several associations and have strong loyalties to certain social and cultural groups. These groups often have worldviews and interests that run counter to those of governments and other similarly organized social and cultural groups. This is so because membership in one group usually dictates an association with a particular activity and/or a commitment to certain values that unite members and at the same time separate them from members of other competing groups. Despite the fact that no two individuals follow identical development paths, people do not feel fully human without belonging to a community, "because our deepest individuality somehow demands fully articulated unity."[14]

Due to this, domestic conflicts are usually multifaceted, involving many issues, groups, and socio-political and cultural relationships. They often include issues related to political legitimacy, ethnicity, race, culture, religion, justice, equality, and socio-ecological ideas. Because governments, regardless of their popularity and political culture, tend always to resist change, they have become party to every political conflict. In addition, governments' claim to legitimacy and control of power and the right to impose sacrifices on constituencies have enabled them to become the principal arbiter in all non-political conflicts. Yet as a result of the non-inclusive nature of the modern nation-state, governments lack the basis to be fair and often lack the means to achieve social justice.

Regimes use varied methods to deal with problems and maintain control. Regimes that feel weakened and threatened by domestic pressure may move to solidify their power base by creating an outside enemy. The classic approach to solidifying internal unity and undermining legitimate dissent is to invoke collective memories of the past and demand individual sacrifices, which serve to create a common perception of vulnerability and question the patriotism of the political opposition. Such regimes may also act to suppress dissent, divide the opposition and play ethnic and cultural groups against each other, thus strengthening their own role as arbiters of domestic conflict. Regardless of the action taken, the result is more likely to accentuate social and political conflict and weaken the society's long-term ability to meet the national and international challenges.

Despite the importance of state structure in causing conflict and determining the right approach to conflict analysis and resolution, there is also a need to understand the ideas, values, and images that make people engage in conflict. Edward Azar said, "It is the denial of human need, of which ethnic identity is merely one, that finally emerges as the source of conflict, be it domestic, communal, international or inter-state."[15]

Regardless of their political structure, states have been more successful in dealing with political conflict than with social conflict, particularly political challenges that questioned the legitimacy of the regimes in power. In contrast, most states have failed to deal with social conflict, especially as related to ethnic, religious, and racial disputes. The record regarding international conflict is mixed because results were influenced more by the regional balance of power and the state's own military power and less by state structure.

In dealing with political conflict, states have used one or more of the following tools:

1. Suppression of dissent to control or eliminate the opposition. This method was and still is the most favored by authoritarian rulers of the Third World, as well as the tool used by the governments of the former communist countries. In 1992, for example, the democratic process in Algeria was halted and a new government was formed by the army, which employed force to suppress and control an Islamic movement that challenged its authority. Meanwhile, a democratically elected president in Peru suspended the constitution and used the army to deal with a Maoist challenge that sought to change the system.

2. Appeasement of certain socio-political forces to quiet dissent and mollify the opposition's popular leadership. This method is most effective when the true challenge comes from a small elite whose primary objective is to effect more political participation or gain economic advantage. Oil-producing states, particularly the Arab Gulf states and Mexico, have resorted to appeasement to buy the elite and weaken the ability of the popular opposition to mount serious challenges to the establishment.

3. Democracy, to facilitate political participation and integrate the opposition into the main political stream. This method has recently been used to resolve certain protracted conflicts in a manner that preserved the dignity of all adversaries and restored stability to shattered nations. In Nicaragua, elections were helpful in resolving conflict inside the country and with the United States, while in Cambodia, elections have seemingly put an end to a civil war that lasted nearly two decades. In the process, democracy was established,

and the legitimacy and interests of all parties, including the state, were safe-guarded.

Suppression, though effective in the short run, often fails to resolve serious conflicts in the long run. Unless followed by democracy, it often serves to harden the opposition, driving it underground and toward violence. The example of Algeria, whose government moved in February 1992 to suspend elections and suppress the opposition, demonstrates the futility of oppression as a means to deal with legitimate dissent and popular demands for change. The Algerian move was itself illegitimate and led to increasing social tension and political violence by a much hardened Islamic opposition.

Appeasement, meanwhile, works more effectively in rich countries or where the majority of the masses are illiterate and largely indifferent to political control. When the opposition is composed of several groups contending for power, appeasement does not work. And in all cases, appeasement leads usually to the spread of corruption and the waste of valuable resources and opportunities, some of which are unrecoverable. For example, in Mexico, corruption was institutionalized and even legitimized as a tool to sustain domestic political balance and keep the ruling party in power, wasting valuable resources and opportunities and condemning the majority of the Mexican people to a life of perpetual poverty.

Democracy, however, is most effective when stability and prosperity prevail and when the opposition consists of several political groups contending for power. In such situations, democracy becomes the vehicle to facilitating change while maintaining stability, inviting political participation, and reducing tension. It also tends to help control corruption, demand accountability, and legitimize and regulate dissent. As R. J. Rummel writes,

Where there are civil and political rights, free and secret elections, the governing elite are dependent upon the electorate for their power and continuance in office. Moreover, their power is limited and divided among different elites and groups, and they constantly have an official opposition looking over their shoulders for the slip, the mistake, the misuse of power that could be used to wrest authority from them in the next election.[16]

Democracy is often ineffective and could even become counterproductive when dealing with conflicts related to ethnic identities and rights of minorities, as will be explained later. Regardless of the circumstances, democracy has limits because "democratic decision making is usually, if not always, based on the interests, values and needs of a ruling elite."[17]

Conflicts that reflect internal power struggles are neither totally national nor international in nature. Nevertheless, they almost always have an important international dimension and are seldom settled or sustained without active outside intervention. The power struggle in Afghanistan in the 1980s, for example, had invited Soviet and subsequently American intervention. Political conflicts in Angola, Cambodia, Ethiopia, Lebanon, and Nicaragua have also invited the intervention of regional powers as well as the superpowers. Power struggles that rely on violence to achieve objectives have been easy to provoke, difficult to contain, and almost impossible to resolve. In most cases, no solutions were found before the near-total destruction of the state structure and of most national institutions and basic group and ethnic relationships.

Nonetheless, the end of the Cold War, the discrediting of communism, and the emergence of an active global movement promoting democracy and respect for human rights are expected to discourage power struggles in many parts of the world. The movement toward democracy and more respect for human rights in particular has provided realistic political frameworks for legitimizing dissent and facilitating political change and participation. Meanwhile, the demise of communism and the end of the Cold War have reduced the importance of almost all Third World countries from a strategic viewpoint. This in turn has vastly weakened the superpowers' incentive to instigate and sustain domestic conflicts, as well as their will to intervene decisively to end them.

The new global developments regarding the fate of communism and superpower relations have had a positive impact on power struggles within states. For ethnic- and value-related conflicts, however, they seem to have had a negative impact. While conflicts caused by power struggles in countries such as Angola, Mozambique, Cambodia, and Lebanon were being settled, ethnic conflicts in countries such as the former Yugoslavia, Turkey, India, Georgia, Azerbaijan, and Russia were either starting or intensifying.

The removal of superpower support of most Third World authoritarian regimes and the discrediting of communism have served to weaken central authority in many countries. At the same time, they have undermined the ideological bonds that used to tie peoples together. Because the economic pie has generally been shrinking while most minorities were being victimized by the old authoritarian regimes, national, ethnic, and religious minorities began to demand that their rights be fully recognized and respected. Such a recognition and respect, most minorities maintain, can only come through territorial separation and political independence. "After two centuries," wrote Arthur Schlesinger recently, "nationalism remains the most vital political emotion in the world, far more vital than social ideologies such as communism or fascism or even democracy."[18]

Nationalism, however, is not only a socio-political force to effect change but also an instrument to create new nations. It is a powerful tool that relies on collective memories to awaken, unify, and activate old nations. Because of this, nationalism has been a motivating force that smaller nations and ethnic minorities are increasingly using today to strengthen group consciousness and restore self-confidence. At the same time, it is a socio-political movement that threatens the political integrity of most multiethnic states, while endangering the power and privileges of those in control.

The modern state, as mentioned earlier, claims absolute sovereignty but has little or no constitutional provisions or even political frameworks to respond positively to the demands of national and ethnic groups under its control. Thus, calls to strengthen international law as a way to deal with international conflict, particularly conflict caused by ethnic disputes, are unhelpful, if not harmful, as long as the nation-state remains the basic unit of analysis. Such a move to strengthen international law will certainly lead to consolidating the powers of the nation-state, whose major prerogatives are increasingly becoming more of a problem in dealing with both domestic and international conflict.[19]

In light of the spread of nationality conflicts and the revival of national rivalries and ethnic enmities, the limits of the nation-state were exposed. As the bases of conflict began to shift away from ideology and strategic matters related to security toward ethnic and nationality issues related to unsatisfactory group relationships, it became clear that both the structure and the prerogatives of the nation-state were in need of an overhaul.

In addition, the universally recognized right of national self-determination has emerged in the new era as a contributing factor to intensifying and multiplying ethnic conflict. In claiming such a right, many ethnic minorities began to call for independence; respecting that right, certain states moved to recognize declarations of independence that were prematurely pronounced. Because no territory claimed by a minority is completely free of other ethnic groups, declarations of independence signaled the beginning of new grievances to add to the old ones, only the roles were reversed. Most minorities under the old system emerged as majorities within the newly created states after independence, and remnants of old majorities began to suffer the fate of old minorities. The Yugoslavian case demonstrates the process of political fragmentation caused by nationalism and the cost of ethnic conflict that fails to attract proper international attention. It also demonstrates that known tools of conflict analysis and resolution are inadequate.

When Croatia declared its independence, the German government moved very quickly to recognize the newly created state, despite European and American calls for caution. The ruling coalition and the major opposition parties in Germany invoked the principle of self-determination to justify their recognition of Croatia's independence. By making that move, however, Germany and the other states that followed its lead have in effect circumvented, if not violated, the rights of other minorities that lived within Croatia at the time.

Croatia's declaration of independence invited Serbia, the largest state within the old Yugoslavian federation, to attack the Croatian state under the pretext of protecting the rights of the Serbian minority in Croatia, committing untold atrocities. The declaration of independence by Bosnia-Herzegovina was also followed by international recognition that failed to protect the new state from Serbian aggression. The war and the atrocities committed by the Serbs seem to indicate that little has been learned from past atrocities and that no real solutions to ethnic conflict exist.

In light of the above, international conflict must be viewed as an outcome or a manifestation of an outdated nation-state system and unjust international order, both of which have failed to understand or meet the basic needs of people, particularly those related to group identity.

The Conference on Security and Cooperation in Europe issued at the end of its summit meeting in Paris in November 1991 what it called the "Charter of Paris for a New Europe." The declaration stated that "the era of confrontation and division of Europe has ended" and called for European relations to be founded on respect and cooperation. The declaration stated that "the intention of participants was to seek effective ways of preventing, through political means, conflict which may yet emerge, [and to] define in conformity of international law, appropriate mechanisms for the peaceful resolution of any disputes which may arise." The charter also affirmed that "the ethnic, cultural, linguistic and religious identity of national minorities will be protected and that persons belonging to national minorities have the right freely to express, preserve and develop that identity without any discrimination and in full equality before the law."[20]

If every ethnic group has the right to develop its identity in full equality with others, every ethnic group will probably seek to establish a state of its own, causing the number of states in the world to double or even triple in a matter of years. "The world," as Louis Kriesberg asserts, "is made up of many more nations than there are states. Few states control territories that locate a single people within those borders and nowhere else."[21] Thus, allowing each cultural minority to pursue independence would lead to changes in most international treaties and laws, creating a world beyond recognition and a situation beyond control. At the same time, if the modern nation-state is to be allowed to maintain its current prerogatives and claimed sovereignty, no ethnic minority or small nation will be able to regain freedom and reclaim lost rights.

Therefore, the circumstances created by the global developments of the last few years demand that the concepts of national sovereignty and self-determination be redefined. They must be made less exclusive and more modest to accommodate the political needs of small nations and provide other ethnic minorities with justice, equality, and respect for their cultural and religious rights and identities. "The disorders in the entire international system are many and profound; the structures for resolving them are obviously inadequate, and the failure to deal with them is disastrous," states Robert Pickus.[22]

Until a few years ago, ethnic conflict was largely treated as an internal problem left for the state to deal with. Even when outside forces intervened, the intervention was undeclared and was considered illegal under international law. Because of that, and the fact that ethnic conflicts were limited in number, minority suffering was tremendous and was largely ignored by most outside powers. However, the global developments that accompanied the communications and information revolutions and that followed the end of the Cold War have changed all of that. Kenneth Boulding writes, "Advancing technology is creating a situation where in the first place we are developing a single world system that does not have the redundancy of the many isolated systems of the past and in which therefore if anything goes wrong, everything goes wrong."[23] The civil war in the former Yugoslavia, for example, has had far-reaching consequences in most European countries, as well as in the United States. Some of these are moral, others are economic, and most are political.

The re-emergence of German nationalism and rightist radicalism has largely been in response to the hundreds of thousands of Yugoslav and Romanian refugees who fled political persecution and economic dislocation in their countries. "Although it is not inevitable that ethnic, religious, or tribal violence in one country will spread to its neighbors, there are usually significant spill-over effects: The refugee flow from the Balkans and Eastern Europe provides a pretext for the revival of neo-Nazism in Germany and for less violent unrest elsewhere in Western Europe," writes Edward Luck.[24]

Therefore, ethnic conflict is also an international conflict that has invited outside intervention and will continue to affect the political and social conditions in many other countries of the world. Its impact is certainly more negative than positive and is destined to challenge our physical and intellectual resources in ways unknown before. In fact, the new global developments that have ended superpower conflict for the time being have "shaken the foundations of most of the work on conflict and peace over the past forty years," leaving states, policy makers and concerned organizations at a loss regarding future direction.[25]

## THE ROLE OF CULTURE

Cultural backgrounds, belief systems, and social values play a vital role in shaping people's ways of thinking and influencing their perceptions of themselves and others. People belonging to different cultures tend to have difficulty communicating with each other and find it even harder to understand why they often fail to communicate. This happens because different cultures place different values on the same things, causing people's expectations and beliefs of what is important or what is right to be different or contradictory.

In all conflicts and conflict-resolution processes, culture largely defines the values and interests that are at the core of each conflict. As they shape people's perceptions of themselves and others, cultures affect the formation of states' policies to deal with friends and adversaries. At the same time, cultures influence the ability to communicate and the tendency to miscommunicate, making the process of human interaction less controllable and its outcome less predictable. Basheer Meibar, in a study of Arab culture, concluded that it is futile to "attempt to resolve conflict involving Arab actors by traditional methods—threat, coercion, negotiation over tangible benefits—while overlooking the symbolic nature of conflict."[26]

Since all forms of human interaction involve ways and means of communication, cultural perceptions are important to understanding others and appreciating their position. Perceptions, however, are not based exclusively on facts but also on images, collective memories, and stereotypes. Stereotypes in turn may be used to dehumanize others, belittle their feelings and justify their mistreatment, forcing them to react in ways that engender antagonism and cause conflict. False images and stereotypes serve to weaken the ability of all parties involved to communicate properly with each other, leading to tension and frustration that could cause serious conflict even over minor issues.[27] Americans, for example, have in their indifferent or casual attitude toward other cultures constructed images and stereotypes of others that are generally negative. Due to this, Americans' ability to develop healthy relationships with most non-Western peoples has been impeded, causing antagonism and conflict to replace friendship, which in turn created a tendency among Americans toward domination rather than genuine cooperation. Even when perceptions are based on proven facts, acting according to normal cultural expectations could lead to miscommunication.

An elderly German woman told me a story about an incident during her first visit to Italy. An Italian man whom she met on the train going to Italy had invited her to his house for dinner. They agreed that he would pick her up from her hotel at 7:00 P.M. The German woman, acting on her perception of the behavior of Mediterranean people in general, expected her host to come late. But as she walked down to the hotel lobby at 7:15 her host was waiting at the entrance and looking at his watch. He told her that he had been waiting there for 20 minutes and that he was about to leave. After apologizing, she told him that she had expected him as an Italian to be late. He answered, "I expected you as a German to be exactly on time."

In dealing with conflict and international relations, experts and policy makers always talk about the political culture of their partners as an important factor in determining their own policies toward the other. They usually make certain assumptions of the others' intentions and possible reactions based upon several factors. Notable among them are previous experiences, factual information, and perceptions of the others' intentions and political culture. However, the political culture of any state cannot be understood in isolation from the wider culture that governs the nation's perceptions of and attitudes toward others and the world at large, which in turn cannot escape the influence of the religious, historical, and economic experience and conditions.

The conventional wisdom in the West claims that diplomats, regardless of their cultural backgrounds and national affiliations, speak the same language of diplomacy, exhibit similar attitudes toward others, and are generally governed by the same rules of rationality. While diplomats may behave in similar ways and feel obligated to respect the same rules of diplomatic protocol, they seldom share a way of thinking or similar worldviews with other diplomats belonging to different cultures. Consequently, they never abide by the same rules of Western rationality. In fact, the concepts of rationality, rational thinking, and rational behavior are relative terms and thus cannot be defined or accurately understood outside the cultural context within which they function. One person's reaction to provocation could differ markedly from the reaction of another person belonging to another culture. This is true because different cultures usually place different values on the same things.

Diplomats, despite the fact that they behave in similar ways and tend to present their views in similar packages, place different values on shared concerns because they are the products of dissimilar cultures. It is this value emphasis that causes the miscommunications that play an important role in instigating conflict and complicating its resolution. In addition, diplomats usually receive their instructions from their home capitals, where they have little influence over the decision-making processes that affect their political positions, activities, and careers. Decision makers are normally separated from their diplomats physically and often psychologically as well. They function within different cultural and political settings, their behavior is usually governed by different rules of rationality, and therefore they respond to different social and economic concerns and environmental issues than do their diplomatic representatives.

Therefore, the behavior of diplomats does not represent and seldom reflects the political culture of their nations, which itself is a product and a component of the national culture. It is this culture that shapes the perceptions of people, influences the formation of government policies, and determines the direction of politics in general. "Political cultures, in brief, cannot be understood in isolation from the wider culture, and it is a pity that this artificial distinction has become widely accepted," writes Raymond Cohen.[28]

During a conference held in Hamburg, Germany, in September 1992, two groups of Iranian and German intellectuals and policy makers discussed issues related to human rights in Islam. The Iranian delegation included ambassadors, former politicians, intellectuals, and three high-ranking religious leaders. The discussion was candid and participants were respectful of each other's views and concerns. At the end of the first day, an Iranian-German, impressed by the level of civility of the discussions, said to me that it was hard to understand how people like those often fail to work together to resolve conflict. Such remarks, though common in similar situations, are nonetheless naive. They fail to understand the role of cultures in shaping people's thinking, and the role of political and social environments in governing rules of behavior. Being in Germany and the guests of an academic institution, both Iranians and Germans behaved similarly. Being the products of different cultures, they thought differently.

Outside the grounds of the institute that housed the conference, a group of Iranians belonging to the opposition demonstrated in protest. Every time members of the group saw the Iranian clergy pass within sight, they began to shout loudly. At the end of the second day, one of the three religious leaders spoke in frustration, expressing anger and dismay. He accused the director of the institute, their host, of siding with the Iranian opposition and violating their rights. He said that the director had allowed the opposition to demonstrate in front of the institute, and that was contrary to their understanding and the spirit of holding a joint conference. The Iranian leader had no idea that the director could neither start nor end the demonstration, and that only German law had that authority. The Iranian political culture and system of government, being different, could not understand the German legal and political environment.

In managing international relations and conducting interstate negotiations, diplomatic messages form the primary means of communications. Messages, written or oral, direct and indirect, are means to send information, convey new ideas, express changed attitudes, and suggest new ways of looking at issues of shared concern. Despite the clarity of most messages, they are almost always subjected to different interpretations. Such interpretations are attempts to evaluate the meaning and rank the importance of the contents of messages in light of previous experiences and conceived perceptions of the other. Thus, interpretations of diplomatic messages, particularly in negotiation, are often misleading and almost always cause miscommunications. They are interpretations that either underestimate or overestimate the value of the message itself, while questioning its timing and sincerity.

In addition, decision makers tend to judge messages, signals, and even freely expressed opinions coming from the other's camp by the standards of their own political culture, not by the standards of the adversary's political culture. Such readings of messages usually hinder an understanding of issues of mutual concern and often complicate the processes of conflict resolution. They may even encourage adversaries to act or react to their own readings of the adversary's messages in ways that harm their own interests, escalate conflict, or deepen mutual suspicion. Because of that, the role of a particular mediator (to be explained in Chapter 7) is very important to ensure proper communications and reduce possibilities of misunderstandings.

For example, an opinion expressed in the form of an article written by a known Middle Eastern expert in the United States that deviates from U.S. public policy carries a substantial weight in the Arab world that could not be justified from an American viewpoint. Since open expression of new and daring political views in almost all Arab countries is unknown, an expression of such political views in the United States tends usually to be interpreted by Arab politicians as a new signal sent by the U.S. government. Consequently, the perceived signals become the subject of careful studying and speculation, often dictating certain actions that reflect new expectations of imminent changes in the American position, changes the U.S. government has not planned or even contemplated.

The great difference in the importance that cultures place on certain human actions or behavior can be further illustrated through a simple story told by Goran Milic, a Yugoslavian television personality. He said that he once was in New York standing at a street corner with his wife and friend. It was pouring rain, they were late for a Broadway play, and needed a taxi badly. He said that New Yorkers had previously told him that it would be almost impossible to get a taxi in New York around 7:30 p.m. Nevertheless, his friend told him that everything in New York was possible for the right price. And while this discussion was going on, a taxi stopped at the traffic light in front of them. The friend walked to the taxi and asked the passenger who was in the car if he would surrender the taxi for $20. The passenger did. Milic added, "In Yugoslavia this would never happen, because it is a matter of pride." Milic maintained that people in Yugoslavia do not kill for money and incidents of armed robberies and muggings are seldom. However, people kill for passion and beliefs, even when they are members of the same family.[29]

In July 1993, the *Washington Post* reported that robberies in Baghdad had become common due to the deterioration of economic conditions caused by the three-year-old U.N.-mandated economic sanctions. An Iraqi woman, fearing that she might become a victim, hid her jewelry with frozen food in the refrigerator. While she was at work, the house was robbed and all the food and jewelry were stolen. The next day, the woman found a small package in front of her house with a note that read, "We are not thieves, we are hungry." The packaged contained all the missing jewelry.

In the Palestinian-Israeli conflict, one of the major Israeli concerns is an article in the PLO charter that calls for the destruction of the state of Israel. Israelis, as well as European and American Jews who favor a political settlement to the conflict, have continued to insist that this article be repealed. Anyone who understands Arabic and Islamic cultures, however, also understands that this article had long ago become irrelevant. It was rendered irrelevant once the Palestine National Council, the legislative body of the PLO, accepted U.N. Resolutions 242 and 338 and implicitly recognized the existence of the state of Israel.

According to Western culture, particularly American culture, almost every relationship is contractual and legalistic.[30] Thus, the only way to cancel a legal decision is to repeal it. But according to Arabic culture and the Islamic legal system, there is no need to repeal any undesirable act through a complicated legal process or battle. Legal acts are easily repealed automatically through the enacting of new legislations that supercede the old ones. This is how Islam's holy book, the Koran, was interpreted to explain inconsistencies regarding certain rulings. The last ruling was always accepted as the last word, canceling and replacing all previous rulings dealing with the same issue.

The Palestinian charter, therefore, does not need to be changed and its controversial article need not be repealed, since it has already been superceded by subsequent PNC resolutions. It must be left to historians to analyze the circumstances that led to its adoption; to judge the rationality or realism of the framers of the covenant; to examine their short- or farsightedness; and to evaluate the article's role in the Palestinian struggle for self-determination. Thus, preserving the integrity of old constitutions in the Arab world, just like preserving ancient manuscripts and monuments, is a matter of national pride and historical importance, but of little practical use and political influence.

The importance of culture and cultural symbols in facilitating or hindering cross-cultural communications dictates a need to incorporate cultural attitudes and perceptions into models and theories of conflict analysis and conflict resolution. Models that were produced by Western specialists have continued to lack the proper tools to deal with non-Western nations, and thus they have remained largely irrelevant to those peoples. For example, "the principles of conflict resolution as they have developed under the umbrella of an agreed upon body of law in the

United States cannot be applied easily to international conflicts where no such body of law exists," writes David Newsom.[31] Even if such a body of law existed, it would be different from the American one, reflecting different cultural values and responding to different social needs and political environments.

Consequently, a need has arisen for mediators capable of bridging the cultural gaps that usually separate adversaries and frustrate their efforts to communicate. The new mediator is in reality a communicator working with and across cultures. He is not just a messenger, a facilitator directing dialogue, or a legal or social expert explaining positions. He is all of that and more as he works to initiate, sustain, and enhance communications and negotiations.[32]

An example of the irrelevance of certain Western conflict-resolution concepts to the non-Western world may be given in a small personal encounter. In February 1992, Search for Common Ground (SCG), an American organization that had arranged several meetings between Arabs and Israelis, decided to establish several conflict-resolution centers in the Middle East. Since launching its Middle Eastern project in 1989, it has decided not to deal with the core political issues of the Arab-Israeli conflict. The complexity and sensitivity of those issues, it reasoned, would cripple its work. Thus, seeking success, not goal-oriented performance, SCG decided to limit itself to dealing with minor, non-sensitive issues.

As the president of SCG explained his decision to establish the proposed conflict-resolution centers, he was questioned by members of the board regarding budgets of the proposed centers and about the Arab and Israeli receptivity to the idea. No one had asked about the functions of the proposed centers because of their awareness of such functions in an American setting. As a member of the board participating in that meeting, I asked the question regarding the proposed functions. The centers, it was explained, would train a generation of young professionals whose task would be to help resolve conflicts related to family, community and labor-management disputes—nothing new or different from the functions of a similar American center.

What the president of SCG and his staff had failed to understand is that the need for such functions, from an Arab perspective, does not exist. Even if such a need did exist and justified the money and effort to be invested, the would-be young experts would be ineffective for several reasons.

First, labor-management disputes similar to those in the West rarely exist in the Arab world. The largest employer in every Arab country is the government, whose employees have no right to go on strike and, in most countries, even to organize and form labor unions. Because the private sector is small, the size of companies is still smaller, and unemployment rates are high, a labor-management dispute would be a novelty.

Second, Arabs generally do not acknowledge family problems, even when they are severe. Family problems are supposed to remain hidden and to be handled confidentially by close relatives. Severe problems that become known are usually referred to the symbols of authority in the community or to a respected religious leader. This is why there are almost no marriage counselors and few psychiatric clinics in most Arab countries.

Third, community disputes in the Arab world are more of the type regarding issues of honor between clans and tribes. In such disputes, when conciliation is sought, the person to mediate and, in most cases, to arbitrate, is an old man known for his wisdom and integrity. A young professional would lack the knowledge of local customs and understanding of traditional procedures of conciliation, and would also be seen as lacking the wisdom and experience to command respect. He thus would not be accepted as a mediator, and his judgment would not be as respected as that of a wise arbitrator.

In addition, the SCG proposal came at a time when racial conflict in the United States was at a high point, as demonstrated by the Los Angeles riots. SCG's attempt to export American expertise and wisdom in conflict resolution to the Middle East was like trying to apply a largely unproven treatment to a poorly diagnosed ailment. Theories, models, and rules that assume that people place the same value on the same things or behave according to the same rules of rationality are misleading.

## RELEVANCE OF RATIONALITY

Rationality means using reason to make decisions and being agreeable to reasonable options. A rational person is a realistic one who uses the information he or she has to evaluate the possible implications of his own action or inaction when faced with a decision to make. Since no person can function in a vacuum, the information to be collected and choices to be made have to be relevant to the surrounding environment in its entirety and the cultural values and historical experience of the larger society to which he belongs.

Environments within which people function and cultural values and historical experiences of societies to which people belong are different. Thus, the attributes of rationality have also to be different to reflect the opportunities and constraints of each environment and to be consistent with the particular value system and historical experience of each society. In addition, unexpected events and major developments usually create new circumstances requiring changes in certain rationality attributes. This simply means that to be rational one has to be realistic, and to be realistic one has to take into consideration the following:

1. the opportunities and constraints that the environment offers
2. the value system and historical experience of the society to which the behavior relates as well as the expectations of the people affected
3. the imperatives of time and changed expectations.

As explained, the assumption that all diplomats or negotiators follow the same rules of rationality is misleading because the rules that govern their behavior in New York or London are not the same that govern that behavior in Cairo, Istanbul, or Lima. Therefore, using Western rationality as a criterion to determine the timing and nature of the next move in negotiation and judge possible outcomes of conflict-resolution processes could be very misleading. In addition, to be fully rational and thus realistic, one must take into consideration what the adversary will do when acting in accordance with his own expectations and environmental constraints and in response to what he thinks his own adversary might do. "In deciding what to do," Michael Nicholson writes, "I must not only take into account what my rival will do, but analyse what they will do in terms of what they think I will do."[33]

Rationality viewed from the perspective of two different cultures is similar to the experience of two drivers living in different countries. The first driver is Western, say American; the latter is Asian, say Malaysian. The American drives on the right side of the road and observes traffic laws and state regulations that emphasize safety, environmental protection, and other requirements such as insurance. They are laws and regulations consistent with American cultural values, historical experience, and environmental constraints. In addition, the driver and the rules he observes tend to generally view cars as essential means of transportation that facilitate going to work, moving goods and people around, and enhancing the general quality of life and productivity of the economy.

The Malaysian driver drives on the left side of the road and observes certain traffic rules and regulations that reflect a different set of values and societal needs. They are rules and regulations that reflect both the preferences of the social and political systems and the physical constraints of the environment. In addition, the Malaysian driver views cars generally, not as essential means of transportation, but as a status symbol that enhances prestige and helps identify class affiliation as well as a means of recreation.

Thus, the laws and regulations observed by the American driver, the way he drives, and the attitudes he adopts regarding both American traffic regulations and the perceived functions of the car are different, if not at odds, with those observed and adopted by the Malaysian driver. The behavior and attitude of each driver, viewed from the perspective of his own culture, would appear perfectly rational. Yet viewed from the perspective of the other's culture, they would appear irrational, making rationality a relative term that is governed, not by universal rules, but by specific rules and values relevant to specific cultures. In light of this, the rationality or irrationality of certain human attitudes and behavior ought to be judged not by the Western rules of rationality, but by the rules of the culture within which the attitudes and behavior are expressed.

An old Kuwaiti friend told me that it took him two years and three tries to obtain a driver's license in Indiana where he attended college, despite the fact that he had several years of driving experience in Kuwait before arriving in the United States and that driving in both countries is on the right side of the road. The problem, he explained to me, was not related to his driving skills, of which he had plenty, but to his attitude toward both the car and the law. Another Jordanian friend who studied in England and learned to drive while a student there felt comfortable driving both in England on the left side of the road and in Jordan, where driving is on the right side of the road. His frequent trips to England and residency in Jordan have helped him to understand and observe the rules of rationality in both countries, despite their different cultures and value systems.

As we talk of certain people being bilingual, we need to recognize that there are people who are bicultural. Just as each language facilitates communication in the countries and among the peoples that use it, each culture and the attitudes and values it reflects have total validity only in countries and among peoples where it prevails. Thus, the "bicultural" person is one who lived through two different cultural experiences and was socialized into both. As a result, the bicultural person has the ability to behave rationally in either culture. However, the rational behavior he displays in one culture has few consequences outside that culture and is not typical of his behavior in the other culture.

In addition, rules of the game, or procedures of negotiations, have a direct impact on the behavior of participants and the outcome of negotiations. They are usually designed to meet certain needs, often demanded by the stronger party. Because of that, participants' behavior during negotiations could very well contradict their basic attitudes toward most possible outcomes and thus frustrate all efforts to conclude agreements. For example, the behavior of the Iranian clergy during the Hamburg conference was governed by the rules of the conference and agreed procedures to conduct dialogue. Yet their attitude toward the demonstrators was a reflection of the value and political systems in Iran and thus was at odds with their behavior at the conference.

Dialogue groups and meetings intended to bring antagonists together to talk about shared problems, interests, and dreams have mushroomed. They are of two types. The first is more political and is designed to help adversaries identify shared interests to use them as a common ground or building blocks to develop programs and solutions to shared problems. The latter is more psychological and is designed to temporarily strip antagonists of their official or claimed positions, reducing them to ordinary human beings with basic fears, needs, family obligations and aspirations. The first type hopes to lead adversaries to discuss sensitive issues and find mutually acceptable solutions to end conflict. The latter hopes to engage antagonists in a humanizing process to help them overcome mutual fear and abandon stereotypes. Both groups, however, hope that dialogue will eventually bring antagonists closer to each other, and develop mutual understanding of one another's feelings. The record of both types, whether between Palestinians and Israelis, Greek and Turkish Cypriots, or Russians and people from the Baltic states, indicates unqualified success as far as stated objectives are concerned. Yet in looking at those encounters from the point of their impact on the respective conflicts, their record is one of near-total failure because none of the conflicts was resolved or even substantially diminished.

The explanation for this apparent contradiction is not easy. It nonetheless demands attention to re-evaluate the nature, structure, and procedures of dialogue groups and meetings. Otherwise, valuable efforts will be wasted, meager resources blundered, and huge amounts of information accumulated without practical use. The dual role of the "bicultural" person and the limited and temporary transformations experienced by individuals due to humanization processes provide some, if not complete, explanation.

Chapter 5 is devoted to political dialogue and will further explain the roles of the bicultural person and the humanization processes facilitating human interaction, consensus building, as well as the failure to advance the cause of peace.

## NOTES

1. Morton Deutsch, "Theoretical Perspectives on Conflict Resolution," in John Burton and Frank Dukes, eds., *Conflict: Readings in Management and Resolution* (New York: St. Martin's Press, 1990), p. 38.

2. Edward Azar, "Protracted International Conflict: Ten Propositions," in John Burton and Frank Dukes, eds., *Conflict: Readings in Management and Resolution* (New York: St. Martin's Press, 1990), p. 155.

3. Michael Banks, "The International Relations Discipline: Asset or Liability for Conflict Resolution," in John Burton and Frank Dukes, eds., *Conflict: Readings in Management and Resolution* (New York: St. Martin's Press, 1990), pp. 55–60.

4. Dudley Weeks, *The Eight Essential Steps to Conflict Resolution* (Los Angeles: Jeremy P. Tarcher, 1992), p. 52.

5. Quincy Wright, "The Nature of Conflict," in John Burton and Frank Dukes, eds., *Conflict: Readings in Management and Resolution* (New York: St. Martin's Press, 1990), p. 25.

6. Louis Kriesberg, *International Conflict Resolution: The U.S.- U.S.S.R. and the Middle East Cases* (New York: Yale University Press, 1992), p. 18.

7. Hugh Miall, *Peaceful Settlement of Post-1945 Conflicts, A Comparative Study* (Washington, D.C.: USIP Conference on Conflict Resolution in the Third World, October 1990), p. 14.

8. See A.J.R. Groom, "Paradigms in Conflict," in John Burton and Frank Dukes, eds., *Conflict: Readings in Management and Resolution* (New York: St. Martin's Press, 1990), pp. 88–89.

9. James H. Laue, "Contributions of the Emerging Field of Conflict Resolution," in W. Scott Thompson et al., eds., *Approaches to Peace* (Washington, D.C.: United States Institute of Peace, 1992), p. 302.

10. A.J.R. Groom, "Paradigms," p. 89.

11. Louis Kriesberg, *International Conflict*, p. 18.

12. See Bryant Wedge, "The Individual, the Group and War," in John Burton and Frank Dukes, eds., *Conflict: Readings in Management and Resolution* (New York: St. Martin's Press, 1990), p. 103.

13. See Dudley Weeks, "Eight Essential Steps," pp. 37, 61.

14. Michael N. Nagler, "Ideas of World Order and Maps of Peace," in W. Scott Thompson et al., eds., *Approaches to Peace* (Washington, D.C.: United States Institute of Peace, 1992), p. 380.

15. Edward Azar, "Protracted International Conflict: Ten Propositions," in John Burton and Frank Dukes, eds., *Conflict: Readings in Management and Resolution* (New York: St. Martin's Press, 1990), p. 146.

16. R. J. Rummel, "Deadlier than War," *Institute of Public Affairs Review*, 41, 2 (August-October 1987): 30.

17. John Burton, "Unfinished Business in Conflict Resolution," in John Burton and Frank Dukes, eds., *Conflict: Readings in Management and Resolution* (New York: St. Martin's Press, 1990), p. 332.

18. Arthur M. Schlesinger, *The Disuniting of America* (New York: W. W. Norton Co., 1992), p. 47.

19. See Michael Banks, "Four Concepts of Peace," in Dennis J. D. Sandole and Ingrid Sandole-Staroste, eds., *Conflict Management and Problem Solving: Interpersonal to International Applications* (New York: New York University Press, 1987), pp. 264–5.

20. Dennis J. D. Sandole, *Conflict Resolution in the Post-Cold War Era: Dealing with Ethnic Violence in the New Europe* (Fairfax, Va.: Institute for Conflict Analysis and Resolution, George Mason University, 1992), pp. 20–22.

21. Louis Kriesberg, *International Conflict*, p. 18.

22. Robert Pickus, "New Approaches," in W. Scott Thompson et al., eds., *Approaches to Peace* (Washington, D.C.: United States Institute of Peace, 1992), p. 237.

23. Kenneth E. Boulding, "Future Directions in Conflict and Peace Studies," in John Burton and Frank Dukes, eds., *Conflict: Readings in Management and Resolution* (New York: St. Martin's Press, 1990), p. 41.

24. Edward C. Luck, "Making Peace," *Foreign Policy* (Winter 1992–93): 139.

25. W. Scott Thompson, Introduction, in W. Scott Thompson et al., eds., *Approaches to Peace* (Washington, D.C.: United States Institute of Peace, 1992), p. xxiv.

26. Basheer Meibar, *Political Culture, Foreign Policy and Conflict* (Westport, Conn.: Greenwood Press, 1982), p. 178. For a more detailed analysis of attributes of Arab culture, see pp. 161–75.

27. See Dudley Weeks, "Eight Essential Steps," p. 44.

28. Raymond Cohen, *Negotiating Across Cultures* (Washington, D.C.: United States Institute of Peace, 1991), p. 11.

29. Jack Anderson and Dale van Atta, *The Washington Post*, December 29, 1991.

30. Raymond Cohen, *Negotiating*, pp. 23–26.

31. David D. Newsom, "Diplomacy and Negotiation," in W. Scott Thompson et al., eds., *Approaches to Peace* (Washington, D.C.: United States Institute of Peace, 1992), pp. 38–39.

32. Mohamed Rabie, *The U.S.–PLO Dialogue, Secret Diplomacy and Conflict Resolution* (Gainesville, Fla.: University Press of Florida, forthcoming), Chapters 3 and 17.

33. Michael Nicholson, *Rationality and the Analysis of International Conflict* (Cambridge, England: Cambridge University Press, 1992), p. 47.

## Chapter Three

# CONFLICT MANAGEMENT

A few decades ago, particularly in non-Western, non-democratic societies, social and political systems were generally moving more toward
domination and away from equilibrium. But the increasing complexity
of life has caused systems to become interlinked, making change difficult
to observe and nearly impossible to control. Because of that, systems
within societies have begun to move more toward equilibrium and less
toward domination. Competing individual and group interests in a fast-
changing economic and technological environment have caused balances
of power to change and become themselves instruments of change. This
in turn has created new equilibria while undermining the status quo and
hindering long-term domination by any party or social force.

In the colonial era, the colonial nation used military power to control
its colonies and ensure domination. The main objective of colonialism
was economic exploitation, and the main tools of domination were military and political in nature. Conflict between colonial powers and indigenous peoples was managed through the use of force and coercion,
causing the roots of conflict to deepen. As A.J.R. Groom says, "Where
there are values at issue, the use of coercion to pressure in any form, to
force an opponent party to compromise is likely to be disfunctional in
that it will tend to promote protracted conflict, even after a settlement."[1]

During the Cold War era, superpower competition and a policy of
containment were the instruments that replaced power and coercion as
a vehicle to secure influence and achieve objectives. The main objectives,
however, were strategic in nature, and military and economic tools were
employed by both superpowers to secure influence and defend interests.
The strategic objectives of both superpowers were simply the contain-

ment of the enemy's military power and political influence and the undermining of the power of its ideology. Smaller and weaker nations were used as tools by the powerful ones, and their economic and political interests were either ignored or undermined.

A policy of economic exploitation during the colonial era dictated the maintenance of tight political control over the colonies and their populations. The objective of the policy was to prevent the colonized peoples from initiating socio-political and economic processes and adopting policies that could weaken the grip of the colonial power and move the colonized nations closer to independence. As a result, Third World nationalism emerged as a force to unite people under foreign control, induce them to self-awareness and help them regain self-confidence and move toward freedom. National freedom, meanwhile, was viewed generally as gaining political independence and achieving economic independence. But in most cases, when independence was granted or secured, the new arrangements were made to facilitate continued domination through the creation of new balances of power inside and among the new states. Because of that, most conflicts were not resolved, and many became protracted, causing much damage to all parties involved.

The post-1945 era, while ending European domination, witnessed the emergence of the United States and the Soviet Union as the only superpowers competing for global dominance. The United States, being the leader of the West and the assumed defender of Western values, felt an obligation to adopt a foreign policy to protect Western interests and preserve the global status quo. Meanwhile, the inherent attributes of communism as a revolutionary, anti-imperialist and anti-capitalist ideology, led the Soviet Union to adopt an active foreign policy to undermine the global status quo, which was viewed as serving the interests of the West and perpetuating injustice and causing conflict in most parts of the world.

As a result, the two superpowers found themselves competing for global dominance that was viewed by both sides as a zero-sum power game. The gains of one side were thought to be losses for the other, making hurting the enemy the only way to achieve one's objectives. Consequently, conflict became the major characteristic of superpower relations, and waging a war of attrition against each other the main tool of managing that conflict.

In the process, the Soviet-American political and ideological conflict was expanded to include most parts of the Third World, which had largely become an object of superpower contention. To avoid direct military confrontation between the two superpowers, particularly in Europe, many Third World countries and regions were suddenly transformed into battle zones to settle superpower conflicts and competing geopolitical interests.

The so-called Cold War, which could be described as such in regard to Europe and Japan, was a hot and bloody war as far as most Third World nations were concerned. It was a real war for which most Third World nations were made to pay a heavy price in material and human terms as well as in lost opportunities, and from which they had nothing to gain. While Europe and Japan enjoyed almost 45 years of continued relative peace and economic prosperity, the Third World suffered the killing of an estimated 25 million of its own people, more than the combined numbers of those killed in the two world wars.

In addition, Third World conflicts created by the colonial era and others precipitated by the Cold War created new enmities, deepened ethnic and tribal hatred, and encouraged extremism and violence in many countries and regions. Arms, which both superpowers generously supplied to client states and Third World dictators, were used to fuel the killing machines in countries such as Somalia, Angola, Liberia, Palestine, the Sudan, India, Turkey, El Salvador, Peru, the Philippines, Burma, Sri Lanka, and many others.

During the Cold War era, both superpowers had sought the building of military alliances and the recruitment of friends and agents among states and rulers, particularly in the Third World, to facilitate the achievement of their objectives. While Third World agents and client states sought and received financial assistance and military and political support, the superpower benefactors in return sought and received economic advantages and military and political influence. Due to these arrangements, most client states and rulers were able to gain enough military power and political backing to pursue their own objectives, which often included the violation of the human rights of their subjects. As a result, the largely unjust arrangements that emerged from the era of colonialism were perpetuated during the Cold War era, and most conflicts that were supposed to be resolved by ending colonialism were either intensified or transformed into internal power struggles.[2]

The end of the Cold War and the decline of the strategic importance of all Third World nations witnessed also the virtual withdrawal of the military and political backing provided by superpowers to their client states. It also witnessed the exposure of the limits of military power in general and its use as a tool to achieve strategic objectives in particular. Consequently, most oppressed nations and deprived minorities felt that the time had come to pursue long-denied rights and long-suppressed national objectives, giving rise to narrow nationalism and the spread of ethnic conflict. Doug Bandow wrote recently that "post-Cold war instability should not come as a surprise. For decades the superpowers suppressed cultural, ethnic, linguistic, nationalistic, and religious differences within allied states. However tragic their consequences, many of the disputes surfacing around the world have legitimate causes and could not be put off forever."[3]

During the Cold War, both superpowers recognized the need to manage international conflict to avoid the escalation of disputes and possible direct confrontation between themselves. Conflict-management techniques were developed to undermine the influence of each other and to enhance their own interests, particularly in regions considered of vital importance. Many poorer and weaker states, as mentioned earlier, were used as battlegrounds to wage superpower wars by proxy and to deter the other from achieving its global goals. Thus, causes of conflict were increased and deepened, and conflict management was transformed into a process to maintain rather than change the relationships that characterized superpower conflict in general.

Conflict-management techniques that were developed and successfully used to manage international disputes during that period were largely the product of a particular mentality and limited experience. The mentality was that of the Cold War, which sought the maintenance of a balance of power between the two superpowers and viewed the Third World in general as a tool to be manipulated to achieve strategic objectives. The limited experience was that of managing superpower relations on the one hand and the relations of each superpower with its allies and client states on the other.

Dealing with the other from "a position of strength" was the main lesson learned from that experience. "Real arms control with the Soviets," wrote Charles Krauthammer, "came as a result not of signed agreements but of the geopolitical defeat of the Soviet Union, which occasioned a burst of unilateral and bilateral cuts in weapons. We did not talk the Soviets into disarming. We forced them into it."[4] Today, neither American, Russian, nor Israeli power can manage, let alone resolve, minor conflicts, such as the lack of order in Somalia, ethnic disputes in Georgia, and a largely peaceful Palestinian uprising in the West Bank and Gaza. The exposure of the limits of military power, which represents the core element of strength, has rendered such power largely ineffective as a tool to achieve strategic objectives.

Conflict-management techniques developed in the West were largely legal and based on a perception that conflict is primarily the result of competing interests, rather than clashing values. Because of that, it was thought that both individual and state behavior could be altered using the right material incentives. Moreover, the Western legal system was and still is a tool to address individual grievances and protect individual rights rather than group rights, which emerged in the post-Cold War period as the main source of grievances and the major cause of conflict.

Edward Azar has argued that the principal unit in conflict analysis ought to be the group, not the individual or the state: "The professional debate over the question of the appropriate unit of analysis has dwelt on the differences between focusing on the individual, state or system and their implications. It has ignored the group totally."[5]

The post-1945 period was shaped by superpower competition, and all conflicts in the world were made to abide by the rules of the Cold War. The United States in particular felt that it had to intervene in almost every conflict in order to protect its own perceived interests and to deny the Soviet Union the opportunity to enhance its influence. Consequently, most conflicts were kept alive for years, their causes deepened and their negative consequences multiplied, polarizing internal ethnic relations as well as external interstate relationships. The new socio-political balances and power centers that were subsequently created left most nations with little to lose from the continuation of conflict and still less to gain from ending conflict. To most people who perceive themselves as the victims of unjust systems, fighting to regain lost rights and recognition has become a matter of pride, not just politics or material gain.

R. J. Rummel estimated the number of people killed in this century to be about 155 million, and more than 95 million of them were killed by communist regimes. Of the remaining 60 million, the number of people killed in all international wars was less than 29 million. The rest, or about 31 million, were killed in civil wars and murdered by authoritarian governments in the Third World.[6] The stability brought by the post-1945 settlement and the Cold War was a stability under oppressive conditions that led to the perpetuation of violence, not peace, and ripened conditions for more conflicts, not conflict resolution.

Nevertheless, the post-1945 period witnessed the success of the superpowers, and at times the United Nations, in managing international conflict in general and in containing certain violent regional conflicts in particular. In Europe, for example, violent conflicts were not allowed to happen because of their serious impact on superpower relations and the possibility of nuclear confrontation. However, in the Third World, violent conflicts were permitted to happen and escalate, transforming many regimes, through superpower financial support and arms supplies, into killing machines that victimized the innocent and rewarded criminals. While this may not have been the intention in most cases, it often was the only result.

As the Cold War finally came to an end, ethnic antagonism became more apparent and violent, and the need for developing the concept of conflict resolution and tools of international conflict management was heightened. But the global developments that caused the acceleration of ethnic conflict and emphasized the importance of conflict-management techniques have also exposed their shortcomings. The lessons gained in the field of international conflict management during the Cold War were largely drawn from superpower experience in dealing with a limited number of conflicts, notably the U.S.-Soviet adversarial relationship and the Arab-Israeli conflict. Since none of those conflicts were really resolved, the conclusions drawn were not based on the results of genuine and conclusive conflict-resolution processes. In addition, the end of the superpower conflict has, as W. Scott Thompson says, "shaken the foundation of most of the work on conflict and peace over the last forty years."[7]

Conflict management and conflict resolution are two different concepts. Conflict management is a process to bring conflict under control, while conflict resolution is a process to end it. Therefore, conflict management could be a step toward resolving conflict by making it manageable, but it does not necessarily lead to ending conflict. In fact, conflict management may serve as a tool to keep conflict from being resolved.

The post-Cold War era is witnessing today a reversal of conditions that governed European and Third World conflicts in general during the previous period. Central and Eastern European nations, wrote three European intellectuals, "seem to be receding into a state of growing anarchy, collapse of political authority, economic misery and even the horrors of civil and interstate wars and re-enactment of extermination programs in the guise of ethnic cleansing. We are witnessing with helpless horror the return of processes that led to Europe's darkest hours."[8]

In the Third World, however, the withdrawal of superpower military and financial backing has forced many older conflicts to move toward resolution while paving the way for the eruption of new, more passionate ones. With the removal of the Soviet threat, "local and regional quarrels are no longer of vital concern" to the United States and Western Europe, making it less likely that they will draw great-power attention and commitment to facilitating their resolution.[9]

## STRATEGIES OF CONFLICT MANAGEMENT

Conflict, as explained earlier, is an integral part of individual life and of intergroup and interstate relationships. Conflict can never be eliminated; it can only be managed to minimize its negative impact, reduce its intensity, and facilitate its positive role in human development. Basheer Meibar stated that "conflict resolution or eradication is not an alternative because it translates into the elimination of choice and perceptual difference. This goal is neither feasible nor desirable. The best we can do is to learn to live with conflict."[10] Meibar equates conflict resolution with conflict eradication by stretching the meaning of the word "resolution" too far. Conflict resolution is not a process to eliminate conflict but to vastly moderate its intensity and impact, eliminating the negative and reducing conflict to a subconscious force that continues to motivate people but does not dominate their outward attitudes and intergroup relationships.

There are two approaches to conflict resolution, described by Morton Deutsch as competitive and cooperative.[11] Competitive processes are usually adversarial, rely on the use of force, are mutually perceived by antagonists as zero-sum in nature, and can readily, but not necessarily, lead to destructive results. They tend to be identified with the "realist" approach to politics at all levels. Cooperative processes are non- adversarial, usually perceived as non-zero-sum in orientation, and often lead to constructive outcomes.[12]

Nevertheless, conflicts are seldom objective, meaning that the gain of one party is the loss of the other. Most conflicts, argued A.J.R. Groom, are subjective in nature if not in perception, "because the parties can change their goals, and the importance of one value in terms of other actual or potential values is always, at least theoretically, subject to reassessment."[13] While this conclusion may accurately describe situations in most Western, democratic societies, it does not reflect situations in traditional societies where social change is slow and largely controlled by rigid value and belief systems.

Conflicts are seldom resolved but often managed, that is, contained and regulated. Depending on the level, intensity, complexity, and importance of the conflict, strategies to deal with it include crisis prevention or avoidance, crisis management, control and containment, and conflict resolution.

### Crisis Avoidance

During the height of the Cold War and after it became apparent that each superpower possessed enough nuclear weapons to destroy the other several times, both powers moved toward adopting a strategy of crisis prevention. Because both superpowers had an interest in avoiding direct confrontation, they began to cooperate to contain serious international conflicts and ignore others as not important. For example, the United States and the Soviet Union showed clear willingness to cooperate in managing the Arab-Israeli crisis precipitated by the October 1973 War. They were subsequently able to contain the ongoing Arab-Israeli conflict and avoid new crises that could have forced them to confront each other. Superpower intervention was one of conflict management, not conflict resolution, and it therefore fell far short of addressing any of the conflicts' causes.

Stuart J. Thorson said that "disputes are often resolvable when an efficient solution together with a mechanism for implementing that solution can be identified."[14] Superpower management of the Middle East conflict had sought neither an efficient solution nor even an agreed mechanism to manage it. The superpowers sought only mutual understanding to restrain their allies and prevent crises from erupting again, leaving conflict to fester at a lower level and mutual enmity to grow unchecked.

Crisis prevention and conflict avoidance are two different things. The first describes a policy and a mechanism to prevent conflict from reaching the level of crisis. The latter describes a general attitude to avoid dealing with conflict by ignoring it and pretending that it does not exist. Conflict avoidance thus "is expressed in the denial of conflict and in the suppression of awareness of the conflict, as well as in the shying away from dealing with the issues of conflict."[15] Conflict avoidance is more of a state of mind that largely describes individual attitudes, while crisis prevention or avoidance is more of a state of political affairs that is largely applicable to states and interstate relations.

The outbreak of civil war in the former Yugoslavia and the renewal of ethnic hostilities in countries such as India, Georgia, and Kazakhstan have given credence to the idea of crisis prevention. Because this requires special systems to monitor conflict on a continuous basis in order to anticipate trouble and activate the proper mechanisms to avoid hostilities, no single outside power could be seen as credible or capable of performing this task. International organizations and forums, particularly the United Nations and the Conference on Security and Cooperation in Europe (CSCE), have emerged as the political bodies that are most likely to be able to build and manage systems capable of avoiding international crises.

During the last decade, the great powers have developed systems to avoid crises from dominating their relationships. This was accomplished through unilateral, bilateral, and collective acknowledgments of differences and mutual interests on the one hand, and instituting better and more efficient communication systems to identify and deal with unexpected problems, on the other. A system to avoid great-power confrontation, however, was also a system to contain serious, non-great-power conflicts by minimizing the need for intervention to resolve them. This in turn caused less serious conflicts to become less important, giving most local and regional powers added freedom to act on their own. Thus, the non-intervention principle, which the strategy of crisis avoidance embodies, is by itself an invitation for the escalation of certain conflicts, particularly self-contained ethno-national conflicts of the type increasingly found in the former communist nations and certain Third World states.

Crisis avoidance is a process to deal with conflict either by freezing it or by creating larger political or security structures to prevent its escalation and the outbreak of serious hostilities.

One way to avoid crises while using the measures to do so as stepping stones toward conflict resolution is to limit the proliferation of certain conventional and all unconventional weapons, particularly nuclear, chemical, and biological weapons. However, the most effective way to accomplish this task is through the creation of conditions that eliminate the need for such weapons in the first place. That can only be accomplished by fostering peace, promoting democracy, and building pluralistic communities bound together by common interests.

## Crisis Management

Crises in society tend to occur when a major social system or a basic relationship undergoes drastic changes that undermine its relevance or threaten its very survival. Crises may also come as a result of continued deterioration in the overall conditions of an order without invoking equal interest to reverse the process and arrest the deterioration. The civil war in the former Yugoslavia is an example of an ethnic crisis caused by the destruction of the bond that used to tie people together, while the civil wars in Liberia and Somalia are examples of crises caused by the continued deterioration of the socio-economic and political conditions in both countries. This means that crises are either manifestations of largely ignored socio-economic conditions reaching their climax or the products of dysfunctioning basic systems reaching the breakdown point. While conflict is a normal product of social and political interaction among human beings and their institutions, crises are not. They are manifestations of failure to resolve or regulate conflict and characterize major conflicts at the point of explosion. Crises related to international relations represent interstate conflicts in their advanced stages that may involve violence and war.

Thus, dealing with a crisis means generally dealing with a serious conflict that has reached a breakdown point. The first steps to be taken in a crisis situation are usually measures to stop the escalation and stabilize the situation, while other efforts are being made to diffuse the crisis. This means that the action at this stage is one of crisis management rather than conflict resolution. Crisis management consists of political and/or military measures to arrest the escalation of a serious conflict and stop hostilities with a view to stabilizing the conflict at the pre-crisis level.

U.S. handling of the Cuban Missile Crisis in the early 1960s and the American-Soviet joint management of the Arab-Israeli hostilities following the outbreak of war between Israel and its Egyptian and Syrian adversaries in 1973 are good examples of crisis management. Both crises were defused quickly, and the situations were restored nearly to their pre-crisis levels. What followed was a process to manage the ongoing U.S.-Soviet and Arab-Israeli conflicts through the application of conflict control and containment measures. Thus, crisis management, though different from both conflict containment and conflict resolution, may serve as an initial, solid step toward achieving either goal.

In response to crises, governments and sometimes the international community may decide that the first priority is to restore law and order. Such was the response of the Turkish government toward the Kurdish rebellion and the response of the international community to anarchy in Somalia. This may lead to preventing further loss of life and the absence of hostilities, or what Galtung called "negative peace." As Dennis Sandole writes, "This is not, however, conflict resolution: a durable agreement that deals with, to the satisfaction of all concerned, the issues that lead to the violence. Accordingly, the parties should move toward positive peace: the absence of structural violence, and pursuit of social justice for all concerned."[16]

A true strategy of crisis prevention or crisis avoidance eliminates the most serious causes and changes the conditions that promote or facilitate conflict in the first place: "Prevention of an undesired event by removing its causes and by creating conditions in which it cannot occur."[17] This can only be done when positive rather than negative peace is pursued and when a strategy of crisis avoidance includes a strategy of conflict resolution that addresses the real causes of conflict.

In situations requiring the application of crisis management techniques, outside powers, particularly the great ones, tend generally to have vested interests in restoring stability and avoiding further escalation or possible confrontation. As a result, they often intervene to protect their own interests and contain the forces that threaten to harm such interests. Because antagonists engaged in hostilities are seldom capable of stopping the escalation of conflict on their own, intervention by outside powers becomes at times critical to crisis management. The intervention may be political, to persuade antagonists to de-escalate, or economic and military, to compel them to cease hostilities. Economic and military measures could also come in the form of positive and/or negative inducements, using military measures as a threat and economic ones as an incentive to induce cooperation.

Cooperation between global and regional powers in situations requiring crisis management tends often to arise spontaneously, forcing traditional antagonists to collaborate to contain a common threat. A mutual perception that the crisis represents a common threat is usually a precondition for antagonists to cooperate and actively intervene to end the crisis. Crises that are self-contained and do not represent an immediate threat to outside powers rarely induce international cooperation to end them. For example, Ethiopia, Sudan, Liberia, Cambodia, and the former Yugoslavia experienced such crises, inviting little outside intervention.

Antagonists' cooperation to manage crises and preserve a threatened status quo rarely continues beyond the initial containment of the intended crisis. Conflicting interests normally prevent antagonists' spontaneous cooperation from becoming permanent because institutionalized cooperation rests usually on shared values or long-term objectives, not on passing temporary threats. For example, during the Persian Gulf crisis of 1990–91, U.S.-Syrian cooperation to face the Iraqi challenge was necessitated by the nature of the crisis, not by shared values or common long-term objectives. Consequently, it failed to survive the conclusion of the war to expel the Iraqi forces from Kuwait, a fact that freed both states to pursue old antagonistic policies months later.

In crisis management, cooperation among antagonists has one objective: to protect states' interests and restore the status quo. Thus, states and political elites tend to follow policies to minimize the possibility of damage caused by the crisis to their own interests, and to maximize their chances of political survival. Long-term implications are usually of little concern, forcing the threatened regimes and elites to form alliances with whatever power is willing to help restore the status quo.

When political survival is at stake, the price to be paid is never too high to prevent collaboration, even with the devil. West European and American collaboration with the Soviet Union to face Nazi Germany in the 1940s, Iraqi attempts to cooperate with Iran during the Persian Gulf crisis, and Iran's cooperation with Israel during its war with Iraq in the 1980s are good examples of state policies to ensure survival and contain common threats at any price.

Preventing conflict rather than reacting to crises requires forums for dialogue and joint problem solving, acknowledgment of the legitimacy of interests of all parties, and an understanding of the historical and psychological dynamics at work. Building long-term collaborative relationships requires addressing mutual grievances and aspirations of conflicting parties and creating new frameworks that encourage them to cooperate and view their problems, interests, and futures as interlinked. R. J. Rummel says: "The peaceful, non-violent pursuit and fostering of civil liberties and political rights must be made mankind's highest humanitarian goal. Not simply to give the greatest number the greatest happiness, not simply to further the efficiency and productivity of a free society, but also and mainly because freedom preserves peace and life."[18]

## Control and Containment

Conflicts may be major or minor, tolerable or intolerable, threatening or non-threatening. Conflicts that are major, intolerable, and threatening represent crises. Conflicts that are major, threatening, but tolerable represent serious, ongoing conflicts. While crises are dealt with through the application of crisis-management techniques, serious ongoing conflicts are often dealt with through the application of crisis-control and containment techniques. These are measures to contain conflict, keep it under control, and prevent its escalation from reaching the crisis level.

Conflict control and containment consists usually of several well-integrated measures to manage an ongoing conflict with a view to addressing its most threatening aspects. Measures of conflict containment include political and non-political courses of action to mitigate the conflict, control it, change its direction, and remove its unpredictability. Such measures may be of a coercive or non-coercive nature, such as military and economic sanctions and inducements to encourage adversaries to change or modify their behavior and attitudes to be less confrontational and more cooperative. This is a necessary component of any strategy to control and contain conflict because "cooperation tends to breed the conditions for further cooperation, while competition tends to breed the conditions for further competition," which serves to heighten conflict.[19]

During the long years of the Cold War, the behavior of both superpowers toward each other was one of conflict control and containment. Both adversaries used measures of deterrence, assurance, unilateral declarations of non-hostile intentions, bilateral political moves, and signed agreements to reduce tension and improve communications. Agreements signed and political understandings reached during the 1960s and 1970s were instrumental in removing the element of surprise from superpower relations and thus served to stabilize the conflict at a manageable, non-threatening level until the end of the Cold War in 1989. Understandings that the superpowers reached between themselves included also the adoption of new policies toward allies and client states in general to limit their freedom of action, particularly actions deemed capable of endangering the uneasy superpower relationship.

Measures to contain a conflict and facilitate its continued management work also to change its focus and often manipulate the forces and players most involved in it. Manipulation and change of focus, however, may be steps to strengthen the position of one party at the expense of its adversaries, or measures to mitigate and diminish the importance of the conflict in a process to resolve it.

For example, the United States, in managing the Arab-Israeli conflict, has resorted to manipulation and coercion to generally weaken the Arab position vis-à-vis Israel. Soviet policy toward the Indian-Pakistani conflict sought to strengthen the Indian position vis-à-vis Pakistan. The manipulation and application of policies to strengthen its own allies and weaken allies of the adversary were seen by both superpowers as an integral part of managing their own conflict.

The concept of security is probably the most important factor influencing the behavior of states and the perception of minorities in conflict situations. Actions taken by states to enhance their security are often perceived by neighboring states as threatening. Such actions usually include the development and acquisition of modern arms, the acquisition of territory by force, or interference in neighbors' affairs with a view to dominating them. To validate the measures taken, states often invoke history to legitimize occupation, and tend to exaggerate security needs to justify the purchase and development of new arms, which in turn leads to heightening mutual fear, suspicion, and enmity. Neighboring states feeling the threat usually move to counter those measures by adopting similar ones and at times seek outside assurances and protection.

As Nazli Choucri writes, "Security, as defined by the theory of lateral pressure, has three dimensions: the military or strategic dimension, namely the security of borders; the political dimension, namely the security of the regime; and the structural dimension, namely the security of the society with respect to its population-resource balance."[20] The security issue is thus at the core of international conflict, particularly when one's added security is perceived as the other's weakened security. Because issues related to security matters are in a constant state of change, conflict control and containment have increasingly been perceived as a constantly evolving and challenging process, particularly by the great powers and international organizations such as the United Nations and the CSCE.

### Conflict Resolution

Conflicts seen as serious, intolerable, and unwinnable are usually ripe for resolution. For such conflicts to be resolved, adversaries must engage in serious peace processes with the declared objective of resolving conflict. A serious peace process would deal directly with the roots of conflict with a view to undermining and eventually eliminating the real and perceived major causes of conflict. Conflict resolution therefore is a process to end a hostile relationship that feeds hatred and violence and to replace it with a new one that promotes cooperation, inspires confidence, and fosters peace.

Conflicts that are ripe for resolution are not always resolved because adversaries seldom have the courage and willingness to communicate their convictions to their adversaries regarding the unwinnability of the conflict and the desire to resolve it. Domestic political considerations and fear that expressing such a desire might be interpreted as a sign of weakness often inhibit most adversaries from talking to each other directly. Due to this, third party mediators are often needed to establish contact, initiate a peace process, and provide certain guarantees for their proper functioning.

Mediation may come in the form of outside intervention by powers whose interests and/or international statures are threatened by the continuation of conflict or stand to benefit from its resolution. Most outside interventions, however, lack the ability to be effective because outside powers seldom have the political will or resources needed to resolve conflict. In the absence of crises, it is hard to persuade influential outside powers to intervene forcefully, and it is harder to induce them to employ the positive and negative measures needed to resolve conflict, particularly in cases requiring sustained efforts for extended periods of time.

A genuine peace process must not concentrate on claims and counterclaims only. It must go beyond that point and be prepared to deal with the real and perceived issues of conflict, issues that divide people and prevent them from working together to create political conditions for peaceful coexistence. Moving toward peace thus must include changing the negative perceptions that govern antagonistic relationships and creating cooperative arrangements to tie people together. This, as Harold Saunders says, must include, "changing the perceptions of each party of the other's character and intent."[21] No matter how important this task is, it has to be approached cautiously in order not to be perceived as brainwashing or cultural imperialism. It must be attempted through the changing of competitive states of mind and political and economic affairs, as well as the establishment of new ones. Proposed arrangements must be future-oriented yet retain a sensitivity to the roots of past conflicts.

Conflict resolution as a peace process is a comprehensive approach to ending conflict and nearly eliminating its causes. The process moves in three different, yet complementary directions simultaneously:

1. Dealing directly with the real causes of conflict, not only with its symptoms
2. Changing people's mutual perceptions of the adversary by explaining the other's grievances and legitimizing his basic demands
3. Envisioning and gradually building integrative relationships that separate interest from values, emphasizing interests and recognizing values while promoting cooperation and fostering peace.

Conflicts generated by unsatisfied basic group needs often invite outside intervention and are very difficult to resolve without active mediation. Processes to resolve such conflicts need to create political frameworks to help antagonists to mutually identify and recognize grievances. This should be followed by leading antagonists to develop alternative methods to address grievances and satisfy needs. Conflict would be resolved when the antagonists agree to make the necessary structural changes that eliminate or vastly weaken the causes of conflict and create new frameworks that encourage and promote cooperation.[22]

In short, crisis management and conflict control and containment are policies to manage an ongoing conflict and keep it under control. They usually reflect a general conviction that the continuation of conflict at a low level is not threatening or desirable, or that the conflict is not ripe for resolution. When conflict containment is administered by outside powers, particularly powers that do not believe that the conflict is ripe for resolution, the result is often its prolongation and possible complication, causing all concerned parties to eventually pay a heavy price.

By maintaining conflict at tolerable but costly levels while a balance of power is sustained, a policy of conflict control and containment usually attempts to persuade the parties concerned that the conflict is unwinnable. This in turn is more likely to make the conflict ripe for resolution. But if such a policy is not followed by a peace process to resolve the conflict, control and containment are more likely to deepen mutual suspicion, perpetuate conflict, and create long-term instability.

The U.S. management of the Iran-Iraq war, which lasted eight years between 1980 and 1988, was intended to prolong the conflict, weaken both warring parties, and enhance U.S. influence in the Gulf region. Despite the fact that both Iran and Iraq were convinced after a few years that the conflict was unwinnable, mutual hatred and fear prevented them from making the necessary gestures to start a peace process. This was the case because states and groups in conflict, particularly their elites, "regularly develop a kind of anxious concern for their status and prestige manifested by the double symptoms of assertion of strength and fear of humiliation if there should be any retreat" from publicly declared positions.[23]

Crisis management and conflict containment may also reflect a conviction that a comprehensive solution to the conflict is either undesirable or impossible. A conflict is judged as unresolvable when the adversaries' mutual hatred is too deep and the resources required to resolve it are beyond the ability of parties involved in its management to muster. The superpowers' management of their own conflict reflected a mutual conviction that it was desirable to contain and sustain conflict. Both adversaries were content with the status quo, which provided them with the ways and means to continue to dominate allies and maintain superpower status.

During the long Cold War years, the relationship between the two superpowers was unhealthy but not dangerous. While conflict prevented superpower cooperation in fields that could have benefited all mankind, it gave elites in both states a pretext to justify their global strategies and worldviews. They used mutual hostility to enhance their military capabilities, promote their ideologies, recruit allies and client states around the globe, and inflame Third World conflicts, particularly those conflicts that were seen as weakening the influence and credibility of the other superpower. Because of this, both superpowers failed individually and collectively to resolve Third World conflict during their enmity years. They only tried with apparent success to manage most conflicts and manipulate the major players involved in them to their own advantages. The end of the Cold War, which exposed the internal weaknesses of both superpowers, seems to indicate that no international conflicts are harmless and all serious conflicts have bad, at times disastrous, global consequences in the long-run.

In contrast with crisis management and conflict containment, a conflict-resolution strategy reflects a general conviction that the continuation of the conflict is costly, undesirable, and dangerous. It tries to construct a process to facilitate dialogue between adversaries, while articulating a vision to change the status quo, eliminating the main causes of conflict and the major sources of tension.

Crisis management, as explained, tries usually to end the crisis and restore the status quo, the situation that preceded the escalation of hostilities. Conflict control and containment, on the other hand, tries to preserve the status quo through the continuous manipulation of the major forces that sustain it. Conflict resolution, in contrast, works to change the status quo and alter the conflicting parties' perceptions of it.

Conflict resolution moves to create peace processes and facilitate the establishment and maintenance of peace. Crisis avoidance, crisis management, and conflict containment move usually to prevent or stop war, while sustaining conflict and manipulating its real causes.

John Burton wrote recently that "in the most developed of countries there are increasing gaps between rich and poor, decreasing social incomes, class-ethnic conflicts, street violence, drug and other alienation problems, environmental problems and greater pressure in the maintenance of even existing living standards. These trends cannot continue without major social disruptions."[24] The difficulty of dealing constructively with issues identified by Burton and the reasons for governments' failure to recognize their seriousness have led to increasingly intractable communal conflicts. Today, writes Richard Rubenstein, "the trend toward communal violence transgresses all established theoretical categories. Intergroup warfare appears in industrial, semi-industrial, and agrarian states; in capitalist and communist polities; in imperial centers and in the nations of the periphery."[25]

## MODELS OF MANAGING ETHNIC CONFLICT

Ethnic conflict is primarily a value-related conflict that has socio-cultural as well as political and economic causes: "It is intractable, partly because it is highly conducive to zero-sum outcomes—I win, you lose. It has high symbolic content [that] is not amenable to the manipulation of material benefits that so often constitutes the stuff of modern policy-making."[26] Thus, ethnic conflict does not lend itself easily to the conflict-management strategies described earlier.

The literature on ethnic conflict has identified three models to deal with this type of conflict: the consociational model, the control model, and the shared homeland model.

## The Consociational Model

This model was originally developed by Arend Lijphart based on the Netherlands' political experience, and was called "consociational democracy."[27] It is a power-sharing model that views different cultural groups as partners interested in overcoming their differences to make the system work and therefore willing to negotiate and make compromises. It also assumes that intergroup negotiations are done by the leaders of the groups who have "the ability to avoid the dangers of intergroup conflict through negotiation."[28] Consequently, political settlements that the negotiation or bargaining processes produce tend usually to be different depending on such factors as democratic traditions, the nature of conflict, and level of societal developments and needs. However, all settlements share two things in common: an ability to stabilize the system, and a tendency to weaken or eliminate the principle of majority rule.

Nevertheless, the consociational model assumes the existence of a legitimate leadership to represent each group, that this leadership is aware of the dangers of conflict, and that it is willing to compromise to facilitate intergroup accommodation. However, the experience of many nations does not support these assumptions. For example, under communism, Third World dictatorship, and Zionism, the political elite in power has systematically eliminated the potential group leadership of the other through cooptation, repression, expulsion, and even physical liquidation. Even in Germany, four years after the reunification of the country, the legacy of communism has hindered the emergence of a legitimate and knowledgeable leadership in the eastern part of the country to bargain with the leadership of the western part on behalf of its constituency. And Lebanon has produced traditional group leaderships that control their constituencies rather than honestly represent them, and negotiate with each other in a pattern similar to that of Mafia bargaining. Their sole objective is to enhance their own interests and ensure, through unilateral and collective action, constituency control.

## The Control Model

This model was developed by Ian Lustick based on the experience of the Israeli political system in dealing with Israel's Arab minority.[29] It is a model to achieve political stability by allowing the majority to have near-total control over the minority—a system of majority dictatorship to enhance the interests of the controlling majority at the expense of the controlled minority, reducing it to a position of subordination and submission.[30] To achieve this objective, the controlling majority enacts laws and builds institutions that foster discrimination, while pursuing policies to ensure minority control in the short run and the perpetuation of majority dominance in the long run.

Under such a system of government and socio-economic relations, intergroup relationships become hostile and not conducive to voluntary cooperation. While minorities are kept outside the centers of political power, without the influence and legal means to effect change, the controlling ethnic groups may experience intragroup democracy. In Israel and South Africa, the Jewish majority in the first and the white minority in the latter have enjoyed Western-style democracy for years, but largely denied it to their non-Jewish and non-white constituencies. The democracy both Israel and pre-1994 South Africa have had was described by Israeli professor Avishai Margalit as a "democracy of masters [in which] the masters enjoy all the advantages of democracy, while their servants merely serve."[31]

The control model is not just a system of government that a majority institutes to control a minority. It is also the model most used by almost all authoritarian regimes in the Third World. In some countries, a minority may seize and maintain power for decades, subordinating all other groups to its control. In most other Third World countries, a small political elite or a family has seized and maintained power for decades without much popular legitimacy. Because of their narrow popular base and lack of legitimacy, the controlling elites in general have not adopted or cannot adopt democracy. However, most are able to stay in power and achieve political stability, often at the expense of individual liberty and socio-economic progress. The means of control by which power is seized and maintained by all Third World elites are: the army, the governmental bureaucracy, the secret service, and the media.[32]

Although the control model is inhumane and anti-democratic, it nevertheless may be suitable or even preferable as a temporary measure to deal with ethnic conflict under certain conditions. However, to make it suitable, the power in control should be foreign, should treat all groups equally and should operate under a U.N. mandate. Its purpose would be to control violence and stabilize the political situation, while new political arrangements are envisioned and negotiated to reorganize intergroup relationships. The U.N. troops in Somalia began in 1992 to play this role, which might provide a precedent for outside intervention in certain power struggles and ethnic conflict situations.

### The Shared Homeland Model

This model was originally developed by Mohamed Rabie to deal with the Arab-Israeli conflict.[33] It recognizes the political reality of ethnicity and nationalism and therefore calls for the political separation of groups unwilling or unable to coexist peacefully under one political system. At the same time, it recognizes the economic imperatives of the time and calls for fostering the economic unity of concerned peoples or ethno-national groups, creating shared homelands for all contending groups to jointly enjoy. It is thus a model to separate the political rights of individuals from their other rights, making the first separate but mutual, and the rest shared and equal. This model will be developed in Chapter 9 of this book.

Despite the apparent differences of the three models, all use structural adjustments in the political and legal systems and in the electoral process to change intergroup relationships. The consociational model resorts to such adjustments to create new, more equal group relationships that foster stability and induce voluntary cooperation. The control model employs the adjustments to ensure the dominance of those in power and the continued submission of those denied access to the centers of power. The stability that is produced is one supported by coercion and therefore not conducive to long-term political tranquility or intergroup voluntary cooperation. Finally, the shared homeland model employs the adjustments to meet the most fundamental needs of ethnic groups for political identity and cultural recognition, while meeting their future needs for security and economic progress.

### NOTES

1. A.J.R. Groom, "Paradigms in Conflict," in John Burton and Frank Dukes, eds., *Conflict: Readings in Management and Resolution* (New York: St. Martin's Press, 1990), p. 88.

2. Mohamed Rabie, *The New World Order* (New York: Vantage Press, 1992), pp. 3–13.

3. Doug Bandow, "Avoiding War," *Foreign Policy* (Winter 1992–93): 165.

4. Charles Krauthammer, "Department of Talk," *The Washington Post*, December 25, 1992.

5. Edward Azar, "Protracted International Conflict: Ten Propositions," in John Burton and Frank Dukes, eds., *Conflict: Readings in Management and Resolution* (New York: St. Martin's Press, 1990), p. 149.

6. R. J. Rummel, "Deadlier than War," *IPA Review* (August–October 1989): 24–27.

7. W. Scott Thompson, "Approaches to Peace," in W. Scott Thompson et al., eds., *Approaches to Peace* (Washington, D.C.: United States Institute of Peace, 1991).

8. Karl Kaiser, Cesare Merlini, and Dominique Moisi, "Hurry to Put European Union Back on the Rails," *The International Herald Tribune*, October 29, 1992.

9. Doug Bandow, "Avoiding War," p. 174.

10. Basheer Meibar, *Political Culture, Foreign Policy and Conflict* (Westport, Conn.: Greenwood Press, 1982), pp. 3–4.

11. Morton Deutsch, *The Resolution of Conflict, Constructive and Destructive Processes* (New Haven, Conn.: Yale University Press, 1973).

12. Dennis J. D. Sandole, *The Conflict Prevention Center: Prospects for Cooperative Conflict Resolution in the New Europe*, unpublished paper, March 1992, p. 2.

13. A.J.R. Groom, "Paradigms," p. 87.

14. Stuart J. Thorson, "Conceptual Issues," in Louis Kriesberg, Terrell A. Northrop, and Stuart J. Thorson, eds., *Intractable Conflicts and their Transformation* (Syracuse, N.Y.: Syracuse University Press, 1989), p. 2.

15. Morton Deutsch, "Theoretical Perspective on Conflict and Conflict Resolution," in Dennis J. D. Sandole and Ingrid Sandole-Staroste, eds., *Conflict Management and Problem Solving: Interpersonal to International* (New York: New York University Press, 1987), p. 38.

16. Dennis J. D. Sandole, *Conflict Resolution in the Post-Cold War Era: Dealing with Ethnic Violence in the New Europe* (Institute for Conflict Analysis and Resolution, George Mason University, October 1992), p. 14.

17. John W. Burton, *Conflict: Resolution and Provention* (New York: St. Martin's Press, 1990), p. 233.

18. R. J. Rummel, "Deadlier than War," p. 30.

19. Morton Deutsch, *The Resolution of Conflict*, p. 42.

20. Nazli Choucri, "Analytical and Behavioral Perspectives: Causes of War and Strategies of Peace," in W. Scott Thompson et al., eds., *Approaches to Peace* (Washington, D.C.: United States Institute of Peace, 1991), p. 286.

21. Harold H. Saunders, "Political Settlement and the Gulf Crisis," *Mediterranean Quarterly*, 2, 2 (1992): 4.

22. Richard Rubenstein, "Unanticipated Conflict and the Crisis of Social Theory," in John Burton and Frank Dukes, eds., *Conflict: Readings in Management and Resolution* (New York: St. Martin's Press, 1990), pp. 222–23.

23. Bryant Wedge, "The Individual, the Group and War," in John Burton and Frank Dukes, eds., *Conflict: Readings in Management and Resolution* (New York: St. Martin's Press, 1990), p. 105.

24. John Burton, "Unfinished Business in Conflict Resolution," in John Burton and Frank Dukes, eds., *Conflict: Readings in Management and Resolution* (New York: St. Martin's Press, 1990), p. 334.

25. Richard Rubenstein, "Unanticipated Conflict," p. 321.

26. Donald L. Horowitz, "Ethnic Conflict Management for Policymakers," in Joseph V. Montville, ed., *Conflict and Peacemaking in Multiethnic Societies* (Lexington, Mass.: Lexington Books, 1991), p. 115.

27. Arend Lijphart, *Democracy in Plural Societies* (New Haven, Conn.: Yale University Press, 1977).

28. Kenneth D. McRae, "Theories of Power-sharing and Conflict Management," in Joseph V. Montville, ed., *Conflict and Peacemaking in Multiethnic Societies* (Lexington, Mass.: Lexington Books, 1991), p. 94.

29. Ian Lustick, *Arabs in the Jewish State, Israel's Control of a National Minority* (Austin: Texas University Press, 1980).

30. Donald Horowitz, "Ethnic Conflict," p. 99.

31. Avishai Margalit, "Halfway to Hell," *Yedoit Ahronot*, April 7, 1987. Translated and published in *Israel Press Briefs*, May-June, 1987, p. 16.

32. Mohamed Rabie, *Religious Fundamentalism and the Rise of Political Islam.* Unpublished paper (Washington, D.C.: Center for Educational Development, 1993).

33. Mohamed Rabie, *A Vision for the Transformation of the Middle East* (Washington, D.C.: The Center for Educational Development, 1990). See also Mohamed Rabie, *Conflict Resolution and the Middle East Peace Process* (Hamburg, Germany: Deutsch Orient Institute, 1993), pp. 39–46.

*Chapter Four*

# THE PEACE PROCESS

The concept of peace, as explained in Chapter 1, ought to be regarded and employed as a process to resolve political conflict, reduce social tension and economic disparities, and create new conditions compatible with the ideas of freedom and justice. It is a process to facilitate, through gradual change, the evolution of people's thinking and institutions in ways that foster stability and encourage the nurturing of cooperative, yet dynamic relationships.

Wars and imposed settlements have rarely solved conflicts. Settlement of conflict through force and coercion has often been at the expense of the poor and the weak and future peace as well. Since the Vietnam War, no military force has been able to end conflict and establish peace. From Vietnam and Cambodia to Afghanistan and the Persian Gulf, wars and settlements arranged by superpowers have neither ended human suffering nor restored security or peace to troubled regions. They could only manage crisis and contain conflicts, reducing their intensity, but often increasing their long-term negative consequences.

The experience of both world wars has demonstrated that imposed settlements to end violence do not end conflict. They can only reduce its intensity, force it to become dormant, and delay its resumption. Conflict cannot be resolved unless and until the positions of all concerned parties are accommodated in a manner that is mutually acceptable and workable, which the settlements to end both world wars have failed to do, as demonstrated by the resumption of ethnic conflict in the former Yugoslavia.

The mutual acceptability of solutions is important to ending hostilities, establishing mutual trust and creating new conditions more conducive to cooperation. Unless they are workable, solutions may fall short of promoting positive peace that endures. Solutions, to work and endure, must address causes of conflict fairly, comprehensively, and realistically. They must take into consideration both the past and the future, transforming perceptions and positions from opposition to managed competition and genuine cooperation. They must also reform existing relationships through institutional, structural, and attitudinal change.

Military force and imposed settlements cannot resolve any conflict. However, they may contribute to conflict resolution if used as a last resort and if they are intimately linked and immediately followed by a genuine political process of peacemaking. While wars are more likely to lead to the destruction of what they intend to protect, peace processes are more likely to reunite adversaries around shared interests, to rebuild what enmity and war has destroyed or postponed.

Morton Deutsch differentiates between the "constructive process" and "destructive process" of conflict resolution: "A constructive process of conflict resolution can be identified with a cooperative social process; a destructive process of conflict resolution, on the other hand, typically has the social and psychological characteristics of a competitive process."[1] Based on our definition of conflict-resolution processes that produce positive peace, however, competitive processes produce no real solutions, only the settlements that coercion and power-based negotiations impose.

A peace process is a political framework for conflict resolution intended to conceive and facilitate the implementation of solutions to end hostilities and change the status quo, creating new environments more conducive to cooperation. The very idea of resolving a conflict embodies an idea of where things ought to be, or what the desired outcome of the process is to look like. This in turn implies that concerned parties are in similar states of mind regarding the framework of the process and the general shape of its outcome. For such a state of mind to emerge, parties must acknowledge the grievances of each other and realize that their perceptions of one another must be altered.

The nature of conflict, the balance of power between adversaries, the desire to negotiate, and the regional and international contexts of negotiations are important factors that influence the structure and purpose of all peace processes. Nevertheless, perceptions of time, the nature and objectives of the enemy, and expectations of future developments are of critical importance, particularly in determining the timing and in choosing the approach and therefore the framework of negotiations, which is the core of any peace process. Without a strategic view or a visionary concept to identify the long-term goals of the process and guide it to its intended destination, negotiations would lack clarity of purpose and often political legitimacy as well.

Accordingly, each process includes certain activities that precede and accompany negotiations and continue after negotiations have been successfully concluded. Negotiation is the direct or indirect political interaction between the major adversaries to find a mutually acceptable solution to their common problems.

Theorists and practitioners of conflict resolution tend to have widely differing views regarding most aspects of processes to resolve conflict. Experts like Henry Kissinger advocate the "step-by-step" approach as the most practical and realistic. Others, like Harold Saunders, emphasize the role of "confidence-building" measures and the need for a general concept of where things ought to be at the end of the process. Still others, particularly those who were involved in the U.S.-USSR unofficial dialogue and are currently engaged in the Arab-Israeli dialogue, stress the role of non-governmental organizations in facilitating human interaction through "Track Two" diplomacy.[2] After facilitating several encounters between Soviets and Americans, Palestinians and Israelis, and Russians and citizens from the Baltic states, Saunders coined the phrase "Public Peace Process" to replace "Track Two" diplomacy.[3]

However, most theorists prefer to construct integrative processes that move from one step to the other leading to peace. One such approach calls for a process that starts with de-escalation and proceeds to negotiation, agreements, and finally to sustaining agreements.[4] This and similar approaches start with procedural matters, move to non-substantive issues and then to substantive issues that form the core of conflict, carefully selecting the issues, initial participants, and timing to launch the intended peace process.

Regarding the framework, both theorists and practitioners seem to be divided between those who advocate a general strategy with clear objectives and well-defined contents, and others who prefer a strategy with vaguely defined goals and contents but well-structured procedures. However, both sides tend to maintain that negotiation is the best way to reach and conclude binding agreements and thus arrive at mutually acceptable solutions to conflict.

The first school maintains that a peace process needs a clear purpose to sustain itself because the parties involved require a sense of what lies at the end of the road. Members of the procedure-oriented school, on the other hand, believe that negotiations usually develop a dynamic of their own to keep them alive and lead the parties eventually to agreement. Thus, a carefully structured framework that encourages adversaries to negotiate and includes built-in factors to sustain negotiations is all that really matters, they maintain. They also argue that emphasis on content, particularly when such emphasis gives special attention to sensitive issues, could complicate negotiations and cause their premature termination. The U.S. government, for example, used this argument in structuring the Middle East peace process, which brought Arabs and Israelis together to negotiate peace at the end of 1991. But despite much publicity and the involvement of the United States and Russia as co-sponsors, this process has failed to live up to expectations.

The Middle East peace process, launched at the end of 1991 in Madrid, was able to gain much credence not because of its accomplishments but because of world interest in it and the willingness of many nations to be a part of it. The continuous media coverage of its proceedings helped trans-form the talk about it into a belief in it and in its potential to achieve peace. Because of that, procedures began to replace principles, and self-nurtured dynamics began to obscure the need to clarify and follow the prescribed "frame of reference" that was supposed to govern the process and its out-come.[5] Consequently, the process faltered and was only kept alive by out-side, primarily American, intervention. A much weakened Palestinian movement and an exhausted and confused Israeli society badly in need of an end to the status quo have continued to cling to it, feeling that it was their own option. In August 1993, after twenty-two months of fruitless ne-gotiations in Washington, both parties declared that they had secretly ne-gotiated an agreement in Oslo, Norway. The Oslo agreement was vague, inconclusive, and limited in scope, leaving all important issues to be ne-gotiated at a later date. It was met with opposition on both sides, and could not be implemented according to schedule.

Since the end of World War II, the United States has shown little or no stamina for conflict resolution. It could only engage in crisis man-agement to end or contain imminent international danger that endan-gered its vital interests or threatened its relationship with the other superpower. Domestic political considerations, presidential election cy-cles, and deep involvement in the Cold War and ideological battles have largely denied successive U.S. administrations the time, power, and con-viction to seriously engage in international conflict resolution and peace-making.[6]

However, the United States was at times able to expand its interna-tional activities regarding conflict management to include containment of major regional conflicts to keep them from spreading and exploding. The management of the Arab-Israeli conflict, the Indian-Pakistani con-flict, and the Iran-Iraq war of the 1980s are examples of successful U.S. efforts to manage or contain serious international conflicts. However, it was a management to control and sustain conflicts at a high cost to all parties concerned that lacked the will to develop a concept of peace to end hostilities and transform relationships between the contending par-ties.

## APPROACHES TO CONFLICT RESOLUTION

Strategies to conflict resolution and peace tend generally to adopt one of several approaches to end conflict and establish peace of either a negative or positive nature. They differ in their operational goals and the means to achieve them. Such approaches may be identified as follows:

1. *The control approach.* This approach, which might also be called the "total approach," considers raw power most appropriate in dealing with conflict. It relies primarily on military power to end conflict through a process to defeat the adversary and destroy his power base. Total defeat of the enemy is usually sought to secure domination and foreclose all other options for political compromise. Because of that, this approach may succeed in ending violence but it cannot establish peace. The best that it can do is to force conflict to become dormant, eliminating some of its manifestations and delaying its eventual resumption.

2. *The step-by-step approach.* This approach calls for partial solutions using a step-by-step process to reduce the level of violence and change the dynamics of conflict. It claims that comprehensive solutions are often too ambitious and too complicated and that efforts to pursue them are more likely to fail. It seeks instead practical and realistic arrangements to contain conflict and eliminate some of its most apparent symptoms and emotional causes. Such arrangements, it claims, would work in the short run to freeze conflict at levels that are tolerable, despite the fact that they might not be the most desirable. While making the renewal of hostilities less likely and more costly, they work in the long run to make progress almost inevitable. Parties that might be tempted to abandon the process or renounce the concluded partial agreements would be viewed unfavorably by the world community, making them liable to lose international sympathy and support. As a result, negotiations become the only option open to the parties, and partial solutions the only way to sustain negotiations and continue the de-escalation process leading to final settlement.

3. *The comprehensive approach.* This approach seeks comprehensive settlements to conflict on the basis of political compromise. A compromise settlement is a solution that asks each adversary to accept less than it had desired and to allow its adversary to get a little more than it had wished, while convincing both parties that compromise is a precondition for ending conflict. Because of its nature and objectives, this approach has been called the "distributive approach," in which benefits and sacrifices are shared. Distributive approaches are more likely to end conflicts that are interest-related, but less suitable to addressing conflicts that are value-related.

4. *The integrative approach.* This approach calls for integrating the interests of adversaries through solutions that meet their mutual needs

without having to sacrifice their basic demands. Such goals may also be accomplished through the building of new cooperative relationships that facilitate the fulfillment of seemingly contradictory goals. Integrative approaches are more suitable for conflicts that are value-related because of their ability to envision new arrangements to integrate the interests of the conflicting parties without undermining their values.

5. *The democratic approach.* This approach, which has lately been gaining more recognition, seeks to resolve certain conflicts, primarily internal ones centered around political power, through the introduction of political democracy. According to this approach, people are given the opportunity to choose their leaders through the ballot box, and adversaries, winners and losers alike, save face. They may even claim victory because of their role in supporting a process to empower the masses.

6. *The shared homeland approach.* This is a new paragraph that will be articulated in Chapter 9 of this book. It seeks to integrate the needs of adversaries and create new relationships to maximize their long-term benefits. It combines a process to address group psychological and political grievances that are causing conflict and provides a vision to build realistic and futuristic frameworks for economic cooperation and collective security arrangements that make long-term stability and peace a shared objective.

The control approach relies on violence and war to deal with conflict. It rejects political compromise and seeks complete domination or total elimination of the adversary. Colonial powers and totalitarian and authoritarian regimes have all resorted to violence and military force to inflict defeat on enemies that dared to challenge them. The control approach has used suppression, imprisonment, and torture to silence political opposition and eliminate dissent. This approach leads to enabling the winner to take all that is there to be taken, and force the loser to lose all that is there to be lost. Since neither victory nor defeat is ever total, grievances are destined to resurface, and conflict is destined to erupt anew.[7]

In the conflict in Bosnia-Herzegovina, the Serbs have opted for a solution employing the much-hated concept of "ethnic cleansing" to drive out or liquidate Muslims who lived in territories the Serbs consider their own. In the process, writes Stephen S. Rosenfeld, "The Serbs are not only inflicting death and misery on others and heavy costs on themselves, they are sowing vengeance and instability on a scale that will plague their national life indefinitely."[8] This means that winners in the short run might be big losers in the long run, making the control approach a means to suppress conflict that increases rather than decreases the suffering of all parties concerned. The time when winners using this approach were able to get away with group murder and genocide is over. Even in the absence of military retaliation by the world community, economic and cultural sanctions are making the price paid by winners intolerable and long-lasting.

After conflict is ended and a winner emerges unchallenged, winners usually move to deal with the aftermath of conflict through a process of either total domination or gradual reconciliation. The first seeks to ensure continued suppression of the adversary, the latter seeks to pacify him. A control approach that is followed by measures to further secure and perpetuate dominance is not a legitimate approach to peace. However, an approach followed by measures to initiate a reconciliation process that leads to integrating all conflicting parties may be an approach to peace.

Domination is a process to reconstruct or modify existing relationships to enable winners to perpetuate control over losers and deny them the opportunity to gain rights to which they are entitled. Examples of domination are to be found in pre-1994 South Africa, where whites still dominated blacks; in Palestine, where the Israelis continue to dominate the Palestinians; in Romania, where a nationalistic majority dominates and discriminates against the Hungarian, German and Gypsy minorities; and in most Third World countries, where democracy is lacking and power is controlled by a dictator or a small elite.

Reconciliation is a process to allay the fears of the defeated adversary and to largely pacify the losers. It is a process to build new relationships that recognize the basic interests of losers and seek their gradual integration into the political and economic systems. In certain cases, reconciliation cannot be achieved except through the adoption of political democracy as a new political and value system to remold the political ideas and social ideals of both winners and losers. Examples of this approach are to be found in the aftermath of the civil wars in Nigeria and Zimbabwe, and in U.S. dealings with its German and Japanese enemies after the end of World War II.[9]

In the cases of Nigeria's civil war in the 1960s and the black population's struggle against apartheid in Zimbabwe, the winners in both cases adopted a policy of reconciliation and integration based on fair and reasonable representation and equal rights. In the Nigerian case, a new federalist system was constructed and more powers were given to states in dealing with all matters that affected the daily life of the people.[10]

After the end of World War II, the United States moved quickly to adopt a policy toward its former enemies that combined domination and reconciliation. On the one hand, it imposed on the Germans and Japanese settlements that denied both states the opportunity to rebuild their armed forces, while forcing them to accept military occupations and new constitutions that strengthened democracy. In Germany, the new constitution sought also to weaken the powers of the central government. On the other hand, the United States conceived and implemented economic, political, and security programs to integrate the German and Japanese security and economic systems into the Western military alliance and the world capitalist system.

Domination, though workable in the short run, is neither fair nor lasting in the long run. It works not to address the real causes of conflict and bring peace closer to reality but to control conflict and suppress its causes. Consequently, when circumstances change, conflict usually erupts again, causing great damage to the interests of winners and losers alike. In contrast, reconciliation has proved to be both successful and humane, restoring stability and building new mutually beneficial relationships that have generally fostered peaceful coexistence and encouraged cooperation.

The step-by-step approach is closest to the total approach, which seeks domination of adversaries and control over conflict. It is an approach based on Realpolitik that uses power to reduce the level of conflict through partial solutions that create stalemates, making the renewal of hostilities more difficult. Partial solutions usually ask or compel the weaker party to make the most concessions needed to conclude agreements and thus tend to reward the stronger party or the aggressor at the expense of the weaker one. Partial solutions enable the strong to make concrete gains and force the weak to accept partial defeat. They thus acknowledge, though discretely and indirectly, a change in the latter's status from contender to loser. This outcome is usually the result of a balance of power that places the stronger party in a position to exploit the need of the weaker one for a settlement to end conflict through political compromise.

The step-by-step approach, therefore, is a political process that largely seeks to institutionalize and legitimize the outcome of conflicts that produce clear but not total winners and losers. It gives little consideration to matters of fairness and justice and does not seek to establish mutually acceptable and workable relationships. Such a process, no matter how successful it may be in the short run, is unlikely to end conflict and promote peace in the long run. The Egyptian-Israeli peace treaty of 1979 ended their conflict but failed to resolve the wider Arab-Israeli conflict, causing Israeli-Palestinian, Israeli-Syrian, Lebanese and Iraqi enmity to increase and mainfest itself in renewed hostilities.

The distributive approach is based on the premise that no claims made by adversaries are totally legitimate or illegitimate, and that political compromise is the most feasible solution to conflict. To reach compromise, advocates of this approach support the idea of negotiation, which they consider most suitable for concluding mutually acceptable and binding agreements. They also value the role of third-party mediators who act as initiators and facilitators of negotiations. In the context of Western culture, where most conflicts are interest-related, compromise has proven its practicality and workability in resolving most conflicts and restoring stability to troubled relationships.

However, when the conflict is over values, not interests, compromise seldom works because values tend to be non-negotiable; and what is non-negotiable does not lend itself to compromise. Even where conflict is over interests, the idea of compromise does not always encourage people to negotiate, knowing in advance that a solution demands some sacrifice. Certain cultures, particularly traditional and non-Western cultures like Islam, view the notion of compromise in negative terms. To such cultures, compromise means more an abandonment of principles and less an acknowledgment of reality that includes a recognition of the legitimate claims of the adversary.

When the conflict is over interests and between peoples or states of similar cultural backgrounds that view the idea of compromise in positive terms, the distributive approach is of great help in resolving conflict. But when the conflict concerns values and is between peoples or states that view the idea of compromise in negative terms, the distributive approach is of little or no help at all in resolving conflict. Edward Azar has stated, "Human needs and long-standing cultural values will not be traded, exchanged or bargained over. They are not subject to negotiations."[11] They must be acknowledged and accommodated if conflict is to be permanently resolved.

The integrative approach seeks alternative options to dealing with conflicts that are capable of integrating the basic needs and interests of adversaries. It is an approach that relies heavily on innovation and believes in the necessity of building mutually beneficial relationships to tie adversaries together. It thus "seeks to help overcome the dilemma that often arises when parties are forced, through distributive techniques, into concessions" that might not satisfy them for long.[12]

This approach, though quite well developed technically and practically in the field of business relations, is still little known in the international arena.[13] This is probably due to its inability to prescribe the kind of options and integrative relationships to deal with international conflict, particularly value-related conflicts. It is hard for this approach to resolve value-related conflicts, particularly ethnic ones, because the values of adversaries tend usually to negate each other, not to complement or even be neutral toward each other. Nonetheless, it is an approach that encourages adversaries to look forward and seek future advantages through cooperative relationships, not only retribution though punitive measures.

The control and step-by-step approaches produce winners and losers; the distributive approach produces no winners and no losers. In contrast, the integrative approach tries to produce only winners and no losers.

The democratic approach calls for the adoption of democracy as a political system and a social value to deal with conflict. Advocates of this approach claim that democracies are less likely to resort to the use of force to resolve conflict, particularly against other democracies. They also claim that democratic societies are more likely to accept compromises and resolve their differences peacefully.[14]

Although research has proven that such claims are inaccurate, democracy has nevertheless been helpful in resolving conflicts caused by power struggles. Elections, which are the essence of political democracy, have been used repeatedly to manage the transition from civil war to peace in countries such as Nicaragua, Cambodia, El Salvador, and Angola. Robert L. Rothstein, however, says, "Democracy is hardly a panacea and it will not by itself either resolve profound domestic problems or necessarily generate an international order that is more peaceful or prosperous."[15]

Governments, past and present, have either ruled by force and coercion or by political legitimacy fostered by popular support. Democracy is a political system and a social ideal that often allows societies to elect governments that represent the people and protect their interests, while providing for the peaceful resolution of political and non-political conflicts.[16] Despite the apparent shortcomings of democracy in several countries, it remains largely superior to all other political systems, particularly in regard to human rights, accountability, economic efficiency, and ability to mitigate power struggles and avoid civil war.

Democracy, while helpful in dealing with domestic conflict and civil wars caused by power struggles, is rather unhelpful when dealing with a domestic conflict caused by ethnic disputes. In such cases, democracy is most likely to lead to concentrating power in the hands of the majority, often leaving minorities with no power or adequate representation in government. In certain cases, it might lead to majority dictatorships that violate the spirit and true values of democracy itself. John Burton wrote recently that "democracy, meaning majority government, is proving to be most undemocratic in multi-ethnic societies. It is also proving to be corrupt when pressure groups exert a greater influence than does the electorate."[17]

The shared homeland approach calls for the separation of interest-related issues from the value-related ones that cause conflict. In ethnic-related conflicts, interests and values work together in a complementary way to cause and sustain intergroup conflict. It is an approach that seeks to separate the value-related political and cultural rights of conflicting parties while integrating their economic and security interests. It proposes to do this by granting antagonists the right to separate along ethnic lines, while tying them together by new economic and security arrangements across political lines. This approach is most suitable when dealing with ethnic conflict and resolving problems related to minority rights. The shared homeland idea was initially developed by the author in 1989 and was subsequently published in several countries.[18]

The above approaches to conflict resolution fall under the two general categories of competitive and cooperative approaches. The total approach, and to some extent the step-by-step approach, use violence and coercion to settle conflict and therefore fall under the competitive category. The other approaches seek solutions through the use of political tools that call for dialogue and negotiation and therefore fall under the cooperative approach.

## PHASES OF THE PEACE PROCESS

Peace processes dealing with international and ethnic conflict have generally three phases but four components. The phases are the initiation of the process, the negotiation to conceive and conclude agreements, and the implementation of agreements. These three phases also constitute three of the four components of each peace process, with mediation being the fourth component. While it is theoretically possible to separate the first three components or phases and identify the start and the end of each one, mediation is the component that generally ties all other components together, integrating them into one peace process.

The first phase of the peace process is the initiation phase, or the political dialogue phase. It is the phase through which communication is established and political dialogue is conducted to persuade adversaries to talk to each other and explain their differences. During this phase the structure and objectives of the peace process are explained and completed, and preparations for negotiations are finalized. It is often called the "pre-negotiation" phase and usually sets the tone for the phase to follow. Understandings reached or frameworks imposed to govern the subsequent phase are more likely to determine the fate and outcome of negotiation.

The second phase is negotiation to conceive and conclude agreements to settle conflict. During this phase, antagonists deal with substantive matters that cause conflict and hinder peace with a view to reaching mutually acceptable agreements that provide for building new, more cooperative relationships. Negotiations are likely to be conducted directly, but they could also be carried out indirectly and secretly.

The third phase is the implementation of agreements. During this phase, attention is focused on creating conditions to end hostilities and build new relationships among adversaries more conducive to peaceful coexistence and long-term cooperation. In regard to today's conflict, implementation has become a complicated and costly process, often requiring massive international support in the form of peacekeeping or even peace-making military intervention.

Mediation, however, is in itself a political process that is more likely to accompany all phases of the peace process, tying them together and integrating their functions to conceive, conclude, and implement agreements. It usually begins before other phases are launched and continues after they are concluded.

In international conflict resolution, great emphasis is placed on negotiation to conclude mutually acceptable agreements to resolve conflict and thus avoid outside imposed settlements that rarely work. Negotiation, says David Newsom, "is not the core of the problem but the final stage in a process that involves profound understanding of other cultures, sensitivity to the internal politics of one's own country as well as those of others, and a judgment of the relative effectiveness of unilateral and multilateral intervention."[19] In other words, conflict resolution requires well-structured peace processes that include negotiation as well as political dialogue and mediation.

Peace processes are not easy to initiate and sustain, but they represent the best hope for resolving conflict, restoring stability, and achieving peace. Since conflicts are different in their causes and intensity, peace processes have also to be different regarding the focus, timing, and methods. While flexibility is necessary to minimize chances of failure, clarity of purpose is a precondition for launching peace processes and maximizing the chances of success.

During the Cold War, the management of international and ethnic conflicts was rather easy; most conflicts were suppressed and the grievances of the weak repressed. Strategic considerations dominated great-power relations, particularly superpower relations, allowing many states, elites, and ethnic groups to violate the rights of others and escape punishment. Some violators were even rewarded for oppressing and humiliating others. For example, "countries with oppressive human rights records were shielded from pressure if their government was aligned with one or the other superpower."[20] Conflicts were seldom resolved but often managed; aspirations of oppressed minorities were seldom addressed but often suppressed; and peace processes were seldom launched and almost always failed.

The end of the Cold War ended bipolarity in international relations and paved the way for the emergence of a new world order governed by a multipolar system. While the old system was dominated by geopolitical considerations, specifically military-security matters, the new system is gradually shifting toward economic and financial matters, with political influence dispersed among several powers led by the United States, the European Union, China, and Japan.[21]

The dispersal of political influence seems to imply also the dispersal of responsibilities for managing the new world order and international conflict. Because the major Western powers, in the absence of the Soviet threat, are having difficulty agreeing on issues related to economic policy and international conflict management, the new world order is slowly emerging in forms that manifest more disorder than order. World powers with proven ability to intervene in international and ethnic conflict situations are increasingly becoming reluctant to commit the resources and prestige required to manage conflict on their own and are at the same time too constrained by competing global interests to find workable formulas for collective action.

International organizations with intervention capabilities such as the United Nations and NATO are nothing more than clubs of states that cannot act without the consent of their members. Their members exhibit reluctance, constraint, and confusion. For example, as Yugoslavia began to collapse, "the United States government stood by like a spectator while casualties mounted and evidence of atrocities accumulated."[22] Other nations, particularly members of the European Union, were unable to agree on a unified, effective policy to intervene and stop the killing, making the union look helplessly divided, selfishly short-sighted and conscienceless.

Former British Prime Minister Margaret Thatcher used harsh words to criticize the West for not acting forcefully to stop the atrocities in Bosnia, accusing Europe of having lost its conscience. In fact, Europe may not have lost only its conscience; it may have also lost an opportunity to construct a framework to define collective security and develop an effective mechanism to defend it.[23]

Swedish Prime Minister Carl Bildt was also quoted saying that the crisis in the Balkans represents a "Western intellectual crisis and a massive failure of Western policy."[24] He added that "the West is much poorly equipped to deal with situations such as Bosnia and Somalia in a global media age in which even the remotest desert town can suddenly become the center of the world."[25] In 1994 NATO threatened to use air power to silence the Serb guns which devastated Sarajevo, creating new conditions for renewing peace-making efforts.

Moreover, "the gulf between American and European geopolitical interests is likely to widen as some issues that worry the Europeans, like the civil war in the former Yugoslavia, have no discernible impact on the United States."[26] It has thus become less likely that consensus on many issues in the absence of the Soviet threat would emerge. Neither NATO nor any other regional alliance has the power and authority to become the new vehicle for collective security.

In addition, the proliferation of advanced conventional weapons, missile technology, and chemical and biological warfare has given several regional powers more latitude to pursue their own interests. This in turn has narrowed the political options and increased the military risks of great-power intervention.[27] Edward Azar reported that conflict situations he examined between 1979 and 1984 indicated that "elites and their leaders show a serious contempt for international and regional arenas. They see these arenas as mere opportunities for scoring points with their own domestic constituencies."[28] The absence of active great-power intervention is more likely to encourage rather than discourage regional actors to disregard international public opinion in favor of satisfying domestic social or political needs, as the leaders of Serbia and Iraq have demonstrated.

Nevertheless, the great powers shoulder a particular responsibility to intervene to manage conflict and foster peace because of their power to influence global change and state behavior on the one hand and their need to protect global interests on the other. "America," wrote Roger Morris, "cannot simply deal with domestic needs and then later turn to the world's anguish. Either we Americans begin anew to heal both, or it may well not matter for our grandchildren if we make ourselves prosperous."[29] Even making themselves prosperous is no longer an option that Americans can pursue alone. All nations' economic interests have become inextricably linked in so many ways that their separation has become impossible and harmful.

Global developments, domestic considerations, and historical experiences have made effective great-power cooperation to manage international conflict more difficult than before. Meanwhile, certain ethnic conflicts have become hard to manage, let alone resolve, because they tend to exhibit irrational behavior and lack precedents to guide peace processes to resolve them. "Abnormal psychology is a subject statesmen will have to master in the new disorderly world," says Jim Hoagland.[30] International and ethnic conflict in the post-Cold War era has created an urgent need for new ways of thinking, organizing, and acting at all levels. To deal with international and ethnic conflict more justly, realistically, and futuristically, we need:

1. To strengthen and invigorate the United Nations and other international organizations, giving them more authority and freedom to mediate conflicts and act as a force of peacekeeping and peace making.

2. To rely more on peace processes that have clear purposes and are backed by the international community, specifically the United Nations and the great powers, using both positive and negative incentives to encourage antagonists to negotiate in good faith and make the compromises necessary to resolve conflict.

3. To envision new ways to negotiate and build new models to resolve conflict

that respond to the imperatives of the time without ignoring the historical dynamics at work.

4. To encourage the development of a global civil society based on the principles of democracy, respect for human rights, and the right of self-determination, not only for states but for ethnic and national groups as well.

5. To declare a strong and honest international commitment to helping the poor nations and to narrowing the disparity between social classes, states, and regions of the world.

Peace as a higher human goal demands a stronger international commitment to ending conflict. Peace and conflict have become two interlinked states of mind and political affairs that affect the lives of all peoples and states. Because of that, peace can solely rely neither on the past nor on national historical experiences. In dealing with international and ethnic conflict, it is important to gain a proper historical perspective of the causes and dynamics of conflict, but it is more important to gain a realistic and futuristic perspective of human change and socioeconomic development. Otherwise, solutions that might be found to address grievances in the short run could very easily fail to meet the post-conflict human needs in the long run. Solutions that are not realistic and futuristic will certainly fail the test of time.

## NOTES

1. Morton Deutsch, "Theoretical Perspective on Conflict and Conflict Resolution," in Dennis J. D. Sandole and Ingrid Sandole-Staroste, eds., *Conflict Management and Problem Solving: Interpersonal to International* (New York: New York University Press, 1987), p. 42.

2. Joseph V. Montville, "Transnationalism and the Role of Track-two Diplomacy," in W. Scott Thompson et al., eds., *Approaches to Peace* (Washington, D.C.: United States Institute of Peace, 1991), pp. 255–71.

3. Gennady I. Chufrin and Harold H. Saunders, "A Public Peace Process," unpublished paper, April 1993, p. 2.

4. Louis Kriesberg, *International Conflict Resolution, The U.S.-USSR and the Middle East Cases* (New Haven, Conn.: Yale University Press, 1992), pp. 3–15.

5. Mohamed Rabie, *Conflict Resolution and the Middle East Peace Process* (Hamburg, Germany: Deutsches Orient Institut, 1993), pp. 39–44.

6. William B. Quandt, *Camp David, Peacemaking and Politics* (Washington, D.C.: The Brookings Institution, 1986), p. 8. Also see by the same author, *The Middle East Ten Years After Camp David* (Washington, D.C.: The Brookings Institution, 1989), pp. 357–86.

7. Louis Kriesberg, "International Conflict Resolution," p. 3.

8. Stephen S. Rosenfeld, "Saving Lives in a Fatally Scrambled Land," *The International Herald Tribune*, November 17–18, 1992.

9. Donald L. Horowitz, "Ethnic Conflict Management for Policymakers," in Joseph V. Montville, ed., *Conflict and Peacemaking in Multiethnic Societies* (Lexing-

ton, Mass.: Lexington Books, 1991), provides a good explanation of the reconciliation process in Nigeria and its positive contribution to political stability and ethnic peaceful coexistence on pages 120–41.

10. Hugh Miall, "Peaceful Settlement of Post 1945 Conflicts, A Comparative Study: The United States Institute of Peace's Conference on Conflict Resolution in the Third World," unpublished paper (Washington, D.C., 1990), pp. 3–7.

11. Edward Azar, "Protracted International Conflicts: Ten Propositions" in John Burton and Frank Dukes, eds., *Conflict: Readings in Management and Resolutions* (New York: St. Martin's Press, 1990), p. 147.

12. Rothman, Jay, *A Pre-Negotiation Model: Theory and Training*, Policy Studies No. 40 (Jerusalem: Leonard Davis Institute for International Relations, Hebrew University of Jerusalem, 1990), p. 11.

13. Ibid., p. 10.

14. R. J. Rummel, "Political Systems, Violence and War," in W. Scott Thompson et al., eds., *Approaches to Peace* (Washington, D.C.: United States Institute of Peace, 1991), pp. 350–65. See also by the same author, "Deadlier than War," *Institute of Public Affairs Review*, 41, 2 (August–October 1987).

15. Robert L. Rothstein, "Weak Democracy and the Prospects for Peace and Democracy in the Third World," *Proceedings of the United States Institute of Peace Conference on Conflict Resolution in the Third World* (Washington, D.C., October 1990), p. 3.

16. Robert J. Samuelson, "The Luckiest Accident," *The Washington Post*, January 7, 1993.

17. John Burton, Introduction to John Burton and Frank Dukes, eds., *Conflict: Readings in Management and Resolution* (New York: St. Martin's Press, 1990), p. 10.

18. Mohamed Rabie, *A Vision for the Transformation of the Middle East* (Washington, D.C.: Center for Educational Development, 1990). See also by the same author, *The New World Order* (New York: Vantage Press, 1992), pp. 168–86; *Conflict Resolution and the Middle East Peace Process* (Hamburg, Germany: Deutsches Orient Institut, 1993), pp. 39–44; "A Vision for the Transformation of the Middle East," *American Arab Affairs* (Spring 1991): 73–86; "A Vision for the Transformation of the Middle East," *Vierteljahres berichte, 123* (March 1991): 39–50; "Arab-Israeli Peace: A Vision for the Transformation of the Middle East," in *Asien, Afrika, Latin-Amerika* (Berlin, Germany: Akademie Verlag, 1991), pp. 705–16. The peace model was also published in Austria, Egypt, Israel, and the former Czechoslovakia.

19. David Newsom, "Diplomacy and Negotiation," in W. Scott Thompson et al., eds., *Approaches to Peace* (Washington, D.C.: United States Institute of Peace, 1991), p. 39.

20. Richard Falk, "New Dimensions in International Relations and the Infancy of Global Civil Society," paper presented at the 90th Anniversary Nobel Jubilee Symposium, in Oslo, Norway, December 6–8, 1991.

21. Richard Falk, "In Search of a New World Model," *Current History* (April 1993): 145–49.

22. Ibid., p. 147.

23. Margaret Thatcher's criticism was first reported by news services and most newspapers in the United States on April 14, 1993.

24. Don Oberdorfer, "Eagelburger's Last Lap: All Eyes Still Look to America," *The Washington Post*, December 20, 1992.

25. Ibid.

26. Doug Bandow, "Avoiding War," *Foreign Policy* (Winter 1992–93): 168–69.

27. Myers S. McDougal, "Law and Peace," in W. Scott Thompson et al., eds., *Approaches to Peace* (Washington, D.C.: United States Institute of Peace, 1991), pp. 131–66.

28. Edward Azar, "Protracted International Conflict," p. 150.

29. Roger Morris, "New Era, New Foreign Policy, New Practitioners," *The International Herald Tribune*, December 11, 1992.

30. Jim Hoagland, "Force of the Irrational," *The Washington Post*, May 10, 1993.

*Chapter Five*

# POLITICAL DIALOGUE

Processes to settle conflict and end hostilities are complicated tasks that require hard work, perseverance, and much preparation. All approaches to conflict resolution, with the exception of the total approach, view negotiations as the best method to conceive and conclude mutually acceptable and binding agreements. But negotiations as a political process are difficult to initiate and sustain. Experts in conflict resolution tend generally to think that the success of negotiations depends to a great extent on the phase that precedes negotiations. This is the phase during which antagonists agree to negotiate and issues of procedure and structure are discussed and finalized. Henry Kissinger once called the preparations for negotiations as important as what is negotiated in any peace process.[1]

The term most often used to identify this phase is "pre-negotiation," although Louis Kriesberg prefers to calls it "de-escalation."[2] In view of the functions and objectives of this phase, neither term seems adequate. As a result, this phase will be called "political dialogue," and a brief explanation will be provided to justify calling it as such.

"Pre-negotiation" is a term that implies that this phase is different and separate from the phase to follow, and that at the end of it negotiations will start. This in turn implies that pre-negotiation is a set of acts and moves to prepare the stage for negotiations. Janice Grossman writes that pre-negotiation begins "when one or more parties consider negotiations as a policy option and communicates this intention to other parties. It ends when the parties agree to formal negotiations or one party abandons the consideration of negotiations as an option."[3]

In almost all cases, this phase of the peace process involves activities

to persuade adversaries to negotiate, and thus it starts before negotiations are considered a policy option. It also includes efforts to arrange
or construct a suitable framework within which to conduct negotiations,
not merely getting all parties to agree to negotiate. As a result, it does
not begin when one or more parties considers negotiations as a policy
option but includes work to persuade them to do so and help to shape
the process of negotiations itself. From a technical viewpoint, "pre-
negotiation" does not end when one or more parties abandons negotiations as an option, because if negotiations do not follow, what precedes
could not be called pre-negotiation.

This simply means that the term "pre-negotiation" does not accurately
describe the nature and objectives of efforts to initiate negotiations. It
describes only the arrangements to prepare the stage for negotiations
after an agreement is reached to negotiate. If such an agreement is not
in place, nothing could be attributed to something that does not exist.
The term "pre-negotiation" thus falls short of describing the nature and
complexity of efforts and activities to make negotiations a policy option
and integrate them into a political process to deal with conflict.

"De-escalation," however, is a term that seems even less suitable than
pre-negotiation to describe the nature and objectives of activities that
often precede negotiations. It implies a process to contain a conflict that
has reached the crisis level or a serious stage; it defines neither the intention nor the nature of efforts to set the stage for negotiation. As a
result, "de-escalation" as a technical term fails to give real meaning to
the type of activities that usually precede negotiations, prepare for them
and make them an option to deal with conflict. The term fails to imply
any connection to negotiations, the phase that may follow and be made
feasible by the actions of "de-escalation." In addition, if de-escalation
efforts were to succeed, they could reduce the intensity of the conflict to
a non-threatening level, causing antagonists to temporarily abandon the
search for a solution to end conflict, and thus consider negotiations as a
policy option.

Therefore, it is clear that both "pre-negotiation" and "de-escalation"
do not properly describe the kind of activities that precede negotiations
and, most important, make negotiations both a policy option and a tool
to advance the peace process. In addition, the proponents of both terms
tend to include in this phase certain activities and decisions that cannot
be carried out without the active involvement of the adversaries themselves, a few of which are an integral part of negotiation itself. As a
result, there is a need to identify a different term to properly describe
the nature of activities to initiate a peace process and prepare for negotiations.

The term that seems most appropriate to us is "political dialogue,"
which describes all activities and arrangements to persuade adversaries

to negotiate, prepare for negotiations, and help construct a potentially successful process to settle conflict peacefully. It is a term that can and usually does eliminate the need to artificially separate the negotiations phase from the activities that precede it, prepare for it, and are likely to accompany it to enhance its chances of success. In addition, "political dialogue" reflects the nature of the private and public interaction involving adversaries before the start of negotiations, as well as informal interaction during negotiations and possibly after their conclusion to build trust and facilitate implementation.

## POLITICAL DIALOGUE AND PRE-NEGOTIATION

Calling for a "larger theory of negotiations," Harold Saunders has emphasized the role of the pre-negotiation phase. He argues for a larger theory of negotiation that includes three pre-negotiation stages: defining the problem, developing a commitment to negotiate, and arranging the negotiations.[4]

Antagonists may develop a commitment to negotiate without outside intervention based on their convictions that the conflict needs to be resolved and that no unilateral solutions are feasible. But it is doubtful that antagonists could, acting unilaterally, define the problem that ties them together in terms that establish new or foster existing channels of communications, particularly when issues of conflict are more value- than interest-related. Thus, outside intervention often becomes necessary to define common issues of contention and to facilitate communication. Arranging for negotiations is also a difficult function to perform without outside help, particularly when negotiations involve the recognition of one party's ethnic identity or political and national rights as a precondition.

Jay Rothman defines this pre-negotiation phase as "an integrated process in which highly placed representatives of parties in conflict prepare for negotiations by jointly framing the issues of conflict generating various options for handling them cooperatively, and interactively structuring substance and process of future negotiation."[5] It is clearly a definition that sees pre-negotiation as a process but does not recognize the complexity of the tasks it is asked to perform. It also underestimates the sensitivity of issues that prevent joint framing of issues of conflict and hinder cooperation to generate options and structure both the substance and process of future negotiations.

As a process, pre-negotiation is often hard to initiate without outside help, which only a third party possessing certain qualities could launch. Because many issues of conflict preclude cooperation between antagonists, indirect and unofficial dialogue is often needed first to encourage antagonists to interact and subsequently define their shared problem in mutually acceptable terms, develop a commitment to negotiate, and arrange for future negotiations. Arrangements for negotiations that maximize the chances of success must include a definition of the larger objective sought, an explanation of the structure of the process and its rules of engagement, an identification of issues to be negotiated, and, at times, a time frame for completing negotiations as well.

It is evident, therefore, that the magnitude and nature of tasks to be performed before negotiations can start often require the antagonists' direct or indirect engagement into political dialogue, leading to a mutual understanding regarding the objective, substance, and procedure of negotiations. It is an engagement into a sustained process to identify shared problems and objectives, define issues of mutual concern, change perceptions that cause conflict, and equip antagonists with a framework and a common language to communicate. Anthony de Reuck has stated that "the aim must be to help the parties to redefine their situations so that they both perceive it as a shared predicament to be solved jointly, and to equip them with a common language to create for themselves a common universe of discourse in order to cooperate."[6]

Political dialogue activities in general have the express purpose of bringing together representatives of conflicting parties to directly or indirectly work jointly to explore new ways to narrow the gaps and reduce the contentious issues that separate them, while preparing for negotiations to resolve conflict. It is a process of human and political interaction between antagonists seeking an explanation to mutual fears and fair solutions to shared problems.

In July 1991, while moderating an Israeli-Palestinian meeting sponsored by the Foundation for Global Community and the Stanford Center on Conflict and Negotiation, Harold Saunders voiced for the first time the concept of a "public peace process" to describe the nature of activities involved. He later defined the new concept as being a "sustained action by citizens outside government to change the fundamental relationship between groups in conflict."[7] He added that the process "centers on bringing together in systematic dialogue—not negotiation—individuals from conflicting groups to probe the dynamics of their conflictual relationship, to think together about obstacles to changing it, and to design a sequence of interactive steps that might remove those obstacles."[8] Because decisions to implement steps to remove obstacles and resolve conflict cannot be taken by individuals, the so-called "public peace process" cannot produce peace. Peace making in fact is a highly sensitive and complicated matter that lies outside the public's domain and strictly within the domain of governments. Consequently, the concept of the public peace process could be misleading, giving the wrong impression that a private dialogue is a potential substitute for official negotiations and structured peace processes.

A peace process, of which political dialogue is a component, starts usually before negotiations, works to define the nature and course of negotiations, and proceeds beyond negotiations to build mutual trust, help achieve real peace, and change antagonists' perceptions of each other. Political dialogue, as a phase in a peace process, works to create an environment conducive to negotiations, involves activities to sustain negotiations, and provides guarantees to facilitate mutually acceptable and binding agreements.

A peace process may be short or long, lasting from a few weeks to several years. For a political process to qualify as a peace process, it has to have well-defined objectives and involve credible participants committed to peace. Political dialogue is the first, and perhaps the most important, component of that process; it is the component that makes it possible and viable. Because of its informal, largely unstructured nature, it tends to be flexible regarding most issues to discuss, procedures to construct, and frameworks within which to conduct negotiations. Its flexibility includes issues of timing, procedure, substance, and whom to involve in negotiations and at which stage of the peace process.

While "pre-negotiation" and "de-escalation" tend to emphasize timing in determining when that phase and the phase of negotiations should start, political dialogue may start at any time, in any place, and by any party possessing certain qualities to initiate a peace process. For political dialogue, timing is not an issue because dialogue between antagonists may change pace and focus, but never stops. It only becomes more active and focused when a consensus emerges among antagonists that view conflict as a shared problem to be resolved jointly. Such a process usually starts by creating an environment conducive to negotiations, accelerating when adversaries show more willingness to compromise, and slowing down when emotions prevent progress from being made. With political dialogue as a component, the peace process acquires flexibility to work with issues that appear more promising than others and with parties that express more willingness to cooperate without losing sight of the larger picture. It can also change focus when faced with serious obstacles, without giving up entirely or abandoning the search for peace.

A viable and focused political dialogue process is one that strives to achieve certain objectives to create a real peace process and prepare for sustainable negotiations. These objectives are:

1. To help or persuade antagonists to articulate their objectives and grievances in terms that lend themselves to political compromise, while helping antagonists believe in peaceful coexistence.
2. To help antagonists develop and accept a shared goal to be further defined and mutually adopted through negotiations.
3. To persuade antagonists to agree upon a framework to guide negotiations and

govern its ultimate outcome. Such a framework, as will be explained later, may be a frame of reference that has legal status, a set of general principles agreed upon by the adversaries, a precedent solution to a similar conflict to be emulated, or a proposed settlement that adversaries accept in principle as a basis for negotiations.

4. To persuade all major parties to acknowledge the grievances of their adversaries and thus to totally or partially legitimize their demands.

Conflicts that are ethnic in nature and emanate from a deep sense of injustice and a strong desire for recognition, demand more from political dialogue than the above. They also demand:

5. Mutual recognition that injustices were committed in the past and that it is in the interests of all to end all forms of injustice.

6. Acceptance of moral responsibility for past injustices by the party or parties most responsible.

7. Mutual acceptance of the other's basic demands for recognition, economic equality, or social justice.

8. Mutual recognition that history cannot be re-created and that the new global political and economic reality demands new inter-group and inter-state relationships and institutional arrangements.

## FUNCTIONS AND OBJECTIVES

In almost all cases of international conflict, the creation of a peace process cannot be accomplished without outside help. Third party intervention consequently becomes necessary to initiate the process and integrate its different phases. Well-structured processes dictate, furthermore, much preparation that takes into consideration the views of all concerned parties.

Third party intervention can take a legal form using means provided for by international law and organizations, such as arbitration and adjudication. It may also take an official form, employing the political influence of other states to initiate a peace process and facilitate negotiations. Intervention could also be carried out by non-governmental organizations active in the field of mediation and conflict resolution to start a direct, though non-official, dialogue among adversaries. Such organizations tend usually to use political, educational, and psychological means to prepare antagonists for productive dialogue and the reaching of certain understandings to facilitate and guide negotiations.

The third party in question may be "an individual, a group, a government or an international organization that is not party to the conflict and that either tries to facilitate a resolution of the conflict or is authorized to determine a settlement."[9] The role of such a party may also be limited to helping adversaries directly or indirectly engage in a focused political dialogue to activate or advance a stalled peace process. This is usually done through the creation of specially designed forums to facilitate communications, encourage personal interaction, and bridge such aspects of the cultural and/or political gaps that separate antagonists and hinder progress.

Third party intervention is particularly "helpful when distrust is a serious obstacle, such as in armistice or peace agreements or agreements seeking to resolve complex and emotional ethnic or religious conflicts."[10] One way to establish trust is to arrange for mutual acknowledgement of grievances and to recognize the dignity and honor of the people offended by the actions or inactions of the other party. Negotiations to resolve conflicts and establish justice and peace cannot proceed without first restoring moral equality between adversaries, particularly when establishing military parity is not possible. Political dialogue is the way to open the door for mutual recognition of grievances, to arrange for the acknowledgment of wrongs committed by the stronger party, and to create a degree of mutual trust.

Third party intervention, legal instruments, and political frameworks to conduct political dialogue serve also to strengthen the position of the weaker party, creating some balance to the peace process. Joseph A. Scimecca has argued that the concept of empowerment, or the enabling of the powerless to gain enough power to correct the imbalance in group relationships, has tremendous implications.[11] In international conflicts, granting antagonists equality in status provides for honest and frank dialogue, facilitates communications, and encourages mutual acknowledgment of grievances.

It is important that adversaries develop a sufficient degree of mutual trust and respect to feel comfortable negotiating with enemies. However, trust is not a precondition to initiating negotiations and making progress. Of more importance are efforts to structure the negotiation process, to guarantee its continuation and sustenance, and to keep it focused on substantive issues. Defining the objectives of the process, settling procedural matters regarding form and representation, and choosing the proper framework to govern deliberations and possible outcomes are essential elements of any efficient and successful negotiation process.

Negotiations to resolve international conflict cannot proceed smoothly and make meaningful progress without having all concerned parties define their objectives in clear terms. Objectives that are mutually exclusive can and often do hinder progress, which in turn causes frustration, stagnation, and possibly the termination of negotiation. Objectives of adversaries, therefore, must be clear and amenable to political compromise. In cases involving ethnic conflict, only third party intervention and an engagement in serious political dialogue can help antagonists define their objectives in clear terms that lend themselves to mutual accommodation, not compromise, because values are non-negotiable.

Peace processes that accept all declared objectives without challenge and proceed to bridge the gaps that separate them are both misguided and unfair. Such processes tend unwittingly to legitimize all objectives, regardless of their legality or illegality, rationality or irrationality, fairness or unfairness. All declared objectives must be analyzed before the initiation of negotiations, using international law and UN resolutions, the UN Charter, human rights declarations, precedents, and the spirit of the time as criteria to judge their objectivity and feasibility. Declared objectives that violate accepted law, norms, and social limits must be rejected as unacceptable and non-negotiable.

Objectives that lend themselves to political compromise tend usually to be definable, fair, and more interest-related than value-related. The phase of political dialogue that precedes negotiations is the proper forum to encourage adversaries to define their objectives and modify them, if needed, to be fair, more interest-related and amenable to compromise. At the same time, political dialogue provides a convenient environment to conceptualize and articulate shared objectives to tie adversaries together and jointly pursue the shared objectives toward peace.

Political and procedural frameworks that guide negotiations are always important because they affect the peace process and tend to influence its outcome. The outcome of the process itself, however, or the larger objectives it seeks to accomplish are much more important than other considerations. They are more important because they tend to determine the approach to negotiations and define the framework to be followed. When the general outcome is defined in advance, the framework would be less of a problem and matters of procedure would become of little importance. Time will be spent discussing substantive issues related to the conclusion and implementation of agreements. Thus, clearly defined and shared objectives are important to placing conflict in its proper perspective, facilitating negotiations, and enhancing their prospects. Negotiations that start without a well-defined framework and before a shared objective emerges are more likely to get stuck in procedural matters that amount to little more than "talk about talk."

An example of such a process of negotiation was initiated by the United States after years of hard work to settle the Arab-Israeli conflict. The process started at the end of October 1991 with the Madrid Conference in Spain. The process promised to conclude a Palestinian-Israeli agreement for Palestinian self-rule within one year, an objective Palestinians had accepted in advance. Nevertheless, the lack of a well-defined framework to guide the process led negotiators to waste much valuable time discussing procedural issues, and more than twenty-two months later, no progress was reported.

Former U.S. Assistant Secretary of State Alfred Leroy Atherton criticized the procedural structure of the Middle East peace process as one-sided. He said, "The formula for Israeli-Palestinian negotiations was designed to protect the Likud claim to all of Palestine against the Palestinians' objective of establishing their own state in the Israeli-occupied West Bank and Gaza."[12] A process that is designed to protect the position of the stronger party fails not only to empower the weaker one, but also to be fair and conducive to progress.

On October 29, 1992, the first anniversary of the Madrid Conference, Edward Djerejian, then assistant secretary of state for Near Eastern affairs, said that Jordan and Israel were "very close to final agreement on an agenda [concerning] topics to be included in negotiations for a peace treaty between the two countries."[13] As for the Israeli-Palestinian and Lebanese talks, no progress was reported, assuming that close agreement on an agenda—a purely procedural matter—could be considered progress.

In the Israeli-Syrian negotiations, an unnamed U.S. official was quoted by *The Washington Post* saying that "both Syria and Israel are trying to work out a statement of principles that would preserve their basic position, while allowing them to proceed to substantial negotiations."[14] But if "basic positions" were to be preserved, it would be difficult to conduct substantive negotiations, unless the term "substantive" is used here to signify procedural issues, and not the core issues of the conflict itself.

The two statements made by U.S. officials clearly indicate that the political dialogue that preceded negotiations settled neither the procedural issues of negotiations nor the framework to define the course of negotiations and guide its deliberations. As a result, what took place during the first two and one-half years of Israeli-Arab direct encounters in Washington was not negotiations but an extension of the political dialogue that had started several years earlier. Spending more than thirty months trying to agree on an agenda for negotiations or a joint declaration of principles to guide its proceedings was a waste of valuable time and political capital by all parties concerned, including the United States.

On October 31, 1992, Israeli Prime Minister Yitzhak Rabin of the Labor Party criticized the structure of the peace process. *Washington Post* reporter David Hoffman wrote on November 1, 1992, that Rabin "criticized the basic approach set at the opening conference in Madrid, saying that it had not produced results." Hoffman added that "Rabin stopped short of calling for change in the procedure, but his remarks today reflected deepening frustration with the year-old peace process."[15] We later learned that his frustration led him to negotiate secretly and directly with the Palestine Liberation Organization (PLO), creating a new process both in structure and substance.

Well-structured and seriously conducted negotiations are political processes to deal with the core issues of conflict, not with procedural matters. Because core issues cannot be avoided and must be dealt with sooner or later, it is better to place them at the top of the priority list of negotiations rather than at the bottom. If core issues are settled first, it will be easy to deal with other issues, and compromises that might be required will be possible to make and defend. If core issues are left to subsequent stages while emphasis is placed on non-core issues, there is no guarantee that the conflict will be settled. Negotiations could easily fail after having settled all non-core issues, wasting much time and effort and causing frustration on all sides.

Procedural matters must therefore be settled during the political dialogue phase, which provides the flexibility and time needed to review all options and set specific agendas for real negotiations. A seriously conducted and focused dialogue process could easily eliminate several non-core issues by merely changing antagonists' perceptions of each other. For example, the Arab-Israeli dialogue, which lasted several years before the Madrid conference was convened, accomplished important things without negotiations. It helped convince most Arab officials, including the Palestinians, that military power was not an option, encouraging them to tacitly recognize and deal with the Israeli political reality. At the same time, it helped convince most Israeli intellectuals that the "transfer" of Palestinians out of their homeland was not a realistic option, encouraging them to tacitly recognize and deal with the Palestinians of the West Bank and Gaza as a people with a distinct national identity.

Antagonists whose objectives are exclusive and whose perspectives collide cannot hope to negotiate successfully without first entering into a political dialogue. The first objective of dialogue in such cases is to dispel most misconceptions regarding the intentions of the enemy and to encourage antagonists to agree on shared goals to be achieved through negotiations. In addition, the dialogue should strive to convince all concerned parties that most possible outcomes of negotiations are preferable to the existing situation. For such a conviction to prevail, the timing and procedure of both dialogue and negotiations have to be right.

Choosing the right time to launch a peace process or to reactivate a dormant one is an important decision because the right timing usually improves chances of success. Nevertheless, waiting for the right time to arrive can be costly, because waiting often means being at the mercy of future developments that no one can control. Such developments, in the absence of hope and political action, are more likely to add to the complexity of issues involved, to create new, largely non-negotiable facts, and to distort people's collective memory and conscience regarding the other.

Choosing the timing, therefore, is a strategic decision that must be determined by a clear criterion. The one criterion that we believe most appropriate is the adversary's willingness to negotiate, because this implies a conviction on his part that the status quo is either damaging to his interests, no longer tenable, or contrary to perceived long-term objectives. It may also imply a conviction that the use of force to settle conflict is no longer applicable or capable of achieving desired goals. However, such a criterion presupposes that all antagonists are looking for a political solution to their shared problems and are willing to negotiate from a position of relative strength expressed in military advantage, political legitimacy or moral standing vis-à-vis the other. It also presupposes that antagonists recognize the existence of each other and acknowledge that each party has legitimate grievances and unfulfilled needs. They are important matters that cannot be dealt with except through sustained and focused political dialogue.

## TRACK-TWO DIPLOMACY

Track-two diplomacy is a people-to-people type of interaction among adversaries, usually promoted and conducted by individuals and nongovernmental organizations. Sponsoring parties of such an interaction are more likely to be foreign organizations interested in peace and the resolution of conflict. The primary objective of such organizations is not to produce solutions but to help adversaries overcome psychological and political problems, particularly problems related to perceptions of the other and his intentions. They also provide a direct, though unofficial channel of communications to exchange views and ideas regarding shared problems.

According to John Burton, the term "track-two diplomacy" was first used by Joseph Montville to describe communications between adversaries at an unofficial level to discuss matters usually negotiated officially. Burton defines track-two diplomacy as "unofficial, informal interaction between members of adversary groups or nations which aim to develop strategies, influence public opinion, and organize human and material resources in ways that might help resolve their conflict."[16]

Sponsoring organizations pursue their objectives by bringing adversaries together in settings that permit open dialogue and encourage personal interaction. They usually try to stay neutral, providing little or no new ideas of their own, often limiting their intervention to matters of procedure to keep the process on track and focused. Because of that they are called "dialogue groups" whose objectives and functions are to facilitate informal political dialogue and personal interaction among adversaries. Dialogue groups are largely facilitators of human interaction, not mediators of disputes between states.

David Newsom says that "to assume that the road to peace lies largely in the technique of mastering the art of bargaining is to rule out the intricate problems involved in bringing disputing parties to the table in

the first place."[17] Dialogue groups consider the mere gathering of antagonists under conditions that facilitate fruitful interaction in itself a success that reflects the essence of their mission.

The experience of most dialogue groups has largely been obtained
from two major exercises. The first is the U.S.-USSR dialogue; the second
is the Israeli-Palestinian dialogue. Both were conducted under the auspices of a small number of non-governmental organizations, often competing with each other to attract the same participants and the same
funds available to finance such endeavors. The overriding objective of
all dialogue activities, however, is to facilitate mutual and better understanding of concerns, grievances, perspectives, and objectives of conflicting parties.

The U.S.-USSR dialogue was conducted directly between American
and Soviet groups whose members were either former officials or intellectuals close to decision-makers in their respective countries. Third
party intervention by an outside party was seldom needed because both
Americans and Soviets had no problem meeting with each other. Meetings were held in both countries for several years without difficulty. The
major objective of the U.S.-USSR dialogue was to lessen mutual fear,
build confidence, and expand channels of communications. By so doing,
the dialogue groups hoped to and probably did help facilitate new arms
control agreements, inspire new Soviet thinking and enhance mutual
trust.[18]

The Israeli-Palestinian dialogue groups, in contrast, have recently begun to proliferate and become active. The experience of the U.S.-Soviet
dialogue encouraged a few American professionals to establish organizations or programs to facilitate Israeli-Palestinian dialogue. Several
churches, women's organizations and universities both in Europe and in
the United States have also entered the field as active participants. The
European dialogue groups seem generally more interested in educational
workshops to reduce mutual misunderstandings and encourage each
party to acknowledge the basic needs and rights of the other. The American groups, on the other hand, seem generally to be more interested in
encouraging both sides to adopt certain measures to build mutual confidence and prepare for eventual peaceful coexistence. We will discuss
in more detail the Israeli-Palestinian dialogue in the next section.

Dialogue groups are a special type of third party mediators whose job
is not to produce settlements but to improve mutual understanding and
create a new environment conducive to negotiation. They are accepted
because they provide forums for interaction and opportunities to gain
valuable insights regarding the adversaries' true positions and intentions. American dialogue groups in particular are perceived in the Arab
world as influential, and having strong connections to both the U.S. and

Israeli governments because nearly all of them are controlled and managed by American Jews.

Dialogue groups act generally to encourage elites on both sides of a conflict to create political processes of informal negotiations without prior commitment to the outcome. They are processes to define the problem, clarify issues, express feelings and concerns, and set the agenda for possible negotiations. Effective dialogue can also help antagonists frame their demands in political terms that lend themselves to compromise. Public opinion on both sides of the conflict is also a major target of dialogue processes, which try to change perceptions of the other and humanize the enemy.

Dialogue groups are most helpful when the conflict is stable and the objective is to improve its management, as was the case with the U.S.-USSR rivalry. They provide channels to improve communications, help contain conflict, explain the rules of containment, and convey a desire to keep it under control by mutual consent. Therefore, dialogue groups provide political forums to help antagonists conceive and improve tools of containment to preserve the status quo, while opening new channels of communications to exchange views regarding their shared objectives and the best means to achieve them. They can, as Richard Schwartz maintains, "create mutual understanding and help generate constructive ideas."[19] Nevertheless, dialogue groups are less helpful when conflict is serious and when the need is to find solutions to change the status quo rather than merely to improve it.

During the U.S.-Soviet Cuban crisis in the early 1960s over the stationing of Soviet nuclear missiles in Cuba, the two states had difficulty communicating. After the disintegration of the Soviet Union in 1991, and due to an honest exchange of information, the U.S. and Russian governments discovered that the crisis was much more serious than they had thought at the time, and that the Soviet actions that precipitated the crisis and the American reactions that followed were largely based on misconceptions. Robert S. McNamara, who was during the crisis U.S. Secretary of Defense, wrote that "each nation's decisions immediately before and during the crisis had been distorted by misinformation, miscalculation and misjudgement," all of which could have been improved by political dialogue to better understand the other and improve means of communications.[20] The U.S.-Soviet dialogue, which was launched in 1960 at Dartmouth College, and other forums sponsored by the United Nations Association and the Pugwash conference have contributed to that end, preventing new serious crises from erupting again.

## CONFIDENCE-BUILDING MEASURES

In every conflict there are always shared needs, problems, and interests that tie adversaries together. In most cases shared needs and interests tend to be framed in terms that make them incompatible. In other cases, they may even be framed as mutually exclusive demands that negate each other.

In all conflicts, adversaries share an interest to manage their conflict by containing or resolving it. However, the outcome desired by one adversary is often different from the outcome sought by the other, although the management of conflict cannot be performed without joint effort.

For example, Israel's position regarding the Syrian Golan Heights, which Israel captured in 1967, has been incompatible with the Syrian position. While Israel desires to continue to hold on to all or some of that territory, Syria demands total Israeli withdrawal as a precondition for peace. Israel's desire is justified on the basis of its security needs, which maintain that the Syrian army should never again be allowed to be so close to Israeli settlements. The Syrian position, in turn, is justified in political and historical terms that maintain that Syrian territorial integrity must not be violated and that its sovereignty over the Golan Heights must be restored.

Mutual concerns and principles that are used by both parties to justify their incompatible positions could easily be reconciled if good intentions prevail on both sides and perceptions of the true intentions of one another are changed. Israeli withdrawal would restore Syrian sovereignty and satisfy Syria's demand for territorial integrity, and Syria's commitment not to redeploy its forces in the Golan Heights would meet Israeli security needs. (See Chapter 9 for more details).

Power struggle and civil wars provide examples of other shared interests framed in mutually exclusive demands. Groups fighting to control governments usually claim, sometimes with justification, that the other is unfit, illegitimate, or both. They also claim that they are more fit to govern and more representative of the will of the nation. All conflicting groups, moreover, claim that they are fighting to protect the interests of the nation and restore security and dignity to the people. Democracy, which gives the people the right to choose their representatives and the type of government to run the country, can reconcile the apparently mutually exclusive demands of the conflicting parties and thus provide a politically acceptable and humane solution to conflict.

Confidence-building measures are steps to be taken to stabilize conflict after shared interests have been identified and accepted. They are unilateral or bilateral steps to ease tension, or stations to move conflict closer to solution. They are also measures to help change perceptions on both sides by demonstrating a desire by one or more parties to accommodate the other and cooperate to manage conflict or prepare for its peaceful resolution.[21]

Confidence-building measures may be symbolic acts that represent mere declarations of goodwill, or substantive acts that change the dynamics of conflict. Symbolic measures tend to be helpful in easing tension and addressing problems related to perceptions. Substantive measures capable of changing the dynamics of conflict are not always helpful and may even lead to deepening fear and suspicion, especially when attempted before a framework for a solution has been articulated and mutually accepted.

Gestures of a substantive nature by one party may be seen by the adversary as a sign of weakness that could encourage that party to demand more concessions before negotiations. Confidence-building measures that the stronger party may undertake or insist on seeing implemented before negotiations could start are more likely to be interpreted by the weaker party as steps to change the dynamics of conflict in favor of its adversary. Actions and reactions related to substantive measures could easily complicate the peace process, adding new fears and misunderstandings rather than building mutual confidence.

As a means to help manage conflict, confidence-building measures are more helpful in conflicts that are stable and when the conflicting parties show more interest in preserving than changing the status quo. In such situations, they provide an element of mutual confidence, conveying a clear message that antagonists are keen on maintaining existing relationships and have no desire to change the balance of power or escalate conflict. But where one or more of the conflicting parties is interested more in changing the status quo than preserving it, certain confidence-building measures are less helpful and may even be viewed with suspicion, because of their propensity to change the existing balance of power, strengthening the position of one party at the expense of another.[22]

As a result, confidence-building measures of a substantive nature should be avoided before negotiations start and before a general framework for a solution emerges. When such a framework emerges, confidence-building measures would then become steps to hasten the process of reaching a solution that all concerned parties had already accepted in principle and were willing to pursue with diligence. Therefore, an agreement regarding a general framework for a solution should be the first confidence-building measure to be attempted during the political dialogue phase, or the early phases of negotiations.

Every political settlement to resolve conflict involves two main concepts, says Harold Saunders: "First is a picture of the settlement the parties could honorably live with. The second is a scenario of steps—a political process—for moving from the present situation toward that settlement."[23] Without those two concepts, it would be hard to initiate negotiations and harder to conclude fair and lasting settlements that establish durable peace.

Negotiations are very important to reaching mutually acceptable and binding settlements because they are the core of any peace process. Nevertheless, negotiations are only a stage in a long process that "involves profound understanding of other cultures, sensitivity to internal politics of one's own country as well as those of others, and a judgement of the relative effectiveness of unilateral and multilateral intervention," writes David Newsom.[24] Political dialogue is that stage in the peace process where antagonists interact, views are exchanged, fears and concerns expressed, and mutual understandings develop regarding the causes of conflict and the best ways to handle it. Well-timed and well-conceived confidence-building measures are actions and gestures indicating progress and fostering mutual trust after basic understandings have been reached.

## ISRAELI-PALESTINIAN DIALOGUE

During the last two decades, dialogue groups and forums sponsoring and promoting Arab-Israeli, particularly Israeli-Palestinian, interaction have proliferated, increasing the frequency of joint meetings and the intensity of discussions. In 1974, the first meeting between Israelis and PLO members was held in Romania, and in 1983 PLO Executive Committee Member Mahmoud Abbas (Abu Mazin) wrote a confidential memo defending Israeli-Palestinian contacts.[25]

The Israeli-Palestinian experience regarding dialogue groups and forums points to certain unambiguous conclusions that generally support the work of such groups in principle but question their capacity to influence political decisions. They are groups and forums that have demonstrated a capacity to bridge the psychological gap that separates Israelis and Palestinians, but have failed to help the public on both sides of the conflict to live that experience and appreciate its utility. While the Israeli-Palestinian dialogue expanded and intensified, extremist views and groups were being born and strengthened on both sides. Thus, whatever impact the dialogue has had was limited to a small elite group of frequent participants and almost no one else.

Dialogue activities fall under two general categories: consensus building and humanizing processes. The first category involves activities that try to lead antagonists to debate political issues of mutual concern and reach consensus regarding their nature, causes, or methods to deal with them. Because of that, participants are usually people who are recognized within their respective communities, have strong connections to their own political establishments, have a capacity to influence decision-making or public opinions, and are more likely to seek and accept compromise. Herbert Kelman, who pioneered the work of getting Israelis and Palestinians together at Harvard University, says, "Great care must be taken to select participants who, on the one hand, have the interest and capacity to engage in the kind of learning process that workshops provide and, on the other hand, have the positions and credibility within their own communities that enable them to influence the thinking of political leaders, political constituencies, or the general public."[26]

The latter category involves activities to reverse the processes of demonizing and stereotyping and to engage antagonists in processes to humanize the enemy and understand his feelings. To achieve this objective, third party sponsors usually design workshops, initiate social functions, and engage antagonists in joint problem-solving activities to improve mutual understanding and develop new ideas to deal with the issues that separate them. Kelman believes that the role of the third party is to "create an atmosphere, establish norms, and make occasional interventions, all conducive to free and open discussion in which the parties address each other, and in which they listen to each other in order to understand their differing perspectives."[27] The purpose of this is to effect change at the individual level and use it to promote change at both the public and policy levels. But, as mentioned earlier, neither the consensus building activities nor the humanizing ones have had the intended impact at either the public or policy level within the Israeli and Palestinian communities.

The reasons for this apparent failure are many and not easy to explain. Some are political, others are cultural, but most are related to the work and intentions of groups and individuals sponsoring the major dialogue activities.

The process of selecting participants has focused attention almost exclusively on a small group of possible participants on each side who are largely bicultural. The ability to speak good English, the language of discussion, has been a major criterion in determining who is invited to participate. Because language is not only a means of communication but also a way of thinking, a knowledge of English means being socialized into Western culture. This leads participants to observe the same rules of rationality and feel comfortable with a Western setting, which in turn helps facilitate open discussion and often friendly interaction as well.

In addition, participants are citizens who, as Saunders says, "do not have to defend a group interest in the status quo and can explore the resistance of entering a dialogue with less risk, although most will have to work within socially accepted limits."[28] However, they are limits dictated more by the rules of the culture under whose auspices they meet and less by the rules of their own cultures. In almost all cases, the encounters, their outcomes, and the identity of participants are kept secret, making the risk involved very small and the impact still smaller. For example, after more than a decade of workshops arranged by Professor Kelman and sponsored by Harvard University, very little is known about the participants, the discussions, or the outcomes. In addition, no sponsoring party or foundation that provides financial support has done a study to evaluate the work of dialogue groups and substantiate their rosy, often exaggerated claims.

Moreover, in all known documented cases, meetings were held in a foreign country, where participants are free from social and most political constraints, where they can express their feelings freely, and where their behavior is governed by the same rules of rationality. Saunders wrote:

Often the place is a critical factor. Sometimes only a far away, neutral site can help the parties feel safe. The space will also be defined by certain ground rules that make it safe; participants will normally represent themselves—nor organizations; consequently, it is a space for dialogue—not for negotiation; to make the space safe, there is no attribution outside that space to the views of any participant.[29]

The ground rules of the space and the structure of dialogue ensure, though unintentionally, that all participants behave according to the same rules of rationality, thus maximizing chances for agreement and minimizing chances for disagreement. Those who are unable or unwilling to play by the same rules are never reinvited to participate in future meetings, as the practice of more than one sponsor has demonstrated.

Being bicultural, as soon as the participants return home, they usually and almost instantly revert to the old rules of rationality dictated by their own cultures. As a result, their experience of interacting with the enemy becomes an adventure largely removed from reality, or a behavioral aberration to be regretted and not repeated, leaving no lasting impact on their lives or ways of thinking.

In addition, some of the best-known U.S. groups and forums have consistently avoided dealing with the core issues of the Israeli-Palestinian conflict, preferring side, non-urgent or non-issue issues. Issues like water, the environment, future economic relationships, and possible joint use of port facilities cannot be seriously and realistically addressed without first addressing the core, politically sensitive issues that cause and sustain conflict.

Kelman has argued that dialogue groups that use interactive problem-solving techniques are more likely to lead to building coalitions across conflict lines—coalitions between subsets of conflicting parties interested in opening a path toward negotiation and peaceful settlement of conflict.[30] He also recognizes that such coalitions are uneasy and subject to change due to fluctuations in the political and psychological climate at home, the use of language that alienates participants on both sides, mutual distrust, or failure to pursue agreed plans.[31]

When issues of conflict are value-related and when group identities are at stake, coalitions across conflict lines often fail to live up to expectations. They are largely bursts of emotions to cooperate with the enemy created under the influence of unique environments and with the help of able facilitators that do not and cannot last. They usually quiet and disappear as soon as participants go back to their homes and begin to resume normal life under conditions of different psychological, cultural, and political settings, giving rise to the other side of the personality of the bicultural person, enabling it to dominate behavior and influence action.

In 1985, Dr. Rudolf Hilf, a German intellectual and retired politician, initiated an effort to bring Israelis and Palestinians together to endorse a set of principles to govern a political settlement of the Arab-Israeli conflict. To develop such a set of principles, Dr. Hilf worked primarily with two people, one Israeli, one Palestinian. The first coordinated with a larger, influential group of Israelis; the latter coordinated with the PLO leadership in Tunis. After four years of hard work, during which more than ten joint meetings of the working committee were held in Germany and countless meetings were held by each member of the working committee with his own party, a seven-point document was produced. In July 1989, a joint meeting was held in Vienna, Austria, to publicly endorse the document. The conference was attended by sixteen prominent Israelis, four of whom were members of the Israeli Knesset; sixteen prominent Palestinians, most of whom were members of the PLO; and more than forty distinguished Americans, Russians, and Europeans.

Since the document was negotiated and accepted by each participant in advance, a shared feeling prevailed that an Israeli-Palestinian coalition across the conflict lines was created. The Palestinian member of the working committee addressed his Israeli colleagues during the conference, saying: "You have to understand that we are now one team; our debate and disagreements are only a practice so we may be better prepared to face the adversary. Our shared adversary consists of all extremist elements on both sides." A plan of action to publicly promote the contents of the document was agreed, but after participants went home, no party took action to implement the plan, and even news about the meeting was largely denied by both sides.

Richard D. Schwartz, who initiated and coordinated the work of several groups that sponsored Arab-Jewish dialogue in the United States, reported that almost all groups were successful. Participants showed interest, were tolerant, and learned much about the feelings and concerns of the other.[32] The reasons for the success were not explained; they were assumed as an inherent quality of grass-roots dialogue.

Given the rules, structure, and type of participants, it would have been a surprise if such groups were to fail. Arab and Jewish participants in the United States are the product of one culture, even if the cultural accent is different. They share an interest in helping their own people resolve their conflict but have little or nothing to lose from being involved or uninvolved. To them, the dialogue is a way to define and preserve their cultural identity, not to influence events in far-away places. In living in one community, they have much to lose from being antagonistic and more to gain from being accommodating.

Among the other notable American dialogue groups and forums are the Institute for Social and Economic Policy in the Middle East of Harvard University, the Institute of Global Conflict and Cooperation of the University of California, the Brookings Institution, and Search for Common Ground in Washington, D.C. These organizations have sponsored many conferences, seminars and workshops, using several countries as stages to conduct their work and enhance their international image.

A careful review and an honest evaluation of the work of both the European and American dialogue groups will reflect the following:

1. They have largely involved Israelis and Palestinians of similar outlook only. Those who participated in meetings but appeared unwilling to show an understanding of the other's sensitivities and fears were never reinvited.

2. Most of those who continued to participate were people willing to play by the rules of the sponsoring organizations, which were and still are rules meant primarily to give the appearance of success and keep the process going. Those who pushed for a more serious and substantive dialogue aimed at tackling the core issues of the conflict were excluded from subsequent gatherings.

3. Their contribution to resolving the Middle East conflict has been negligible at best. Because participants are people who have largely accepted to meet with the enemy, knowing in advance that very little, if anything, would be accomplished, they have generally avoided publicity. As a result, the meetings and their modest outcomes have failed to change Israeli or Arab public opinion or influence policy on either side in a meaningful way.

4. Due to the lack of political accomplishments, almost all forums, particularly the major American ones, have begun to issue or plan to issue joint studies concerning the conflict with added emphasis on regional economic and environmental issues. This policy has been pursued to give the appearance of progress while avoiding the core political issues and the need to envision plans for a comprehensive settlement that guarantees fairness, peaceful coexistence and lasting peace.

As a result of the above, the number of all Palestinians and Israelis who have become regular participants in all forums does not exceed today thirty to forty people on each side. The number of their American and European counterparts, including the Russians, is probably fewer than forty. An international club of fewer than 100 similar-minded, bicultural intellectuals and a few former politicians and army generals was formed. They meet regularly to entertain each other and provide the rationale for the continued existence of certain organizations, organizations whose primary objective is to enhance the prestige of a few social entrepreneurs seeking self-promotion, almost all of whom are European and American Jews.

Harvard's Institute for Social and Economic Policy in the Middle East, for example, has held several seminars and formed working groups to develop a plan to deal with the most important economic aspects of a future Israeli-Palestinian relationship. An outline for a "Seminar on Economic Cooperation in the Middle East" identified the following areas for study: labor, data, health, and water. As a part of what it called the "Economics of Transition," it identified Palestinian economic administration, monetary affairs, fiscal affairs, agriculture, industry and trade, and foreign aid. Each of the eleven areas of investigation was assigned to a distinguished economist, almost all of whom, just like those in charge of the dialogue groups, are American Jews.

Contrary to the claimed intention of the study to facilitate "economic cooperation in the Middle East," not a single Arab or Arab-American economist was assigned to lead the work of any group. In addition, the * political framework of the future Arab-Israeli relationship, which is a basic assumption for any realistic study, was not defined. But to guarantee the participation of some Arab economists, each participating researcher was given the freedom to set his or her own assumptions regarding the political future of the occupied Palestinian territories.

Because of their lack of balance and political sensitivity, the studies were perceived as biased even when they were objective from a strictly technical viewpoint. And because economic policies do not function in a vacuum and cannot ignore the political context in which they operate, the absence of a unified political frame of reference made the studies a purely intellectual exercise. Finally, because individual researchers were permitted to set their own political assumptions, the studies lacked coherence and therefore produced no clear recommendations. Allowing each individual researcher to pursue his own political agenda amounts to allowing certain radical positions on both sides to be expressed and legitimized.

The failure of such forums to produce concrete results has increasingly served to marginalize participants, particularly the Palestinian ones. By marginalizing known and credible representatives, most forums have unwittingly contributed to alienating and undermining moderation in general, and consequently have deepened Arab intellectual frustration and increased popular suspicion of the West's view of justice and fairness, particularly that of American Jews.

Harvard's Institute for Social and Economic Policy in the Middle East sponsors other joint activities to promote mutual understanding and the humanization of the enemy. Every year it brings a number of Arab and

Israeli professionals together as fellows to attend a special management program, at the end of which fellows receive a master's degree. As part of working, learning, and interacting together, all fellows are required to live and socialize with each other. It is a process to strip them of their titles and induce them to behave as normal people unconstrained by their official positions. A Jordanian fellow in 1991 refused to socialize with his Israeli colleagues. When pressured by the program director, he wrote the crown prince of Jordan and the president of Harvard University, bitterly complaining and threatening to leave the program. In fact, the pressure placed on him drove him to the verge of losing his mind.

Every group of fellows included at least one Palestinian from Israel or an Israeli-Arab. Two of those Israeli-Arab fellows told me that they knew their Jewish colleagues before attending Harvard University as co-workers in the Israeli health system. They also told me that their experience at Harvard had an adverse effect on their relationships with their Israeli-Jewish colleagues. It was an experience that made them view Israeli Jews more negatively and feel less inclined to trust them and cooperate with them than before. It seems that activities to humanize the enemy had worked as planned, reducing all fellows to ordinary people responding to their respective cultures and to deeply held beliefs and fears felt by their own peoples. As a result, Israeli Jews were forced to see their Israeli-Arab colleagues as ordinary Palestinians, not as fellow co-workers, and Palestinians were forced to see Jews as Israeli occupiers, not fellow citizens and co-workers.

Political dialogue as the first phase in a conflict-resolution process must perform certain tasks to create a new environment more conducive to negotiation by preparing concerned parties to negotiate. Such a preparation also includes clear understandings regarding the framework to guide or govern negotiations and the general shape of the final settlement to be sought. Notable among the tasks that a serious political dialogue would be required to do are:

1. To define the problem, explaining its real causes that need to be considered.
2. To help adversaries frame or reframe their positions and demands in political terms amenable to compromise, while changing certain value-related issues to interest-related ones when possible and as needed to facilitate progress.
3. To encourage all parties to express their concerns, air their grievances, and make their feelings known to others.
4. To persuade all concerned parties to acknowledge the identity of the other and recognize his fears and legitimate demands.
5. To create new and reliable channels of communications among adversaries that can be used before and during negotiations.

6. To design a negotiation process that is focused and well-defined, allowing no party to gain substantial control to determine the pace of the process and greatly influence its outcome. This requires that

   a. The focus should be on dealing with the core issues of conflict, not with its symptoms only.

   b. The process should have a clearly defined objective that all parties share and feel that it is in their own interest to accomplish.

   c. A clear framework to guide all discussions toward solving the problem should be articulated and mutually accepted.

Political dialogue should concentrate, when possible, on the future, on current interests and future expectations, not on national memories and collective grievances. History when used must be understood as a source of knowledge to explain mistakes and missed opportunities, to recount grievances and even to provide excuses for previous failures, but not as a guide to shape the future or a model to describe how things ought to be.

Political dialogue is an informal process of interaction between representatives of adversarial groups to overcome certain psychological or political problems that separate them and prevent interaction. Because of that, political dialogue can be official or unofficial. Official dialogue is conducted by representatives of conflicting parties to explore possibilities and review options to construct an official political process to resolve conflict. Unofficial dialogue, on the other hand, is conducted by concerned members of conflicting groups or citizens of conflicting states to reduce tension and suspicion, reverse processes of mutual demonization, improve mutual understanding, expand and upgrade channels of communications, and create new environments more conducive to cooperation and the peaceful resolution of conflict.

Official dialogue is a phase in a peace process to resolve conflict. It is that phase through which mutual misunderstandings are clarified, procedural matters are discussed and settled, and a framework for negotiation is articulated and approved.

Because issues and causes of conflict are a living and constantly recurring phenomenon, political dialogue never ends. It is needed to continue to explain feelings on both sides of conflict, to counter stereotyping, ease growing tension, and facilitate cooperation. While constructive and focused political dialogue may prevent the escalation of conflict and hostilities, it cannot resolve conflict by itself. It remains a political tool to prepare for negotiation or envision new ideas and options to manage the status quo and improve chances for peace.

## NOTES

1. Henry Kissinger, "The Vietnam Negotiations," *Foreign Affairs*, 47 2 (1969).

2. Louis Kriesberg, *International Conflict Resolution* (New Haven, Conn.: Yale University Press, 1992), pp. 4–8.

3. Jay Rothman, *A Pre-Negotiation Model: Theory and Training* (Jerusalem: Leonard Davis Institute, Hebrew University of Jerusalem, 1990), p. 3.

4. Harold Saunders, "We Need a Larger Theory of Negotiation," *Negotiation Journal* (1985).

5. Jay Rothman, *A Pre-Negotiation Model*, p. 4.

6. Anthony de Reuck, "A Theory of Conflict Resolution by Problem Solving," in John Burton and Frank Dukes, eds., *Conflict: Readings in Management and Resolution* (New York: St. Martin's Press, 1990), p. 186.

7. Gennady I. Chufrin and Harold H. Saunders, "A Public Peace Process," unpublished paper, April 1993, p. 2.

8. Harold Saunders, "We Need," p. 2.

9. Richard Bilder, "International Third-Party Dispute Settlement," in W. Scott Thompson et al., eds., *Approaches to Peace* (Washington, D.C.: United States Institute of Peace, 1991), p. 192.

10. Ibid., p. 202.

11. Joseph A. Scimecca, "Conflict Resolution: The Basis for Social Control or Social Change," in Dennis J. D. Sandole and Ingrid Sandole-Staroste, eds., *Conflict Management and Problem Solving: Interpersonal to International Applications* (New York: New York University Press, 1987), p. 32.

12. Alfred Leroy Atherton, "Avoiding Dead Ends with the Palestinians," *The Washington Post*, August 4, 1993.

13. John M. Goshko, "Israel, Jordan Reported Near Peace Treaty Talks Agenda," *The Washington Post*, Nov. 30, 1992.

14. Ibid.

15. David Hoffman, "Rabin Criticizes Peace Talks," *The Washington Post*, November 1, 1992.

16. John Burton, *Conflict: Practices in Management, Settlement and Resolution* (New York: St. Martin's Press, 1990), p. 139.

17. David Newsom, "Diplomacy and Negotiation," in W. Scott Thompson et al., eds., *Approaches to Peace* (Washington, D.C.: United States Institute of Peace, 1991), p. 30.

18. Chufrin and Saunders, "A Public Peace Process." In this article the authors provide a good account of the U.S.-U.S.S.R. dialogue and suggest a five-stage public peace process.

19. Richard D. Schwartz, "Arab-Jewish Dialogue in the United States," in Louis Kriesberg, Terrell H. Northrup, and Stuart J. Thorson, eds., *Intractable Conflicts and their Transformations* (Syracuse, N.Y.: Syracuse University Press, 1989), p. 202.

20. Robert S. McNamara, "Conclusion, 30 Years On: Better a Non-Nuclear World," *International Herald Tribune*, October 15, 1992.

21. Mohamed Rabie, *Conflict Resolution and the Middle East Peace Process* (Hamburg, Germany: Deutsches Orient Institut, 1993), pp. 18–22.

22. Ibid., pp. 18–20.

23. Harold H. Saunders, "Political Settlement and the Gulf Crisis," *The Mediterranean Quarterly*, 2 (Spring 1991): 7.

24. David Newsom, "Diplomacy and Negotiation," p. 40.

25. Mohamed Rabie, *The U.S.-PLO Dialogue, Secret Diplomacy and Conflict Resolution* (Gainesville: University Press of Florida, forthcoming), Chap. 3.

26. Herbert Kelman, *Coalitions Across Conflict Lines* (Harvard University, Paper No. 91–9, 1991), p. 7.

27. Herbert Kelman, *Coalitions*, p. 5.

28. Chufrin and Saunders, "A Public Peace Process," p. 11.

29. Ibid., p. 12.

30. Herbert Kelman, *Coalitions*, p. 8.

31. Ibid., pp. 13–27.

32. Richard D. Schwartz, "Arab-Jewish Dialogue," pp. 186–202.

*Chapter Six*

# NEGOTIATION

In most conflicts, antagonists tend to have difficulty initiating negotiation on their own. International conflicts that are value-related make face-to-face negotiations almost impossible to conduct or even to contemplate. Third party intervention, as a result, becomes imperative if negotiations are to be initiated and sustained: "Negotiation is a set of communicative processes through which individuals or groups try to resolve disagreements that exist among them."[1] Because disagreements are mutual, negotiations are shared processes that bring antagonists together to review conflict and try to settle disputes. But for serious negotiation processes to be launched, mediators often have first to perform tasks to help the major antagonists clarify their positions and construct a mutually acceptable process of negotiation. Noted among these tasks, which are often performed during the political dialogue phase, are:

1. The need to define the respective positions of the antagonists and identify their demands in clear terms.
2. The need to help antagonists perceive those positions and demands as accommodating or bridgeable, meaning that the gulf separating them must be reasonable and of a largely political rather than ideological character.
3. The need to persuade antagonists to accept a frame of reference or a set of recognized principles to guide negotiations and govern their ultimate outcome.
4. The need for all parties to share a larger goal and see the possible outcome of negotiations as mutually beneficial.

In addition, antagonists must acknowledge the grievances of their adversaries and the legitimacy of their concerns. Otherwise, they will be unable to treat their adversaries as equals, at least from a human and cultural viewpoint, or make the necessary compromises that mutually acceptable agreements dictate. In value-related conflicts, failure to acknowledge the grievances of the adversary and treat him with respect would prevent the building of integrative relationships in the future, which are necessary for making and sustaining peace in the long run.

Every international and ethno-national conflict has two major sides. They are different but inseparable from each other and neither one of them makes sense without the other, or can command attention and respectability on its own merits. The first side represents the grievances of a contending party and embodies the goals it seeks to accomplish. The other, meanwhile, reflects its fears and the perceived dangers it wishes to eliminate. But the same perceived fears and dangers of the first party usually mirror the grievances and the goals of the other contending party. Thus, the grievances of all parties tend to be contentious, the goals contradictory, the fears mutual and the conflict a shared problem.

The existence of one side serves to legitimize the existence of the other, and addressing the needs of one party would not be possible without addressing the needs of the other. For example, the Palestinian-Israeli conflict exists because both the Palestinians and the Israelis have a problem that the other's grievances, goals and fears mirror. Palestinians have a problem because Israel's larger goals threaten the political identity of the Palestinian people and the socio-economic means they require for survival. Meanwhile, the Israelis have a problem because the larger Palestinian grievances and goals threaten Israel's continued existence as a political entity and endanger its socio-political ideology.

If Israel were to resolve its problem without addressing the legitimate grievances and fears of the Palestinian people, the Palestinian community would have to cease to exist. If the Palestinians were to resolve their own problem without addressing the legitimate fears of Israel, the Israeli state would have to cease to exist. Since neither community is about to disappear or abandon its communal and national character, neither Palestinians nor Israelis can find a political solution to their shared problem on their own.[2] Only by working together can they resolve the two sides of the problem that separate them; and only when each party acknowledges that the other has legitimate claims and valid fears can a genuine peace process be initiated and sustained. This means that for negotiations to start and be sustained, both sides of a conflict have to: acknowledge that their adversary has legitimate claims; accept the principle of reciprocity; agree upon a certain frame of reference or a guiding principle to direct and advise negotiations; and see negotiations as an opportunity to maximize long-term gains, particularly shared gains.

International negotiation is a "process of communication between states seeking to arrive at a mutually acceptable outcome on some issue or issues of shared concern."[3] Because peoples and states usually have some interests that are shared and others that are contradictory, they negotiate to reconcile differences and conclude agreements to resolve conflicts. Agreements in turn are legal and political instruments to transform certain relationships into more desirable and permanent ones. Negotiations are a diplomatic process of interaction between peoples or states to redefine their relationships regarding issues of mutual concern that cause or perpetuate conflict.

As peoples and states interact, they normally cooperate and compete, developing conflicting interests and nurturing adversarial attitudes. To reconcile conflicting interests and modify adversarial attitudes, antagonists must negotiate on the basis of historical facts, current needs, and future imperatives, not only on the basis of power relationships. This means that standards to guide negotiations must be fair and take into consideration the historical dynamics at work, the facts on the ground, and the imperatives of the future. Although the position and power of the stronger party must be acknowledged, its will must not be allowed to prevail.[4]

## APPROACHES TO NEGOTIATION

The point of departure in conflict resolution may be a mutually accepted set of principles to guide negotiations, a frame of reference outlining the trade-offs required to resolve conflict, an overall political plan serving as a general framework to redefine the overall relationship, or a precedent to be emulated. A serious negotiation process cannot be launched and sustained without the antagonists' acceptance of certain principles and rules to govern the behavior of negotiators, channel deliberations toward the desired ends, and keep the process on course.

Nevertheless, there are politicians, most of whom served in the U.S. government, who advocate an open process of negotiation that is free from regulations and guidelines. They maintain that negotiation processes tend usually to create their own rules and develop certain dynamics of their own that are more likely to change perceptions on both sides and help sustain negotiations. To such politicians, only procedural matters to regulate deliberations have to be conceived and constructed. They emphasize such matters as the selection of the parties to be involved, the issues to be negotiated, the criteria for choosing the timing of negotiations, the place where negotiations are to be held, and the nature and conditions of outside intervention.

History, however, seems to indicate that no open processes of negotiations have succeeded in resolving the conflicts they were intended to resolve. Even the Arab-Israeli negotiations that were established as semi-open have languished for several years without making progress, despite repeated U.S. intervention. They were negotiations that accepted U.N. Resolutions 242 and 338 as a frame of reference but left those resolutions vaguely defined and subject to differing interpretations, vastly weakening their legal authority.

Raymond Cohen writes that "in the Anglo-Saxon tradition great stress is laid on creating the conditions for an equitable contest. A whole vocabulary exists to describe this state of affairs: fair play, level playing field, rules of the game, due process, and so on." In most other cultures people are "less enthusiastic about competition, with its potential for affront and painful confrontation, than about ensuring a result that will protect their cherished dignity."[5] Thus, while an open process of negotiation may be suitable for resolving conflict in the West, it is rather unhelpful when the conflict is placed in a non-Western cultural context. A managed process, therefore, would be preferable to an open one because of its ability to assure antagonists of their dignity.

Nevertheless, U.S. experts and practitioners of conflict resolution as well as diplomats tend generally to favor open processes of negotiation. They feel more comfortable working through an open process because it leaves them with more control over both the procedure and outcome of negotiation. They also feel that a managed process constrains their ability to maneuver and manipulate, using their skills to produce desired results that serve their own interests. To most such experts, negotiation is in fact conflict resolution and the process that determines the shape of future relations. John Burton, for example, has said that "in conflict resolution, nothing more is involved than ordinary negotiation except that the parties are deeply analytical, seeking to get to the source of the problem and find ways of dealing with it."[6]

However, a careful review of negotiation processes to deal with most social, political, and business conflicts in the United States will reveal that such processes are more managed than open. Laws, regulations, established procedures, traditions, and rules of the game have transformed all claimed open processes of negotiation into managed ones. The mere claim that the American system is fair and seeks to empower the weak and disadvantaged makes negotiation processes subject to certain social and/or legal limits. Today there are no games without rules, no elections without procedures, and no court rulings without laws and precedents. There are also no proceedings to settle family or business disputes using mediation, arbitration, and adjudication that are indifferent to established procedures, reject precedents, or violate accepted social limits.

Consequently, it appears that Americans are uncomfortable not with the rules of the managed process but with the concept, or with the message it conveys. It is an attitude typical of situations in which most Western professionals concerned with conflict resolution preach approaches that promote win-win outcomes, while their culture is largely based on values that promote competition leading to win-lose, or winner-takes-all outcomes.

In dealing with international conflict, negotiation is the game, or the political forum to identify problems and seek practical solutions to settle differences. Because of that, they must have certain rules to guide them, guarantee fairness, and ensure outcomes that do not violate legal, moral, social, or political limits.

## DEFINING NEGOTIATION

Negotiation processes may be defined as managed or open. Managed processes are those that accept a binding frame of reference, follow a set of basic principles, accept a proposed peace plan, or follow a precedent solution that served a similar purpose. Open processes, in contrast, accept no limitations on their deliberations and have no clear and binding guidelines by which possible proposals would be judged when the need arises. Examples of managed processes to negotiate or resolve conflict can be found in the experiences of Namibia, Iraq, and Egypt.

In resolving the conflict in Namibia, the process was based on a frame of reference outlined by UN resolutions that called for Namibia's independence and for an end to South Africa's occupation. The white minority government of South Africa rejected those resolutions and ignored the international community's calls for negotiation and compromise. It moved to criminalize the struggle of the Namibian people for freedom and political independence. However, under UN-imposed sanctions and heightened international pressure, the South African government was later forced to negotiate with SWAPO, the political and military arm of the Namibian people, and recognize previously endorsed UN resolutions. U.S. active involvement in negotiations and the use of UN resolutions as a legally binding frame of reference led to a resolution of the conflict and to Namibia's independence in 1989.

After Iraq invaded and occupied Kuwait in 1990, the United Nations was asked to enact resolutions that defined a frame of reference for ending the crisis and terminating Iraq's occupation of Kuwait. When Iraq refused to abide by the UN ruling, the international body used its legal authority to impose economic sanctions and subsequently authorized the use of military force to drive the Iraqi army out of Kuwait.

In 1974, following the October 1973 war between Israel and its Egyptian and Syrian neighbors, the United States resorted to shuttle diplomacy to arrange two disengagement agreements between Egypt and Israel. The point of departure in the American diplomatic effort at the time was the development of a mutually acceptable set of principles, rather than a frame of reference. They were principles negotiated by U.S.

mediators who later used them to guide and subsequently conclude the two disengagement agreements. This approach was dictated by Egypt's former president Anwar Sadat, who told then-U.S. Secretary of State Henry Kissinger that negotiations would not take place before an agreement was reached regarding the principles to guide the negotiation process. As John Burton writes, "Sadat's first move in talks was to tell Kissinger: we first have to agree, you and I, on the principles on which to proceed."[7]

Another approach to negotiation is to base the process on a proposed plan for a political settlement. A proposed plan is a general but clear framework for a comprehensive settlement that prescribes what is to be accomplished, while putting the pieces of the desired peace together in terms of either integration or compromise. In most cases of international conflict, almost all plans prescribe solutions that include compromises for shared interests and integrative arrangements for conflicting values.

Proposed plans that antagonists are more likely to accept are those that third party mediators conceive and present. In the absence of a legally binding frame of reference and/or a mutually accepted set of principles, this approach becomes the most feasible way to conduct and improve chances for concluding negotiations. It usually provides antagonists with a credible theoretical framework that enables them to conceptualize the shape of a fully integrated settlement and envision the benefits of durable peace. Workable plans, however, are those accepted by antagonists in advance as a basis for negotiation, not prescribed by an alien power to be imposed on antagonists.

Mutual acceptance of a proposed plan will help all conflicting parties to overcome problems associated with having to define their objectives in realistic and politically acceptable terms. Negotiators are compelled to deal with issues related to details, stages, and implementation procedures of the proposed plan. Time wasted on making extremist opening statements and debating procedural matters will be largely saved and employed to make real progress toward peace. A mutually accepted plan also resolves three major issues related to the rules of negotiations and principles of peace:

1. It makes procedural matters of little importance, allowing for concentration on substantive issues.

2. It automatically defines the shape of the goal sought by all antagonists, and thus enables them to share an objective and encourages them to launch a joint effort to achieve it.

3. Because of their comprehensive approach to conflict resolution, well-conceived and articulated plans include all parties to the conflict, and thus address all legitimate grievances and fears in the course of one process, which

produces comprehensive rather than interim or partial solutions that seldom work.

Claims are usually made that if the final outcome of a peace process is known and accepted in advance, then there is no need for negotiations. Former Israeli Prime Minister Yitzhak Shamir, for example, used this argument repeatedly to underline his determination to have an open process of negotiations with Israel's Arab adversaries. It was an argument that had the intention of undermining sincere Arab and Israeli efforts to outline a credible framework for a comprehensive and fair peace settlement. After his defeat in the June 1992 election, Shamir said that he had intended to negotiate with his Arab adversaries for ten years without concluding agreements.[8]

A proposed peace plan that defines the shape of a political settlement does not necessarily identify and define its components in clear terms. Rather, it tends to provide a general outline of the proposed settlement, specify the principles to guide negotiations, articulate the shape of antagonists' future relationships, and explain the mutual benefits and virtues of peace.

To reach the desired outcome and realize the shared objective, adversaries are required to discuss the details and identify and define all the components of the outcome. Implementation, particularly in conflicts involving value-related issues, would be carried out through transitional stages and over a relatively long period of time. This in turn opens the way for certain modifications to correspond to changing circumstances, adding new components and removing others, and producing at the end of the process an agreement more conducive to cooperation. The ever-changing regional and international environments, and the increasingly dynamic relationship between all societal processes at the national, regional, and global levels are causing assumptions, perceptions, and even socio-political systems to change rapidly. This dictates vision, flexibility, and adaptability in conceiving and implementing peace plans.

The last approach to conflict resolution is the one that bases the negotiation process on a precedent established by another group of antagonists while resolving a similar conflict. This approach implicitly accepts the principles that governed the process to resolve the other conflict, and considers the precedent settlement worth emulating.[9]

As a result, antagonists concentrate on adapting the precedent to suit their own situation and on devising the means to adopt its outcome to resolve their conflict. Such a process compels antagonists to limit their discussions and suggestions to what is relevant to the precedent and its outcome. Extreme positions are eliminated, recrimination is largely avoided and objectives of the antagonists are implicitly identified and defined in realistic and practical terms.

This approach has lately been used frequently to deal with conflicts caused by internal struggle over political power and legitimacy. The democratic approach to conflict resolution based on elections has established credible precedents in countries such as Nicaragua, Ethiopia, Cambodia, and Mozambique. Negotiations in such cases usually concentrate not on defining the outcome of the peace process but on guaranteeing the fairness of elections and the orderly management of the transition to political legitimacy and stability.

Precedents are also helpful in resolving conflicts caused by territorial disputes and contradictory claims regarding natural resources. International law, the World Court of Justice, and the notion of sharing were instrumental in establishing principles and precedents to resolve several conflicts between neighboring states. The latest conflict to be settled on these bases, as of the writing of this book, was the territorial dispute between Yemen and Oman. Mutual concessions by both countries were finally made in October 1992, and negotiations were concluded after eight years of rhetoric and hard bargaining.

Generally speaking, a managed process has a clear direction and sometimes a known destination as well. A process that is governed by a set of principles is a process with a course and a direction; a process that has a plan to follow is one with a destination. Another process that attempts to adapt a known solution to a similar conflict is one that has a clear direction and a fairly well-defined destination. Without a direction or a destination, which a managed process provides, it is very difficult to move negotiations from one phase to the next on the way to peace.

An open process, in contrast, has a general purpose but no chartered direction or defined destination. Because a purpose is usually limited to declarations of intent, such as commitment to peace, they are not legally binding and have little or no practical use. They are more of a political statement, hard to define and much harder to implement. An open process, moreover, can produce more than one outcome that deviates from the stated purpose, contradicts the intent of the process, or transforms the exercise into an exchange of blame and mutual accusations leading nowhere. In addition, an open process fails not only to tie phases of negotiations together but also to identify and define such phases.

The Arab-Israeli peace process launched in October 1991 was, as mentioned earlier, a semi-open process and, because of that, it failed to live up to expectations. Commenting on its status after twenty months and ten rounds of negotiations, David Hoffman of *The Washington Post* said, "Even after nearly two years of grappling with the issue, the two sides could not agree on such broad concepts as whether the Palestinians' autonomy would apply to individual residents or be territorial."[10]

A member of the Palestinian delegation added, "Out of the practical experience of the last 20 months, it has been difficult to agree on an interim arrangement that leads to something we have an idea about."[11]

Asher Susser, director of Tel Aviv University's Center for Middle Eastern Studies, said that if "Israel gave a clearer idea of where the talks are going, it would be easier for Palestinians to accept a gradualist approach."[12]

A negotiation process that is left open lacks the legal authority that a frame of reference usually provides; it lacks moral power, which sets of principles normally possess, and political clarity and rationality, which plans and precedents tend to instill in negotiation. It is a process that leaves control in the hands of concerned adversaries and the third party sponsors of negotiations. Because the stronger party in any conflict always tries to dictate its conditions, open processes often fail to empower the weaker party and establish the principle of reciprocity. They are processes largely based on power politics rather than ideal politics and thus seldom produce fair settlements that last.

Consequently, the outcome of open processes of negotiations are more likely to reflect the existing balance of power, which in itself is a cause of conflict, while preserving and validating the forces that govern old relationships. Such an outcome is more likely to be unfair and to be perceived by the weaker party as unjust. Unjust and unfair settlements are not sound outcomes, nor do they transform hostile relationships into cooperative ones that foster long-term peace and stability. They are arrangements to contain conflict while its roots and causes are left unattended to.

Open processes of negotiation, moreover, tend to permit the most radical viewpoints to be freely expressed during negotiations and even legitimized by the process itself. Demands that might be made by radicals during an open process are likely to be considered possible options, even when they contradict international law and UN resolutions and conventions. For example, Israeli negotiators have continued until September 1993 to call their Palestinian counterparts "the inhabitants of the territories," denying them the recognition accorded all nations and human communities and reducing them to an environmental problem.

Managed processes, in contrast, permit no extreme demands to be made and no unrealistic opinions to gain legitimacy. Demands and opinions that are in contradiction with international legality and violate universally accepted norms of human rights and state's behavior are rejected. They are neither considered nor allowed to be freely expressed during negotiations. This paves the way for the principles of fairness, equality, and legality to guide negotiations and govern their outcomes.

Dennis Sandole argues that the movement toward conflict resolution is a movement in thought and action away from Realpolitik and toward Idealpolitik.[13] Competitive processes of conflict resolution are normally governed by the logic and power of Realpolitik and tend to seek solutions based on compromises that serve the interests of the stronger party. In contrast, cooperative processes are governed by the spirit and values of Idealpolitik and usually seek solutions based on creating integrative relationships that serve the causes of peace and stability. Sandole writes, "If in any given relationship, trust, confidence and security could be substituted for distrust, suspicion and insecurity, then the chances would be increased for cooperative processes of conflict resolution to dominate the relationship."[14] Such a transformation cannot be achieved through negotiations only and should not be expected to prevail before conflict is resolved. To produce such outcomes, particularly when distrust, suspicion, and insecurity prevail, negotiation processes have to be managed to neutralize the power of Realpolitik and introduce the values of Idealpolitik.

Power plays an important role in conflict management in general and negotiations to resolve conflict in particular. The more powerful party is often able to impose its will on others and influence the outcome of negotiations. Powerful states influence international law more than do weaker ones, and they tend to obey internationally sanctioned rules less than the weaker states. Power may also "impose limits on the equal application of the law."[15] But even if laws are the product of politics and power, their application "cannot be reduced solely to politics and power without negating the idea of law."[16]

Nevertheless, power can be restrained and balanced by counterpower. This is why students of Realpolitik believe that a balance of power is an important factor in respecting international law and maintaining stability. It is also a reason that in negotiations, powerful parties tend to resist intervention from an outside source because of its ability to diminish their capacity to impose their will on their adversaries. Richard Bilder says, "Typically, the party in the more powerful negotiating position might be expected to be particularly reluctant to accept third party intervention, because such intervention may have the effect of counterbalancing or neutralizing its bargaining power."[17]

When the Middle East peace process of 1991 was constructed, Israel insisted that negotiations with its weaker Arab adversaries be conducted face to face, and that no outside power, including the United Nations and the United States, be allowed to intervene without the consent of all parties concerned. Transforming open processes of negotiation into managed ones serves to empower the weaker party and counterbalance the power of the stronger one, creating conditions for a fair outcome.

To summarize, constructive negotiation processes that are meant to resolve conflict and produce durable peace settlements must be guided by the rules and inherent values of one of the following:

1. A legally binding "frame of reference" that relies heavily on international law, the UN charter and resolutions, or previously signed and recognized bilateral and regional treaties and agreements.

2. A clear set of principles that rely on international law and conventions, internationally sanctioned norms of behavior of sovereign states, the right of nations to self-determination, and the spirit of the time, particularly as related to human rights and political, economic, and environmental interdependencies.

3. A peace plan often conceived and articulated by concerned third parties with intimate knowledge of the real and perceived causes of the conflict, the issues disputed, and the positions of the parties involved.

4. A precedent arrangement that was instrumental in resolving a similar conflict and establishing peace.

## STRATEGY AND PROCEDURE

The analysis in this book assumes that dialogue, negotiation, and mediation are three integrative components of one political process whose aim is to resolve conflict and achieve peace. Thus, negotiation has one strategy and one objective. It is an objective to achieve peace based on fairness and a strategy to do so through the conclusion of mutually acceptable and freely negotiated agreements. Strategies that seek to prolong negotiations, buy time, or frustrate efforts to conclude agreements are strategies to use negotiations as a tool to hinder peace, continue hostility, and perpetuate injustice.

The first strategy, the strategy for peace, considers the status quo unhealthy and seeks to change it. The second, in contrast, considers the status quo opportune and seeks to perpetuate it. Strategies that seek peace tend usually to envision arrangements to build new cooperative relationships to end hostility and foster stability. Strategies to buy time tend to envision arrangements to preserve the existing balance of power, facilitate permanent domination, and legitimize both ends through the process of negotiation.

Therefore, any strategy to make negotiations a process in the service of peace and conflict resolutions must be designed to maximize chances for reaching arrangements that change rather than preserve the status quo. Such a strategy should give serious consideration to matters related to the auspices under which negotiations are to be held, the priority of issues to be tackled first, the overall approach to be followed, as well as many other issues that deal with both substance and procedure. Noted among such issues are timing, parties to be involved, level of representation, place of negotiation, third party participation and intervention, and deadlines to be set and respected.

Most negotiations tend to be conducted between two unequal parties. The weaker party shows usually more interest in peace and seeks a quick conclusion to negotiations. However, it is more likely to lack the means to achieve its objectives and thus to express frustration during negotiations. The stronger party shows usually equal interest in negotiations but seeks to prolong the process in order to press the weaker one into making more concessions. It uses its power to create new facts on the ground to foreclose certain options and ensure that future agreements will enable it to maximize benefits at the expense of its adversary.

The weaker party resorts frequently to raising the issue of fairness and calls for just solutions. The stronger one resorts almost always to such tactics as raising issues of procedure and calling for confidence-building measures to create mutual trust before final agreements can be concluded. Therefore, a strategy for peace should have a well-defined objective and credible, built-in means to realize that objective, which in turn dictate a need for a legally or politically binding framework, and often also require the intervention of an impartial and credible third party.

### Timing

Timing is an important element of any strategy for action. When a conflict is ripe, or approaching the point of being ripe for resolution, mediation and/or negotiation should be launched or intensified without delay. Developments that help conflicts proceed and signs that indicate that a particular conflict is ready for resolution are many. Among them are substantial changes in the balance of power, lack of domestic support and international backing for the continuation of hostilities, deteriorating economic conditions and increased socio-political problems at home, regional realignments, a change in political leadership, and in the case of violent and bloody conflicts, a stalemate that makes war unwinnable. Nothing is as important as a drastic shift in the political position of the leadership of one adversary or more.

In 1977, the Egyptian president made a trip to Israel declaring his desire to make peace. It was one of the most dramatic political moves in the history of international diplomacy, leading to profound changes in the perceptions of peoples on both sides of the Arab-Israeli conflict, and consequently to negotiating and concluding a peace treaty between Egypt and Israel in 1979.[18] Gorbachev's ascendance to power in the Soviet Union in 1985 and his unilateral initiatives to reduce tension with the United States and limit the arms race were instrumental to ending the Cold War in four years. In fact, all agreements that the United States and the Soviet Union concluded regarding the arms race and nuclear weapons resulted from changes in one party's political position and dropping certain demands that had prevented progress from being made in the past, not from clever negotiating or better timing. Nevertheless, "sometimes aspects of domestic circumstances, relations between adversaries, and the international context together almost compel agreements."[19]

Despite the importance of timing, conditions to ripen conflict could be engineered to encourage or force negotiation. Whenever attempted, they should be made to reduce the cost of conflict, shorten wars, and avoid violent confrontations caused by civil strife. Careful analysis of the real and perceived causes of conflict, improved communications, honest and skilled mediation, persuasion, economic sanctions, and a well-structured peace strategy are forces capable of leading conflict to conclusion.

However, the American school of Realpolitik claims that the creation of a stalemate is probably the best way to ripen violent conflicts and convince antagonists that war is unwinnable. W. Scott Thompson, for example, argues that some conflicts "ought to be allowed to play out."[20] Others even advocate that conflicting parties be assisted to reach that conclusion, not through political persuasion but through direct military confrontation. They maintain that providing both sides with the means to continue the fight and attain a military balance of power would weaken their will to fight and convince them to negotiate. John Poindexter, national security adviser to President Ronald Reagan (1981–88) used this argument to justify the U.S. arms-for-hostages deal with Iran in the mid-1980s, when Iran and Iraq were at war. In testimony to the U.S. Congress, Poindexter said that Reagan had agreed to sell arms to Iran in order to enhance its fighting capabilities and restore the balance of power in the Gulf war.[21]

In the case of the Arab-Israeli conflict, the same school of Realpolitik and the same U.S. administration argued for a different kind of power relationship. The U.S. Department of State claimed that its support for Israel was intended to enable the Jewish state to maintain a qualitative military edge over its Arab neighboring states, gain the self-confidence necessary for making peace, and induce the Israeli government to make the economic policy changes required to restructure its economy.[22]

Some students of the Realpolitik school promote conflict settlements that reflect power relationships among adversaries. Richard Bilder, for example, says that "to the extent that intervention by third parties typically produces outcomes different from those that would have resulted from negotiations based on the effective power of the disputing states acting solely by themselves, the outcomes and settlements resulting from intervention may distort rather than reflect the real underlying power relationships and be unstable."[23]

Realpolitik is a school of thought that gives little or no consideration to matters of fairness and seeks only political settlements that largely validate rather than fundamentally change the status quo. It is a school that seeks political stability, not fairness, and power and domination, not equality and justice, as the way to deal with conflict. It feels more inclined to use the control model and follow the total approach to re-establish stability and achieve peace—peace being merely the absence of war.

### Party Preference

Choosing the right parties to participate in negotiation is another important element of strategy. In certain conflicts caused by interest-related issues, it might be better to exclude all parties that are not directly involved in the conflict or greatly affected by it. A settlement produced only by the major parties is simpler and easier to implement and would be more likely to endure. Inviting non-essential parties to participate in negotiation often induces those parties to exaggerate their interests and grievances to justify participation and legitimize demands that could complicate and prolong the process. Agreements that may be reached are more likely to be complex and difficult to implement and enforce.

In international conflicts involving more than two nations, the choice usually becomes one of priority rather than preference. It is a choice either between the weak parties, the strong ones, or all adversaries at the same time. The Arab-Israeli conflict provides good lessons in this regard. The first Arab-Israeli peace agreement was signed between Israel and Egypt, the largest and strongest Arab state. All other Arab states have tried but failed to stop Egypt from negotiating and concluding a separate peace agreement with Israel. Because of its disadvantages regarding the larger Arab cause, the Egyptian-Israeli agreement failed to produce real peace or restore stability in the region.

In 1983, following Israel's invasion of Lebanon, the U.S. government mediated an agreement between Israel and Lebanon, the smallest and weakest Arab state involved in the Arab-Israeli conflict. But since U.S. mediation excluded Syria, failing to take Syrian interests into consideration, the Syrian government succeeded in nullifying the Israeli-Lebanese agreement, preventing its implementation.[24] The exercise, however, increased Arab suspicion of U.S. intentions, heightened fear on both sides of the conflict, and intensified the arms race in the region.

These facts seem to suggest that in conflicts where more than two states are directly involved, all parties should be invited to participate in negotiations, and that comprehensive rather than partial settlements should be attempted. Partial agreements and interim arrangements are more likely to be costly and slow, and when successfully concluded, to fall far short of achieving peace and stability.

### Issue Priority

Almost all international conflicts involve issues that are interest-related and others that are value-related. Only territorial disputes and conflicts over natural resources may involve no value-related issues of particular significance. Priority in multiissue conflicts is usually between minor, largely interest-related issues and substantial, largely value-related ones.

In such conflicts, however, interest-related issues tend to be a consequence of the larger, more substantive value-related ones. As a result, a strategy giving priority to resolving the minor issues first may not work because of the fact that they are more likely to be a consequence of the major issues—an aspect of the conflict, not its real cause. Even if the strategy works, it may not produce tangible results to justify the time and effort invested in it. In certain cases, attempts to give priority to interest-related issues that are clearly a consequence of value-related ones could backfire, deepening suspicion and creating more problems.

The Arab-Israeli conflict is also instructive in regard to this point. The United States has tried repeatedly and almost constantly for more than two decades to end the Arab economic boycott of Israel on the one hand, and to stop the building and expanding of Israeli settlements in the occupied Palestinian territories on the other. Nevertheless, all efforts ended in failure and American money and political capital spent to induce Israel and the other Arab states to be more forthcoming were wasted. Attempts have also been made since the 1950s to settle the issue of dividing water resources between Israel and its immediate Arab neighbors without much success. The Arab boycott of Israel, Israeli settlement policy, and the dispute over water resources are a consequence of the larger Arab-Israeli conflict. It is a conflict over value-related issues, primarily the Israeli denial of Palestinian national rights and Israeli violation of the sovereignty and territorial integrity of Syria, Jordan, and Lebanon.

This analysis suggests that priority should be given to dealing with the major, value-related issues that form the core of the conflict. However, negotiating mutually acceptable solutions to interest-related issues but making implementation conditional on resolving the value-related ones could signify progress and provide concrete evidence that negotiations work. This in turn could motivate negotiators to work harder and become more reasonable and careful not to undermine the success accomplished in the interest-related arena while seeking solutions to the more sensitive value-related issues.

### Third Party Intervention

In certain conflicts, particularly when conflict is induced by or cannot be fully sustained without substantial outside assistance, third party intervention in negotiation is very important. The outside power or powers providing the bulk of the assistance needed to sustain conflict assume particular responsibility for taking the initiative to end the dispute. In international conflicts involving war and violence, antagonists should not be expected to initiate negotiations on their own, regardless of circumstances. Self-sustained conflicts tend also to require outside intervention to initiate and sustain negotiations and introduce new ideas to facilitate solutions. This type of intervention, however, falls under mediation and may be launched by concerned non-governmental third parties and not only by outside powers involved in the conflict.

Third party intervention in negotiations, particularly intervention carried out under the auspices of the great world powers or the United Nations, can provide incentives and guarantees to initiate and sustain negotiations. In general, outside intervention can provide several services and inducements, such as persuasion, protection, moral support, economic and non-economic assistance, and guarantees of agreements. It can also provide negative inducements in the form of political, economic, military and media pressure to make non-cooperation costly and self-defeating.

Inducements that can be employed by outside powers and the world community to encourage or compel antagonists to negotiate are many. The most frequently employed ones, however, are: coercion, economic sanctions, media and political pressure, financial and military assistance, and persuasion.

Coercion is more likely to be used by one adversary or a sponsor of negotiations against the weaker party to extract a favorable or quick agreement. It is less likely to lead to peace and stability and may even backfire, causing a regional arms race, a war, or both. Iraq's attempt to use coercion against Kuwait in 1990 led to the Gulf war of 1991 and to the acceleration of the arms race in the Gulf region in 1992 and 1993 by Iran, Saudi Arabia, Kuwait, and others.

Economic sanctions were used by the United States unilaterally against Cuba and by the Western powers collectively against the communist states for most of the Cold War years. They were also employed by the world community against South Africa and Iraq. Military and economic sanctions were also employed against Serbia and the other newly created states in the former Yugoslavia to undermine their ability to fight and continue the Balkan war.

The impact of economic sanctions on South Africa seems to indicate that such measures are effective when employed collectively and allowed to take their course. In a world that has become increasingly interdependent, it is expected that economic sanctions will be used more frequently and will become more effective. Collective sanctions, however, are more effective than unilateral ones, and the most effective of all are UN-mandated sanctions. Economic and military sanctions used as preventive measures before hostilities escalate into open war are more likely to be effective. When employed after hostilities escalate, they are less likely to be effective, and may even serve to penalize the weaker party, as UN-mandated military and economic sanctions did in Bosnia in 1992–94.

Financial and military assistance are measures that could be used uni-laterally by a superpower or collectively by a group of powers through a regional or an international organization. In 1979, for example, to en-courage Egypt and Israel to sign a peace treaty, the United States pro-vided both states with an aid package valued at $5 billion, of which $3.2 billion went to Israel and $1.8 billion to Egypt.[25] U.S. military and eco-nomic aid to both states has averaged more than $6 billion annually ever since, as compared with less than $2 billion in 1977, with Egypt receiving about 40 percent of the total. Military and diplomatic backing could also come in the form of a formal treaty or a memorandum of understanding, guaranteeing agreements to end conflict and ensuring the long-term se-curity of certain states.

In a world characterized by economic troubles, ethnic conflict, viola-tions of human rights, environmental concerns, and retreating great powers, financial assistance and economic sanctions are becoming in-creasingly more effective as tools to facilitate conflict resolution and pro-mote regional cooperation.[26] Without them, dictators will continue to violate the basic human rights of their constituencies, ethnic conflict will escalate, and the ideas of capitalism and political democracy will be dis-credited in many parts of the world.

Persuasion and political and media pressure represent two sides of the same coin, and thus serve the same purpose in a complementary manner. The first provides positive incentives and underlines realism and ration-ality; the latter provides negative inducements and works to weaken the will to resist and the ability to marshal international support.

When the use of inducements appears advisable, it is more effective to use both negative and positive inducements at the same time. Using only one type seems to backfire, causing conflict to be prolonged and costly. Positive inducements alone, as the case of U.S. aid to Israel has demonstrated, are more likely to lead to intransigence. Sanctions alone could deepen the sense of isolation and increase the national will to resist and to go on fighting regardless of consequences, as the case in Serbia seems to indicate.

International and ethnic conflicts are different even when they involve the same issues. They are different because of matters of geography, balance of power, time, international implications, political cultures, his-torical experiences, and value systems of the conflicting parties. As a result, concerned powers, international organizations, and parties inter-ested in initiating peace processes to resolve conflict should start by an-alyzing the symptoms and identifying the real causes of conflict. They should also identify and solicit the assistance of those outside powers that are more interested in helping to resolve conflict, as well as those that are keen to keep it alive. Based on that, a strategy that includes mediation and negotiation should be designed to suit the needs of each particular conflict. Such a strategy would have to answer the following questions:

1. What is the basis that should guide the entire peace process, and govern negotiations in particular?
2. Which antagonists should be involved in the peace process and who should be involved in each stage of negotiations?
3. Which issues should be addressed first—the basic value-related ones or the secondary, interest-related, or all issues at the same time?
4. What is the role of mediators, and what is the authority of the sponsoring international organization or powers?
5. What is the role of outside powers that have a stake in the conflict? How are they to be dealt with, and whose interests are liable to be substantially affected by the possible outcomes of negotiations?
6. Should emphasis in negotiations be placed on procedural or substantive matters, and what are the requirements and possible consequences of each?
7. When and how should the peace process and negotiations be launched?
8. What positive and negative inducements should be used to encourage negotiations and help conclude agreements, and when?
9. What is the role of the confidence-building measures? When should they be used during the different stages of a peace process—before negotiations, during the first phase of negotiations, or at the later phase when the process approaches conclusion?
10. Above all, what is the real and overall objective of the entire peace process and what are the objectives of its components, particularly mediation and negotiation?

Negotiation is a political process to end conflict. It uses all available means to persuade antagonists to negotiate, while trying to create enough pressure to compel adversaries to show more willingness to compromise. The instruments it usually uses include legal measures, psychological pressure, persuasion, economic incentives and sanctions, and political leverage. It is a process that defines the procedure, identifies the substantive issues, reduces uncertainty, and provides assurance along the way to conflict resolution. It further provides promises of change for the better as it persuades antagonists to focus attention on the future, not the past, and to build new cooperative relationships that tie them together.

Agreements, when it is time to conclude them, should be made simple, and the outcome of negotiations should be clear. Otherwise, differing interpretations will follow, reigniting tension and invoking suspicion that could complicate the process of implementation and undermine agreements, as demonstrated, for example, by the Israeli-PLO Oslo agreement. In addition, the agreements should also strive to integrate the interests of antagonists by creating new frameworks and incentives for cooperation. This means that the outcome must be seen by all concerned parties, particularly the major ones, as mutually beneficial and promising. Agreements that are fair and futuristic should change the attitudes of adversaries from being two parties facing each other on conflicting lines to two partners facing the future side by side.[27]

## NOTES

1. Robert A. Rubinstein, "Culture and Negotiation," Elizabeth Warnock Fernea and Mary Evelyn Hocking, eds., *The Struggle for Peace* (Austin: University of Texas Press, 1992), p. 116.

2. Mohamed Rabie, *A Vision for the Transformation of the Middle East* (Washington, D.C.: Center for Educational Development, 1990), pp. 23–25.

3. Raymond Cohen, *Negotiating Across Cultures* (Washington, D.C.: United States Institute of Peace, 1991), p. 7.

4. Roger Fisher and William Ury, *Getting to Yes* (New York: Penguin Books, 1983), pp. 3–4.

5. Raymond Cohen, *Negotiating*, p. 62.

6. John Burton, "Unfinished Business in Conflict Resolution," in John Burton and Frank Dukes, eds., *Conflict: Readings in Management and Resolution* (New York: St. Martin's Press, 1990), p. 328.

7. Raymond Cohen, *Negotiating*, p. 81.

8. Mohamed Rabie, *Conflict Resolution and the Middle East Process* (Hamburg, Germany: Deutsches Orient Institut, 1993). The book explains how these approaches apply to the Middle East peace process and why an open process of negotiation is unsuitable for resolving the conflict.

9. Ibid., pp. 46–47.

10. David Hoffman, "Serious Doubts on Mideast Talks," *The Washington Post*, July 23, 1993.

11. Ibid.

12. Ibid.

13. Dennis J. D. Sandole, *The Conflict Prevention Center: Prospects for Cooperative Conflict Resolution in the New Europe* (Fairfax, Va.: George Mason University, unpublished paper, 1990), pp. 2–5.

14. Ibid., p. 5.

15. Oscar Schachter, "The Role of International Law in Maintaining Peace," in W. Scott Thompson et al., eds., *Approaches to Peace* (Washington, D.C.: United States Institute of Peace, 1991), p. 71.

16. Ibid., pp. 70–71.

17. Richard Bilder, "International Third-Party Dispute Settlements," in W. Scott Thompson et al., eds., *Approaches to Peace* (Washington, D.C.: United States Institute of Peace, 1991), p. 195.

18. For more information about Sadat's trip to Israel and its implications for the Arab-Israeli conflict and future prospects for peace, see William B. Quandt,

*Camp David, Peacemaking and Politics* (Washington, D.C.: The Brookings Institution, 1986), pp. 135–167; William B. Quandt, *Peace Process* (Washington, D.C.: The Brookings Institution, 1993), pp. 270–73; and Harold H. Saunders, *The Other Walls* (Washington, D.C.: American Enterprise Institute, 1985), pp. 95–99.

19. Louis Kriesberg, *International Conflict Resolution* (New Haven, Conn.: Yale University Press, 1992), p. 123.

20. W. Scott Thompson, *Where History Continued: Conflict Resolution in the Third World* (Washington, D.C.: United States Institute of Peace Conference on Conflict Resolution in the Third World, 1990), p. 10.

21. This information was revealed during the questioning of Poindexter by the Joint Congressional Committee that investigated the Iran-Contra Affair, August 3, 1987.

22. Mohamed Rabie, *The Politics of Foreign Aid* (New York: Praeger, 1988), pp. 4–6.

23. Richard Bilder, "International Third-Party Dispute Settlements," p. 209.

24. George P. Shultz, *Turmoil and Triumph* (New York: Charles Scribner's Sons, 1993), pp. 208–19.

25. Mohamed Rabie, *The Politics of Foreign Aid*, pp. 113–16.

26. Mohamed Rabie, *The New World Order* (New York: Vantage Press, 1992), pp. 187–208.

27. Roger Fisher and Scott Brawn, *Getting Together: Building Relationships as We Negotiate* (New York: Penguin Books, 1988), pp. 5–6.

# Chapter Seven

# MEDIATION

---

Mediation is an act of intervention in a conflict or dispute by a third party or an outside power to improve the chances of resolving conflict. It usually seeks to engage the adversaries in constructive dialogue, initiate negotiations between antagonists, or break a deadlock in negotiations. A mediator may be an individual, a small group of individuals, an organization or a government; all of them, however, must share an interest in resolving conflict. "A mediator is essentially a facilitator of communications between the [conflicting] parties, assisting them to engage in a dialogue directed toward the objective of mutual resolution of their dispute."[1]

Individual mediators are persons who either feel strongly about the conflict and volunteer their services to mediate, or are paid professionals whose job is to facilitate communications and negotiations among adversaries. Small groups of individuals are more likely to represent nongovernmental or international organizations that are committed to promoting peace and the resolution of conflict through political means. Governments, however, are less likely to act as mediators out of concern for others. They usually intervene to protect or promote their own interests or because one of the major conflicting parties requests their intervention.

Mediation by a third party is usually launched either at the request of an adversary or at the mediator's own initiative. Adversaries' induced mediation comes usually as a result of a new conviction that the status quo is no longer tenable or desirable and that conflict is not winnable. Such a change in attitude may be due to internal pressure caused by heightened economic or political problems, or external pressure caused by unfavorable change in the balance of power. Change in attitude could also come as a result of an internal political development that brings a new, more moderate leadership to power, as explained in the previous chapter.

Acts of mediation that are induced by a third party's own initiative, called "uninvited third party intervention," tend usually to be the result of new developments that improve the chances for negotiation or ending hostilities. Such developments may come in the form of newly conceived ideas that seem promising, new information regarding a favorable change in one party's attitude, or a combination of both. Third party independent intervention can also come as a result of an international development indicating success in resolving a similar conflict, setting a precedent and providing renewed hope. Such developments serve usually to ripen conflict, making mediation and negotiation essential to initiating peace processes.[2]

Whatever the reasons for change that induces mediation, the change in adversaries' attitudes is more important because it signals a change in perceptions regarding time, its relevance, and its future role in conflict. Such perceptions normally play the role of a resilient socio-political and psychological force in each conflict, affecting attitudes and policies and causing peace processes to be initiated, accelerated, delayed, abandoned, or totally avoided. An adversarial party that perceives time to be working to its own advantage is more likely to wait and reject serious negotiations, even if that party's position is the weaker one. In contrast, another party that perceives time to be working to its enemy's advantage is more likely to seek serious negotiations, even if its position is the stronger one. A party that is weak and sees no chance that time may change to its advantage in the future is more likely to feel desperate and seek mediation, serious negotiation, and show willingness to compromise.

However, a strong party may not be able to clearly see the importance of time and the role it plays in determining its relative position vis-à-vis its enemy in the long run. For example, in the Arab-Israeli conflict, the Likud governments of Israel have always acted as if time were going to be always on their side. They thought that the longer Israel waited, the weaker the Arab position would be, and the more Israel would gain in future negotiations. But a future perceived as such is in fact a point in time that no one can precisely define, and one no party has developed a capacity to recognize upon its arrival.

The Israeli Labor governments, in contrast, have largely acted as if time was on their enemy's side or at least could not be counted upon to further strengthen Israel's position in the long run. As a result, they sought mediation and negotiation, using Israel's qualitative military edge and unqualified U.S. backing to maximize benefits in the short run. Due to a keen awareness of the role of military power during the Cold War and because of undisciplined U.S. backing, Israel was able to gain and maintain a distinctive military edge over its Arab adversaries. But since Labor governments sought a settlement that reflected the existing balance of power between Israel and its Arab adversaries, they failed to engage the Arab side in serious negotiations leading to a settlement.

While power could be used in a positive way to fight evil and convince a menacing enemy to come to its senses, it is often used in a negative way to intimidate and control an opponent that might be neither dangerous nor provocative. When power is used to determine the outcome of negotiations, it is more likely to perpetuate an unhealthy relationship in which one party controls or dominates the other. In such a power relationship, the stronger party not only prevents the subordinated one from making positive future contributions to the relationship, but it also deprives itself of the contributions that the weaker party might be able to make.[3]

In conflicts involving ethnic disputes and ideological issues, time tends to be of less importance. Efforts to preserve cultural identity and defend perceived national interests work usually to reduce the importance of time and the impact of internal and external developments on attitudes toward conflict. In such cases, independent third party mediation becomes more important to initiate a peace process and persuade adversaries to engage in political dialogue that improves communications and contributes to changing mutually hostile perceptions. Morton Deutsch writes that "to induce a constructive process of conflict resolution, we need to have a communication process that is more like the kind of communication that takes place in a cooperative context," which in ethnic conflicts only mediation can provide.[4]

In some cases of regional or civil conflicts that threaten to escalate and draw in other parties,

actors who fear such escalation may seek to reduce the conflict to protect themselves from becoming involved in hostilities. They are actors seldom indifferent to either the outcome of negotiations or the issues and terms that will be negotiated. Mediation in such cases may involve one intervenor, but it may also be a collective endeavor by two or more states acting within the framework of an international organization or outside of it.[5]

Such mediators, as noted, will be motivated more by self-interest and less by concern for others, and therefore are less likely to seek fairness and more likely to work for the restoration of political stability regardless of long-term implications. Even when they seek peace and express deep concern, they are unlikely to lose sight of their own interests.[6]

## THE ROLE OF MEDIATION

Mediation is an act of outside intervention to assist adversaries to resolve a shared conflict. It works to create a peace process to engage adversaries in a constructive political dialogue, or to transform an established dialogue process into a conflict resolution and peace-making one. In so doing, mediation works to initiate dialogue or foster negotiation, integrating it into a wider peace process to resolve conflict. The role of mediation could be defined as helping to achieve peace through a political process that works to:

1. Initiate dialogue among adversaries and induce cooperation between competing groups.
2. Facilitate analysis of causes of conflict and prepare for negotiations to end it.
3. Sustain and foster direct or indirect negotiations through improved or added channels of communications.
4. Bridge gaps between adversaries through the establishment of direct human contacts and help antagonists discover common goals that require joint actions.
5. Enhance the chances of success in resolving conflict through the introduction of fresh ideas and new creative proposals.
6. Simply provide a forum for declaring the acceptance of compromise settlements that could not otherwise be declared.

The first role of mediation applies mainly to value-related conflicts and others caused by power struggle. In almost all international conflicts as well as in most power struggles, adversaries are less likely to initiate negotiations on their own even when the conflict is ripe for solution. Internal politics, ideological convictions, and national commitments to certain outcomes make the other an enemy whose destruction is more desirable than resolving conflict.

In addition, value-related and power struggle conflicts tend to reject the idea of accepting the other as equal or acknowledging the legitimacy of his grievances, two basic conditions for constructive negotiation. John Burton has said, "If there is going to be a resolution to conflict, if there is going to be peaceful change, then probably there is a need for a third party, a nonofficial facilitator, perhaps with official blessing."[7] As a result, mediation by a third party to start a dialogue among antagonists becomes a necessity to prepare for negotiations. Such a dialogue tries to achieve five major objectives:

1. To persuade adversaries to recognize the grievances of each other and to acknowledge that most claims and counter-claims are either fully or partially justified.

2. To accept the other as an equal whose existence, concerns, fears, and demands have legitimacy within the context of conflict.

3. To persuade antagonists that political dialogue and negotiations are the best and safest way to resolve conflict and secure peace.

4. To help antagonists reframe their positions in terms that reflect interests and needs rather than values and ideological convictions.

5. To explain to the parties involved and to their publics that the new global political and economic imperatives make interdependence, partnership, peaceful coexistence, and mutual recognition of political and cultural rights basic conditions for national political development and regional economic progress.

In certain negotiations involving value-related conflicts, communication between antagonists usually suffers from misinterpretation of the messages exchanged and from a lack of adequate communication as well. This is true in direct negotiations, but more so in cases of indirect negotiations that are conducted through outside intermediaries. Mediation in such cases can improve communication, reduce the likelihood of misunderstanding, and add a new, more reliable channel of communication. In such situations, mediation works to achieve the following objectives:

1. To prevent the collapse of negotiations due to misunderstandings or the lack of proper communication.

2. To provide antagonists with a reliable channel of communication to convey their ideas to their adversaries discreetly and informally as needed, and thus to avoid missing any opportunity that might be helpful.

3. To keep antagonists focused on the main issues of the conflict and prevent negotiations from degenerating into declarations of non-negotiable positions, leading to increased suspicion and mistrust.

Antagonists tend to think and act as if the feelings of the other do not matter; some even pursue policies to create more problems for the other, complicating its position. A party that makes the problems of an adversary more difficult to deal with is a party that complicates its own problems. It forces the adversary with whom it has to deal to act in a less rational and predictable manner. Thus, not to acknowledge the grievances of the other and not to accept the legitimacy of its interests are acts that make the opposing party more desperate and more radical, which in turn exacerbate the problems faced by all parties concerned. Since the ultimate objective of mediation is to bring adversaries to a mutual acceptance of standards of fairness and broad equity, mutual acknowledgment of legitimate rights, grievances, and interests serves to establish mutual trust and facilitate constructive dialogue and serious negotiations.[8]

Mediation that provides a sound and reliable channel of communication helps antagonists overcome problems of miscommunication and others caused by differing cultural perceptions. Cultures, as explained in Chapter 2, attach different importance to deeds and attitudes, and at times place contradictory values on the same human and political objectives. In such cases, mediation assumes the task of initiating dialogue, sustaining negotiation, and most important, explaining the positions and intentions of adversaries to each other.

The task of explaining the positions and intentions of adversaries that belong to different cultures is a formidable but important one. It requires intimate knowledge of the cultures of the adversaries and a true understanding of the issues involved as perceived by the adversaries themselves. It may also require equipping adversaries with a common language to communicate and interpret the messages exchanged.[9] Political positions and human intentions could not be fairly explained outside their own cultural contexts, and this in turn requires a certain degree of identification with those positions and intentions. Because no one can honestly identify with the positions and true feelings of more than one adversarial party, mediation in such cases would have to go beyond its traditional role of improving communication and proposing new ideas. This new role of mediation and the way to perform it will be explained in the second part of this chapter.

Nevertheless, anthropological work, says Robert Rubinstein, "shows that there are cultural norms and preferences, but not all individuals from a particular society hold or behave according to a single set of norms. And, of course, such norms are constantly affected by social, political, economic and other events and considerations within the society."[10] Because of that, intimate knowledge of the others' cultures might not be enough to play a successful mediating role. Such knowledge must be complemented by an equal knowledge of internal intellectual developments and socio-economic forces affecting the course of societal change in general.

An enhanced understanding of the role of culture in conflict has increased the duties of mediation, requiring mediators to perform more sensitive tasks. One of those tasks is to help antagonists reframe their non-negotiable positions into matters of interests that lend themselves to compromise. In so doing, mediation also helps antagonists reach agreements regarding procedural matters and other issues related to negotiation, particularly the appropriate approach to be followed.

Mediation should also differentiate between needs and desires in order to reframe and prioritize issues to be negotiated. "In effective conflict resolution," writes Dudley Weeks, "focusing on needs is essential, but so is clarifying which issues are needs and which are desires."[11] Self-determination, or self-assertion through national and cultural identification, is a basic need of all nations and ethnic groups. It is a need that cannot be ignored if conflicts related to international disputes and ethno-national rights are to be resolved. The desire to deny the other the same rights and needs must be explained and placed in its proper context in order to eliminate it or at least minimize its impact on the peace process.

Mediation can also enhance the chances of success in resolving conflict, not only through better communication and guidance of negotiations, but also through the introduction of new ideas. New ideas are usually introduced to facilitate or advance negotiations and suggest creative pro-posals to resolve conflict, provide political guarantees and new options to conceive and build cooperative relationships. The role of mediation in such cases is to make antagonists aware of the existence and relevance of constructive ideas and other practical solutions that were helpful in resolving similar conflicts. Where confidence-building measures are hard to initiate, and where mutual suspicion reduces chances for making con-cessions, mediation, particularly UN and great-power intervention, can provide the guarantees needed to make mutual concessions leading to compromise. The role of mediation in such cases becomes one of building consensus through innovation, persuasion, and protection of antagonists' basic interests.

For such a constructive role to be played by mediation, the mediating party or team must be credible and able to gain the trust of all adver-saries. Trust, as will be explained in the next section, could be divided among members of the mediating party, while being shared by those members; it is not necessary that all adversaries trust all members of the mediating team, but it is necessary that all mediators trust and under-stand each other.

The credibility of the mediator, moreover, can suffer or be enhanced depending on the conditions imposed on one adversary before negotia-tions begin. David Newsom writes,

If, as in the case of U.S. opposition to the participation of the Palestine Liberation Organization in the Middle East Peace Process, such conditions are identified with one of the contesting parties, credibility suffers. Certainly a realistic position requires that a peacemaker relays the conditions that one party may impose on the other; but there is an important distinction between relaying conditions and defining them, as a precondition to mediation.[12]

The United States had continued to oppose PLO participation until Israel recognized the PLO and signed an agreement with it in 1993.

Credible mediation that works to build consensus is more likely to cause perceptions to be transformed on both sides of the conflict. It does so by conducting well-structured peace processes to motivate and guide antagonists to focus their attention on the new ideas and initiatives pre-sented. Such a process, if successful, leads to creating a shared position of two parts: the problem that the conflict and the issues involved in its represent, and a possible solution that the new ideas and proposals suggest. This in turn makes progress toward the resolution of conflict not only feasible but almost inevitable. As Louis Kriesberg writes, "When a shared view of the issues in contention emerges, the parties can envision a mutually acceptable outcome."[13]

The emergence of a shared view of conflict and its possible solution works to motivate all antagonists, while directing their attention toward a settlement to end hostilities. It is also more likely to help antagonists to develop a similar view of a future that provides a mutually acceptable definition of the respective places and roles of antagonists in it, and emphasizes its mutual benefits from minimizing short-term losses to maximizing long-term gains.

Mediators who know the issues involved and understand their true importance, while appreciating the political sensitivity and cultural differences of antagonists, are more likely to contribute to conflict resolution. They tend to make fewer mistakes, miss fewer opportunities, waste less time, and recognize positive change quickly. They also strive with confidence to help antagonists reframe their positions and demands in more politically acceptable terms, emphasizing negotiable interests and transforming perceptions regarding non-negotiable values to ones that are mutually accommodating. These actions serve to improve communication and reduce the likelihood of misunderstandings and recrimination. The introduction of new ideas and options, moreover, works to prevent negotiations from reaching an impasse, while leading them toward consensus building and positive conclusions.

In general, mediators are accepted by antagonists because they tend to be perceived as impartial, knowledgeable, or effective. In fact, their effectiveness is usually a function of their impartiality or their power to influence the attitudes of one antagonist or the other. Thus, a mediator's closeness to one party might imply "the possibility of 'delivering' that party and hence can stimulate the other party's cooperativeness."[14] Regardless of their effectiveness as communicators, however, mediators induce antagonists' cooperation because their intervention promises outcomes that are desired by conflicting parties and often hard to produce otherwise.

Mediators are likely to produce desirable outcomes because they usually possess certain powers and use specific political and/or legal techniques to motivate or force antagonists to cooperate. The powers mediators possess may be political, moral, economic, or simply those of logic and persuasion. The techniques they use may be negotiation to solve conflict, arbitration to settle disputes, or coercion to implement binding UN resolutions and previously signed agreements. Nevertheless, mediation that produces mutually acceptable agreements is more likely to resort to negotiation, and start, with the help of parties concerned, by negotiating a suitable frame of reference and a procedure to manage and guide negotiations.

According to James Laue, three conditions must be met if third party mediation is to be effective:

1. A willingness on the part of the conflicting parties to negotiate or engage in joint problem-solving.
2. The availability of a mutually acceptable forum to conduct mediation activities.
3. The credibility of the intervenor, or mediator, must be recognized and respected by parties concerned.[15]

A study conducted by Hugh Miall covering thirty conflicts that were settled peacefully found that mediation had played an important role in facilitating conflict resolution. Miall wrote that "third parties had an important role in sixteen out of thirty territorial conflicts examined. They were important in half of the conflicts resolved without violence, and in three out of four of the conflicts resolved after major violence."[16] The study also suggests that mediation was almost indispensable in situations involving violence related to ethnic disputes and in power struggles.

International and inter-communal conflicts usually include one or more of the following elements of conflict: clashing nationalistic or ethnic identities and aspirations, deep cultural and religious differences, political and economic disputes, historical injustices, and territorial claims. In such conflicts, mediation is likely to fail unless the underlying political and psychological causes of conflict are dealt with.[17] Because conflict is an integral part of a mutual relationship, the entire relationship must be considered when conflict is reviewed and a resolution is sought. Otherwise, political processes to resolve conflict, including mediation, will become processes to manage conflict and address some of its aspects without resolving it.

The causes of conflict are real as well as perceived. Real causes of conflict cannot be addressed except in peace processes that include negotiations that aim to change the status quo and build new, more cooperative relationships. Perceived causes of conflict can be dealt with through mediation and political dialogue to dispel mutual misconceptions regarding the other. Such misconceptions take one or more of the following forms:

1. Negative impressions and popular stereotyping of the other and its cultural values.
2. State policy and political statements to explain and counter the perceived in-

tentions of the other, using language that lacks sensitivity or intends to hurt the feelings and undermine the credibility of the adversary.

3. Political positions to frame the shared conflict in exclusive terms, and intellectual and media debate to shape public opinion in a manner that rejects and dehumanizes the other.

4. A distorted worldview regarding one's place in history, its destiny, and its duty to change the course of history or realize a perceived fate.[18]

A process to correct misconceptions is in reality a process to create mutual understanding and encourage cooperation. Without the cooperation of antagonists, misconceptions cannot be corrected, and shared views cannot emerge. Given the nature and intensity of most ethnic conflicts in the world, it is hard to conceive of a peace process that has any chance of success without active mediation by a credible third party.

Because of differences in their interests and values, people pursue goals and nurture attitudes that cause constant conflict. The socialization process of living and working together and a need to interact with others to pursue goals and promote values have compelled societies to develop mechanisms to resolve conflict. These are built-in mechanisms that all societies and systems use, often unconsciously, to manage and resolve conflict. At times, systems fail to function, causing their mechanisms for resolving conflict to become dysfunctional, which in turn causes certain conflicts to escalate.

To deal with such situations, new mechanisms are needed to manage conflict and restore balance. Mediation and negotiation are mechanisms that create means and forums to analyze conflict, identify its causes, and propose options to resolve it.

Agreements that antagonists produce to resolve conflict may succeed or fail, depending on their ability to deescalate competition, reconcile conflicting interests, and recognize and legitimize incompatible values. Agreements that endure must accomplish the following:

1. Address the underlying causes of conflict.

2. Be accepted and viewed as satisfactory by all conflicting parties.

3. Be reached jointly without undue pressure or intimidation.

4. Do not compromise values.

5. Establish foundations for new, more equitable relationships.

6. Are not challenged by outside powers that have influence.

7. Have built-in mechanisms and guarantees for implementation and long-term joint monitoring.

## U.S. MEDIATION IN THE MIDDLE EAST

Since 1967 and the adoption of UN Security Council Resolution 242, the United States has assumed the role of the chief mediator between the Arabs and Israelis. In 1979, the United States helped mediate the conclusion of a peace treaty between Egypt and Israel, and in 1983, it helped negotiate an agreement to settle the dispute between Israel and Lebanon. U.S. intervention was also instrumental in reviving the Middle East peace process to resolve the Arab-Israeli conflict in 1991.

The history of the U.S. mediation in the Middle East has been greatly influenced by two major factors: the imperatives of the Cold War as perceived by the American ruling elite; and the power of the Jewish or Israeli lobby in Washington, whose most vocal representative is the American-Israeli Public Affairs Committee (AIPAC).

In all diplomatic efforts that sought to restore stability in the Middle East and settle the Arab-Israeli conflict, the United States sided with Israel and, at the same time, tried its best to exclude the Soviet Union from all serious efforts. When the Cold War ended and the time finally came for the United States to play a role more suited to an "honest broker," it could not escape the influence of the Jewish lobby and thus it could not be fair or neutral. In addition, "when the Cold War ended, many people in the United States, in government and out, on the left and on the right, seemed glad to be relieved not only of the Cold War, but of foreign policy itself."[19]

U.S. intervention became less effective, losing enthusiasm and motivation. The Camp David accords of 1978 and the Egyptian-Israeli peace treaty of 1979 represent the most significant achievements of U.S. diplomacy in the Middle East. But the conclusion of these two agreements was not solely the work of American mediation. Although U.S. mediation and the active involvement of President Jimmy Carter were instrumental in persuading both Egyptians and Israelis to accept the accords, nothing of the sort would have been initiated without the change of perceptions on both sides caused by the Egyptian president's visit to Israel in 1977. Sadat's visit to the Jewish state was in great part due to the failure of U.S. diplomacy to advance the Middle East peace process, and it took the Carter administration by surprise.

William Quandt, then the National Security Council's staff member in charge of Middle East affairs, said that what disillusioned Sadat was "Carter's apparent inability to stand up to Israeli pressure, coupled with evidence that Carter was tired of spending so much time on an apparently intractable problem."[20] Consequently, Sadat concluded that he had "to strike out on his own." Quandt added, "Washington was caught by surprise and once again the United States was obliged to adjust its strategy because of events in the Middle East that had proved to be beyond its control."[21]

After moving into the White House, President Bill Clinton adopted a policy that sought minimal intervention in international affairs. Nevertheless, he seems to have decided not to disengage from policies and activities he inherited from the Bush administration, particularly in the Middle East. Because of that and because of its eagerness not to alienate Jewish voters, the Clinton administration took steps that in effect transformed the U.S. role in the Middle East from that of a proclaimed "honest broker" into an "Israeli cheerleader." It no longer was willing to accept the established rules of the game or respect the principles of international legality. The Clinton administration's attitudes toward the Middle East are similar to those it adopted toward Bosnia, where, as Martin Peretz says, the "administration allowed itself to be party to a military and diplomatic settlement that is not only intellectually unsatisfactory and politically inconclusive, but also morally despicable."[22]

Even when the administration put its Middle East team together, all senior officials appointed were Jewish Americans. Although these American Jews have the right to serve and represent the United States, they could not be perceived by the Arabs as neutral, and in reality they were not neutral. For example, the senior staff member in charge of Middle East affairs at the National Security Council is Martin Indyk. Indyk, before joining the Clinton administration, was the executive director of the AIPAC-affiliated Washington Institute for Near East Policy (WINEP). Dennis Ross, who was appointed chief coordinator of the peace process, is a previous fellow of the Washington Institute for Near East Policy. Days before he was appointed by Clinton, it had been announced that he was selected to replace Indyk at WINEP. Because the ideological orientation and political views of both AIPAC and WINEP are closer to those of the Israeli Likud than to Israel's Labor Party, the U.S. Middle East team was more protective of perceived Israeli interests than the Israeli government itself.

In July 1993, following the conclusion of the tenth round of negotiations in Washington, the American team visited the region seeking the finalization of a proposed "declaration of principles" to govern Israeli-Palestinian negotiations. A leader of the PLO said later that "Palestinians needed an Israeli mediator to intervene with the U.S. team to soften its position."[23] It was the team that was supposed to mediate between Israelis and Palestinians.

As mentioned earlier, U.S. intervention in the Middle East has largely sought ways to manage the Arab-Israeli conflict, rather than to resolve it. It was an intervention to protect perceived American interests and respond to domestic pressures dictated by domestic politics, particularly presidential and congressional elections. No U.S. administration has found the time, motivation, or the energy needed to initiate and sustain a negotiation process to resolve the Arab-Israeli conflict. Today, as in the past, the new ideas and energy needed to sustain the peace process come from the region, not from the United States. In June 1993, a high State Department official said: "We cannot build bridges over oceans, but we can build bridges over rivers."[24] Because of the U.S. failure to properly structure the peace process, only the parties involved were able to suggest new ideas and options to advance the process. "For all of the Clinton administration's spasms of activism in the region, the energy and imagination for the momentum of the peace process now come from Israel," writes Martin Peretz.[25] It was Israeli willingness to allow members of the Palestinian delegation to consult openly with the PLO and subsequent secret Israeli meetings with PLO officials that prevented the collapse of the peace process and led to an Israeli-Palestinian agreement for self-rule in 1993.

U.S. intervention policy in international conflict situations seems to be generally governed by the two lessons learned from involvement in Vietnam and Iraq. The first calls for avoiding military intervention because of its high risk and high cost, regardless of the moral and strategic implications. The second calls for active military intervention in situations that guarantee negligible cost, strategic imperatives, and potentially high returns. As a result, intervention in Bosnia was limited to diplomacy without military backing, causing U.S. policy to lack credibility and, in light of the Bosnian atrocities, morality as well. In Somalia, on the other hand, intervention was limited to military involvement without a parallel diplomatic process to resolve conflict, causing U.S. intervention to heighten tension there and be viewed by some factions as foreign domination. Today, the U.S. intervention policy in international conflict situations opposes military intervention where such intervention is needed and promotes diplomatic intervention where diplomacy alone cannot be effective, making it a policy that lacks coherence and effectiveness.

Paul Goble argues that the Clinton administration's foreign policy is "rooted in three problematic convictions":

1. "An uncritical faith in the virtues of multilateralism," making U.S. foreign policy dependent on others and action hard to initiate.

2. "A profound belief that the end of the Cold War releases the U.S. from its obligation to provide international leadership," leading to isolationism at a time of globalism and increasing interdependence.

3. "An ingrained opposition to use of military power if such use entails significant casualties taken regardless of the issues at stake," which leaves U.S. diplomacy ineffective and perhaps misguided. Its intention is to conceal impotence rather than project leadership.[26]

## MEDIATION—AN INTEGRATIVE MODEL

In conflict resolution, particularly during the early stages of a peace process, antagonists tend unconsciously to divide their objectives into two categories. The first category includes the primary goals that each party wants to accomplish, that reflect the major claims it makes and identify the basic needs it feels it has to satisfy. The second category identifies the goals that each party wishes to deny its antagonists. As a result, the first set of objectives tends to acquire attributes that describe it in positive terms, while the latter acquires attributes that describe it in negative terms.

The negative set of objectives sought by one party is most likely to be a mirror image of the positive set of objectives sought by its antagonist, meaning that the wishes of one party are more likely to represent the needs of the other. For example, Israeli opposition to the establishment of a Palestinian state in the occupied territories mirrors the Palestinian need for political identity. No party would be able to achieve all its objectives through negotiations because this means denying the other party the opportunity to achieve any of its objectives.

A major secret of success in negotiations lies in the ability of mediators to persuade each party to concentrate on the needs or the positive set of objectives it seeks to accomplish and overlook the wishes or the negative ones. A process that seeks to perform this task serves also to legitimize the basic demands of each party and thus effect an implicit acknowledgment of mutual grievances. Therefore, a mutual disregard of the negative objectives, or vastly de-emphasizing these desires, serves to help both parties achieve their primary objectives and emerge as winners.

Overlooking the negative objectives becomes in effect the price each party has to pay to achieve its major positive objectives. In situations where the positive cannot be separated from the negative, such as conflicting claims to the same resources or piece of land, the principle of sharing becomes the most practical, if not the only way to go. Accepting the principle of sharing would transform the negative objectives and unite them with the positive ones, thus enabling both parties to emerge as winners, viewing the outcome in the same positive terms. It would also lay concrete foundations for building cooperative relationships based on principles that promote stability and foster peace.

A mediation strategy that persuades all conflicting parties to overlook the negative objectives can also contain the desire to dehumanize the other and deny his grievances. It can vastly reduce the number of contentious issues, legitimize the basic rights claimed by each party, build mutual trust, and establish the principle of reciprocity. Thus it makes negotiation not only possible, but also sustainable and promising.

In the next few pages, a new model of mediation, called the Integrative

Model of Mediation and Negotiation, is described. William Quandt and Mohamed Rabie developed this model in 1988 while working together to initiate a dialogue between the United States and the Palestine Liberation Organization. Although neither Quandt nor Rabie was aware of the fact that a new model of mediation was being developed, their objective was to enable the United States and the PLO to start a direct political dialogue. To do that, they envisioned a new approach to bring the two parties together, producing the Integrative Model of Mediation, or the Q-R model.

In February 1988, just a few weeks after the outbreak of the Intifada in the occupied Palestinian territories of the West Bank and the Gaza Strip, it became clear that the United States and the PLO needed to talk to advance the prospects for peace in the Middle East. Because previous attempts to communicate indirectly through third party intermediaries failed to produce positive results, Quandt and Rabie felt that the new need was for direct contact.

As stated earlier, in international conflicts requiring mediation, several factors should be present to facilitate mediation and prepare for negotiation. These factors include the need to identify the objectives of the conflicting parties and define their positions in clear terms.

In the case of the Israeli-Palestinian conflict, neither the Israeli, the Palestinian, nor the American positions had been defined in clear and politically acceptable terms. As a result, all efforts to mediate among these three parties before 1988 ended in failure. With the Intifada, however, the Americans and Palestinians began to change and express themselves in more realistic terms.

While the PLO had begun to talk about a two-state solution to the Israeli-Palestinian conflict, the United States had begun to emphasize the "land for peace" formula embodied in UN Resolution 242. The United States also began to talk about the need to address both the "political rights" of the Palestinian people and the "security requirements" of Israel as inseparable.

Meanwhile, the PLO's ability to assert control over the Intifada had removed all lingering doubt regarding its claim of being the sole legitimate representative of the Palestinian people. Several other developments had also contributed to strengthening the PLO's political role and enhancing its legitimacy and international position. Such developments included a declaration of allegiance to the PLO by the Intifada's leadership, a decision by King Hussein in July 1988 to sever all administrative links to the West Bank; increased international sympathy with the Palestinian cause; and a re-energized peace camp in Israel calling for compromise and negotiation with the PLO.

Consequently, the United States began to realize that the intended peace process could not proceed without the Palestinians, and that genuine Palestinian participation could not be secured without the blessing of the PLO. A U.S.-PLO dialogue therefore emerged as a strong possibility to facilitate contact, build mutual confidence, and revitalize the stalled peace process.

While several political developments generated the need for a U.S.-PLO dialogue, the process that eventually led to U.S.-Palestinian engagement was the work of third party mediators. Three parties—the Swedish government, a small group of American Jews, and a two-man team of William Quandt and the author—performed the important task of persuading both parties to say the right things and make the right moves, leading to the opening of a U.S.-PLO dialogue in December 1988. But despite the important role played by the Swedish government and the American Jews, it was the Quandt-Rabie team that conceived the idea, constructed the approach, bridged the political and cultural gaps, and initiated the process that made the dialogue a reality.[27]

William Quandt and I were neither professional mediators nor social entrepreneurs seeking work and money. We were witnesses to a protracted and costly conflict that we fully understood and were committed to help resolve. Our commitment to Middle East peace was the common ground we shared, and our goal to initiate a U.S.-PLO dialogue was our shared objective.

Quandt's knowledge of the U.S. political system and his commitment to the larger American objectives in the Middle East were unquestionable. He had previously been a senior staff member of the National Security Council in charge of Middle Eastern affairs and continued to be one of the most articulate American experts on the subject. At the same time, my intimate knowledge of the PLO system and its leadership and commitment to the Palestinian cause were also unquestionable. I grew up in a Palestinian refugee camp, knew several PLO leaders as classmates and neighbors, and wrote about the Arab-Israeli conflict. In addition, Quandt and I are bicultural men who were socialized in both the American and Arab cultures, which enabled us to view the problems facing our initiative from the perspectives of both parties. This knowledge and commitment made both of us insiders working from the outside rather than outsiders trying to explore the inside, gaining the trust and respect needed to establish our credibility.

We started with a limited goal but an ambitious vision. The goal was to get the U.S. government and the PLO to enter a direct political dialogue that could lead to establishing mutual trust and understanding. The vision, however, was to contribute to peace making in the much-troubled Middle East. While the goal was well defined, the vision was open and complicated. Nevertheless, both objectives required an unusual understanding of the history of the Arab-Israeli conflict and the issues involved in it, and great sensitivity to the cultural and political perceptions of both parties. It also required individual dedication and team-work throughout the process.

Before 1988, U.S. efforts to communicate with the PLO and the PLO's efforts to communicate with the United States were conducted primarily through third parties, which included the Jordanians, the Egyptians, and the Saudis. Despite the credibility of these parties, each had its own po-litical agenda and short-term goals that could not be separated from its relations with either the United States or the PLO. Therefore, it was nat-ural for each party to keep its own interests in mind while passing mes-sages between Washington and the PLO headquarters in Tunis. Because messages were formulated and delivered orally and informally, accu-racy, even if good intentions were assumed, could not be guaranteed. In addition, differences in culture between the United States and the Arab intermediaries on the one hand, and differences in the political culture between the intermediaries and the PLO leadership on the other, caused miscommunication to prevail and trust to suffer.

Messages that were exchanged between the United States and the PLO were distorted and often misinterpreted, regardless of their clarity and the intentions of the intermediaries. Messages that were supposed to build mutual trust were instrumental in accentuating mistrust; commu-nications to facilitate understanding unwittingly served to deepen mis-understanding. Thus, a new channel of communications had to be invented and a new approach conceived to overcome the problems that crippled progress. These problems included the United States' self-imposed ban on talks with the PLO, Palestinian sensitivity toward offi-cial contacts with the United States, third party self-serving manipulative roles, and cultural gaps that seemed unsurmountable.

William Quandt and I tried to provide the answers to all four prob-lems. Being insiders working from the outside, we were able to facilitate contact between the two parties that enabled them to exchange views and debate issues. The new team we created was neither fully represen-tative nor unrepresentative of the conflicting parties. We were like ad-vocates, with each of us representing one side. Unlike advocates, our task was not assigned by others who wanted us to defend their positions and maximize their benefits. Rather, our task was a self-assigned and jointly launched initiative to preserve and integrate the positions of the two conflicting parties and lead them to agreement on issues of mutual concern.

In addition, we possessed certain qualities that, while eliminating the negatives of the old third parties, were able to assemble all that was needed to establish direct contact between the two adversaries and ad-vance the dialogue process. Both of us were knowledgeable of the United States and the PLO systems and the decision-making processes in Wash-ington and in Tunis. We were fully aware of the cultural sensitivities and political difficulties facing policy makers in both capitals, able to argue our case vigorously with both sides as insiders, and we had no political agenda of our own to advance.

When the idea to negotiate a U.S.-PLO understanding for dialogue was conceived, we began by defining the approach to realize it.[28] The first step, we decided, was to identify and define the desired goal in clear terms and create enough interest on both sides to pursue it. This step was an attempt to help both parties perceive the goal we designated as a shared attainable objective. We accomplished this task between February and April of 1988 without much difficulty. We met first with U.S. officials in charge of Middle East affairs at the National Security Council and later met with the PLO leadership in Tunis. Both sides, we discovered, were ready for dialogue but lacked the means to make the necessary concessions and create a suitable framework to initiate it.[29]

The second step was to present both parties with a position paper outlining the terms for a dialogue, rather than asking them to make certain gestures to build confidence. These terms were based on our knowledge of the two parties' positions and the political difficulties they faced. The terms we outlined did not ask either party to abandon its basic position or even make significant concessions. The terms asked instead that each party meet the basic demands of the other in exchange for having the other meet its own. The terms thus provided for each party to achieve its own goals by allowing the other to achieve its own objectives. In so doing, we succeeded in persuading each party to concentrate primarily on its own goals rather than those sought by the other, allowing no mention of any negative objectives by either party. At the end, we helped both parties get to the dialogue table without having to defend the new positions because they were not required to substantially change their old ones. Each party, in effect, was able to claim victory and pronounce the opening of the dialogue as a vindication of its old position.

In conceiving this approach, I drew on my business rather than academic experiences. In business, people make millions of deals every day without first having to go through a process of building mutual confidence, or even negotiating face to face. All that is usually needed to consummate a business deal is to have each party conceive the proposed deal as being in its own interest. A contract spelling out the terms of the deal and guaranteeing performance would be the second thing needed to close the deal and pave the way for completing the transaction.

My and Quandt's involvement in the dialogue initiative provided a strong element of mutual confidence. However, it was a confidence extended by the two parties not directly to each other but through us individually and collectively. Being largely accepted as insiders working from the outside gave us the knowledge to express the two parties' positions with accuracy, while enabling us to argue our case with decision-makers on both sides without much hesitancy. We argued not as intermediaries or traditional mediators, but as committed insiders trying to exploit a valued opportunity to separately advance the interests of both parties while jointly advancing the cause of peace. The process we constructed enabled us to maintain access to decision-makers while giving them the opportunity, the confidence, and the confidentiality to pursue the initiative without much political concern. The mutual trust and respect members of the team had toward one another was employed to prevent miscommunication and misunderstandings.

As we began our work, it was agreed that each of us would be in charge of communications with one party only, the one he knew best and whose trust he enjoyed most. This meant that Quandt would work with the U.S. administration and I would work with the PLO. It was decided further that we would share all relevant information, treat it with confidentiality and use it only to reinforce the desire of the two contending parties to pursue the dialogue initiative.

Dividing the tasks in this manner maximized the team's knowledge and contacts, while giving each member the freedom to maneuver as an insider with his own party. Since each contending party was asked to work only with the person it knew well, trusted most, and believed represented its views, the process was instrumental in conveying to both parties a strong sense of confidence.

Working together, the team developed a two-page position paper containing the basic demands of the U.S. government and the PLO for a dialogue, as understood by the team itself. It spelled out what were thought to be the U.S. conditions for a dialogue with the PLO, and the PLO's demands in return for meeting U.S. conditions. The ideas contained in the paper were first shown to U.S. officials at the State Department and later to the PLO leadership in Tunis. During discussions with the two parties, four main objectives were sought and accomplished:

1. To explain the basic idea of the team's work that each party should know in advance what the other would say, and that what would be said by each party would be acceptable to the other.

2. To develop the position paper prepared by the team into a document that met the fundamental conditions of both parties for dialogue, and that the words used to state those demands would strive to address the political difficulties and cultural sensitivities of the respective parties.

3. To explain the process leading to dialogue by having the PLO first make a declaration that met the basic U.S. conditions, followed by a U.S. declaration welcoming the PLO's move and meeting its basic demands. Both parties, moreover, were allowed to reiterate their traditional positions in order to satisfy their respective constituencies.

4. To encourage the contending parties, after an understanding was reached, to take small steps to build mutual confidence, reinforce the credibility of members of the team, and keep interest in the process strong.

To accomplish these goals, the team expanded its role to include reading the thinking and interpreting the attitudes of both parties. The team articulated all new ideas, suggestions, hints, and its own interpretations in terms that lent themselves to political compromise while addressing the sensitivities of both parties.

Discussions that Quandt held with U.S. officials at the Department of State in early August 1988 led us to modify slightly the original version of the position paper. The modifications, however, were minor and largely limited to changes in the wording and priority listing of points contained; no substantive changes were suggested or made. The document that emerged as a result was more to the liking of the U.S. government, particularly since the suggestions made by the State Department had concentrated on what the PLO was supposed to say. In addition, four days of intensive discussions that I later held with the PLO leadership in Tunis produced other changes that reflected PLO priorities.

During both rounds of discussions in Washington and in Tunis, neither the United States nor the PLO provided exact wordings or asked for specific formulations; only preferences and alternative options were suggested. The final document was the work of our team but the result of much thinking and intensive discussions with both parties. As such, the document gave each party the option to claim it as its own, or to disclaim it as the work of others, without negative political consequences.

By the end of September 1988, the document was implicitly accepted by both parties and a few gestures of goodwill had been undertaken. The discussions that followed in October dealt primarily with the timing of the proposed announcements. The Israeli elections, the U.S. presidential elections, and the Palestine National Council meeting, all of which were held in November 1988, caused the announcements to be delayed. Other political factors had also intervened to delay and even threaten the entire initiative. But having gone that far, both parties could not afford to retreat. Motivated by the intervention of the Swedish government, the announcements were made on December 14, 1988, to start a dialogue. Within forty-eight hours, they were followed by the first meeting between high-ranking U.S. and PLO officials.[30]

In conflict resolution, third party mediation can play a crucial role in initiating peace processes and facilitating negotiation. It can even conceive and initiate a process on its own to resolve conflict. Events and developments beyond the control of concerned parties could cause third party mediators to compete with each other or complement one another to hinder or advance the process. However, the success of mediation depends to a great extent on the clarity of its objectives, on the moral commitment of its initiators, and the initiative's own ability to help the contending parties clarify their positions and define their goals in clear terms that are amenable to compromise. Positions and demands that are not clearly stated make the work of mediators like sailing in an ocean without a compass, and the process loses its sense of direction.

Where conflicting parties lack the ability or willingness to state their positions and goals in clear and politically acceptable terms, traditional mediation may not be of much help. A small team of communicators with intimate knowledge and perhaps a previous association with the contending parties would have to be assembled and given the task of articulating and integrating the positions of the contending parties. Such tasks go beyond the usual work of bridging gaps and devising political compromises because the positions to be bridged lack clarity.

The communicators in such cases go beyond traditional mediation and into the art of helping the contending parties first articulate their respective positions, doing so in a manner that renders those positions amenable to political compromise. Mediation, which will follow, will concentrate on bridging the gaps between the positions that had been articulated from the beginning to lend themselves to political compromise and thus integrate the goals of both parties leading to agreements. People in conflict normally know more about their own conflict than anyone else because they live it and always think about it. Therefore, having a small team of mediators whose members have intimate knowledge of the issues of conflict and maintain association with conflicting parties serves to integrate mediation with negotiation. Members of the team negotiate with each other as advocates of the positions of their associates, while working in a complementary manner to persuade conflicting parties to accept what they had negotiated and settled among themselves.

One lesson we learned from the U.S.-PLO dialogue initiative was that confidence-building measures are important but not effective until a shared goal emerges to tie the contending parties together. Even a vaguely defined goal could be sufficient to start a process and facilitate the employment of confidence-building techniques. Such techniques in turn serve to reinforce commitment to the larger goal and advance the process. Meanwhile, intelligence and constant communications are the key to avoiding misunderstandings, minimizing the negative effects of surprise, and enhancing chances of success.

To summarize, the integrative mediation and negotiation model is composed of four basic elements: a team of communicators, a strategy to deal with adversaries, a process to reach agreements, and guarantees to ensure progress.

### Team

The team, as explained, is made up of two persons working separately with conflicting parties but together to define the strategy, launch the process, and bridge the political and cultural gaps as and when needed. Its members represent the points of view of the conflicting parties but do not work for those parties or maintain official links to them. Each member works with the party he or she knows best, is most trusted by, and with which he shares the same cultural background. In addition, members of the team should be able to work together and communicate freely and informally with each other, share mutual trust and respect, and have no political or personal agendas of their own.

### Strategy

The strategy is to first outline an objective for the proposed process in clear terms and then to convince the conflicting parties to cooperate to advance the process. Second, prepare a paper that best represents the respective positions of both parties, integrating their interests. The paper should also outline a frame of reference to guide the process and govern its outcome. Third, inform both parties of what can or should be said or done to begin a dialogue or negotiation, making sure that each party accepts in advance what would be said and/or done by its adversary before it actually gets done.

### Process

The process to reach agreement consists of each member of the team negotiating with the party assigned to him or her to obtain its approval of the proposed paper. This usually involves helping each party see the advantages of compromise, appreciate the difficulties that its adversary faces, and understand the need to concentrate on the positive side of its own objectives. To accomplish this, team members modify the document to be more sensitive to both parties' positions and situations, while keeping it within the parameters set by the frame of reference originally developed and articulated by the team itself. The document may also outline the steps and set dates to move the process to the point of direct engagement.

## Guarantees

This task involves keeping both parties constantly informed of all developments that are relevant to the process as well as encouraging them to implement certain measures to build mutual confidence. To do that, both members must keep lines of communication with the parties concerned, as well as with each other, open and active at all times. Obtaining the signatures of both adversaries on the final document deepens mutual confidence, diminishes chances of reversal, and provides an element of pressure, forcing both adversaries to proceed as prescribed.

## NOTES

1. Edward F. Sherman, "Applications of Dispute—Resolution Processes in the Israeli-Palestinian Conflict," in Elizabeth Warnock Fernea and Mary Evelyn Hocking, eds., *The Struggle for Peace* (Austin, Texas: University of Texas Press, 1992), p. 102.

2. Genady I. Chufrin and Harold H. Saunders, "A Public Peace Process," unpublished paper (April 1993), p. 6.

3. Dudley Weeks, *Eight Essential Steps to Conflict Resolution* (Los Angeles: Jeremy P. Tarcher, 1992), p. 18.

4. Morton Deutsch, "Theoretical Perspective on Conflict Resolution," in Dennis J. D. Sandole and Ingrid Sandole-Staroste, eds., *Conflict Management and Problem Solving: Interpersonal to International Applications* (New York: New York University Press, 1987), p. 43.

5. Saadia Touval and I. William Zartman, "Mediation: The Rule of Third-Party Diplomacy and Peacemaking." Paper written for conference on " Conflict Resolution in the Third World," United States Institute of Peace, Washington, D.C., October 1990, p. 4.

6. Ibid., p. 5.

7. John Burton, "International Conflict Resolution and Problem Solving," in John Burton and Frank Dukes, eds., *Conflict Management and Problem Solving* (New York: St. Martin's Press, 1990), p. 251.

8. Edward Sherman, "Applications of Dispute," p. 101.

9. Raymond Cohen, *Negotiating Across Cultures* (Washington, D.C.: United States Institute of Peace, 1991), Chap. 4.

10. Robert A. Rubinstein, "Culture and Negotiation," in Elizabeth Warnock Fernea and Mary Evelyn Hocking, eds., *The Struggle for Peace* (Austin, Texas: University of Texas Press, 1992), p. 123.

11. Dudley Weeks, *Eight Essential Steps*, p. 40.

12. David Newsom, "Diplomacy and Negotiation," in W. Scott Thompson et al., eds., *Approaches to Peace* (Washington, D.C.: United States Institute of Peace, 1991), p. 37.

13. Louis Kriesberg, *International Conflict Resolution* (New Haven, Conn.: Yale University Press, 1992), p. 40.

14. Saadia Touval and J. William Zartman, "Mediation," p. 13.

15. James H. Laue, "The Emergence and Institutionalization of Third-Party Roles in Conflict," in John Burton and Frank Dukes, eds., *Conflict: Readings in Management and Resolution* (New York: St. Martin's Press, 1990), pp. 267–68.

16. Hugh Miall, "Peaceful Settlement of Post-1945 Conflicts, A Comparative Study." Paper written for the conference on "Conflict Resolution in the Third World," United States Institute of Peace, Washington, D.C., 1990, p. 11.

17. Edward Sherman, "Applications of Dispute," p. 110.

18. Jay Rothman, *A Prenegotiation Model, Theory and Training* (Jerusalem: Leonard Davis Institute, Hebrew University of Jerusalem, 1990).

19. Martin Peretz, "From Sarajevo to Jerusalem," *The New Republic*, September 6, 1993, p. 21.

20. William B. Quandt, *Peace Process* (Washington, D.C.: Brookings Institution, 1993), p. 268.

21. Ibid., p. 270.

22. Martin Peretz, "From Sarajevo," p. 29.

23. The PLO leader was Fatah's Central Committee member Sakhr Habash, who told the author the same thing during a phone interview on August 20, 1993.

24. Daniel Williams, "Christopher Offers U.S. as Golan Peace Guard," *The Washington Post*, June 16, 1993.

25. Martin Peretz, "From Sarajevo," p. 27.

26. Paul A. Goble, "AWOL Abroad: Clinton's Foreign Policy," *The Christian Science Monitor*, July 2, 1993.

27. Mohamed Rabie, "The U.S.-PLO Dialogue: The Swedish Connection," *Journal of Palestine Studies*, 21/4, 84 (1992): 54.

28. The idea of the dialogue was conceived by Mohamed Rabie, who approached William Quandt asking for advice and cooperation. The full story of the secret contacts between the United States and the PLO and the role of other parties are told in *The U.S.-PLO Dialogue, Secret Diplomacy, and Conflict Resolution*, written by Mohamed Rabie and forthcoming by the University Press of Florida in 1995.

29. For more details, see Mohamed Rabie, *The U.S.-PLO Dialogue, Secret Diplomacy, and Conflict Resolution* (Gainesville: University of Florida, forthcoming).

30. The full story of the U.S.-PLO dialogue is told in a forthcoming book by this author, *The U.S.-PLO Dialogue, Secret Diplomacy and Conflict*, to be published by the University Press of Florida.

*Chapter Eight*

# ETHNICITY AND CONFLICT

Until a few years ago, the conventional wisdom was that nationalism was an outdated concept and a largely resolved problem. On both sides of the Cold War, the trend seemed to indicate that the world was moving toward internationalism rather than nationalism. The threat of nuclear war, emphasis on democracy and human rights, economic interdependence, and gradual acceptance of universal ideologies were slowly evolving as independent but integrative forces promoting individual freedoms, international interdependences, and universal values.

The threat of nuclear war between the two superpowers and the ability of each superpower to destroy the world using its nuclear arsenal made people everywhere more aware of the dangers of friction, narrow nationalism, and war. This in turn made them more amenable to the ideas of cooperation and universal peace. Economic interdependence, meanwhile, linked people, business concerns and states in a web of shared interests and environmental concerns, making political and cultural interdependence a reality. Most ideologies, though different in nature and objectives, were and continue to be powerful forces promoting universalism at the expense of nationalism and particularism. Socialism as a socio-economic ideology and democracy as a political ideology espouse similar social values and attitudes, such as justice, fairness, and equality.

In addition, the economic and political dimensions of individualism as expressed by the two concepts of a free market and representative democracy have weakened group identity, while strengthening and legitimizing individual and institutional competition. Because "they were effective in unlocking the natural resources of the country, writes Raymond Cohen, "they have become almost categorical ideological imperatives. Their demonstrable success has convinced Americans of the universal applicability of their way of life and their duty to spread its benefits around the world."[1]

Francis Fukuyama argued that the two world wars, which were largely caused and led by extremist national movements, have weakened the appeal and rationale of nationalism. He said that the two world wars may have played a role regarding nationalism "similar to the wars of religion in the sixteenth and seventeenth centuries with respect to religion, affecting the consciousness of not just the generation immediately following but all subsequent generations."[2]

However, the decline and subsequent demise of the Soviet empire, the collapse of communism, the end of the Cold War, and the gradual decline of ideology in general under the mounting pressures of economic realities have changed all that. They are working unilaterally and collectively to vastly weaken the motives and undermine the political rationale for universalism. The removal, at least temporarily, of the threat of nuclear war undermines the political forces that emphasized strategic unity at the expense of national identity in the West, the East, and the Third World. Ideas calling for the unity of all like-minded humans are much weakened, particularly after communism was discredited and national capitalism and protectionism began to mount a comeback in Europe and in the United States.

Thus, major social ideas and political forces that tried in the past to change people's thinking and unify their way of life began to crumble almost at the same time. This in turn opened the doors for the re-emergence of narrow nationalism and cultural particularism and intensified ethno-religious rivalries, leading to types of conflict that were unknown for a long time. "Ethnic loyalty," wrote Richard Rubenstein recently, "was expected to disappear in advanced capitalist societies with the emergence of the fully socialized 'economic man' and in socialist societies with the appearance of the class-conscious communist man."[3] No one seems to have expected ethno-nationalism to re-emerge, asserting itself and claiming the future.

For the purposes of this study, conflicts categorized as ethnic or ethno-national will include also religious conflicts. The reason for this inclusion is the fact that most religious groups view themselves as culturally different from the rest of the population, having their own values, belief systems, and traditions. Religious groups, fearing discrimination and/or assimilation have resorted to measures that gave them over time a unique identity centered on religion and religious traditions. Such measures include special education systems, intermarriage, strong community support systems, and, at times, a different language and a tendency toward isolationism, making them almost ethnic minorities. In the former Yugoslavia, for example, Serbs, Croats, and Muslims are divided by religion, not by ethnic background, because nearly all of them are Slavic in origin.

Ethno-national conflict is a dispute between two or more cultural groups that feel different from each other and view their relationship as unfair under existing political orders. It is "opposition among social entities directed against one another," the intensity of which "tends to increase with decreases in the social distance between the groups and with increases in the amount of energy behind them."[4] Changes in the intergroup relationships are the cause and focus of ethnic, national, and religious conflicts. Changes sought usually range from recognition of cultural rights to autonomy to political separation and independence.

Ethnic and national groups tend to be different from each other. Ethnic groups are usually small, do not think of themselves as being nations, and often do not have their own language or homeland. They differentiate themselves from their neighbors on the basis of race, religion, kinship, or tradition. National groups, on the other hand, tend to be large, have a different language and cultural traditions, and often a history of governing themselves as a separate nation in a region or a homeland of their own.

Ted Gurr differentiates between national and minority peoples. He defines the first as "regionally concentrated groups that have lost their autonomy to expansionist states but still preserve some of their cultural and linguistic distinctiveness and want to protect or reestablish some degree of political separate existence."[5] He defines minority peoples as groups having a "defined socioeconomic or political status within a larger society—based on some combination of their ethnicity, immigrant origin, economic roles, and religion—[that] are concerned about protecting or improving that status."[6]

For example, almost all conflicts in Africa are ethnic ones among core groups of tribes and minority peoples. Conflicts in Turkey between the Turkish government and the Kurds, in China between the Tibetans and the Chinese, and in Palestine between Israel and the Palestinians are national conflicts. However, conflicts in India, the Philippines, and Sudan are largely religious and cultural conflicts that fall within the category of ethnic conflict. Conflict in the former Yugoslavia is both religious and ethnic, it evokes memories of group enmity and rivalry.

## BACKGROUND

The democratization process that has recently gained momentum in Eastern and Central Europe, in Latin America and in several other parts of Africa and Asia has demonstrated that the will of the people is stronger than the power of armies and official institutions of oppression and violence. The Palestinian uprising in the West Bank and the Gaza

Strip against Israeli occupation, the popular revolts and ethnic conflicts sweeping the former communist states of Europe, the civil war in Yugoslavia, the retreat of apartheid in South Africa, and the triumph of the Eritrean Revolution in Ethiopia are signs that the time has come for smaller nations and oppressed ethnic and religious minorities to reclaim freedom.

National aspirations and cultural particularism are becoming a power not to be denied, and an urgent problem to be addressed rather than suppressed. Ethnic and religious minorities everywhere view nationalism, self-rule, and self-determination as the only workable frameworks to liberate themselves and revive their cultures. Some also view self-determination as the shortest way to attain political freedom and economic progress and develop statehood institutions to protect themselves and enhance their security against future foreign aggression. Although such expectations may be unrealistic, the convictions and perceptions they represent and the emotions they usually evoke are powerful forces threatening the political structures and territorial integrity of many states. As the Yugoslav experience demonstrated, national movements, in their hasty and almost irrational drive toward separation and self-assertion, have become agents of war and destruction in many parts of the world.

The new wave of narrow nationalism and ethnic hatred is largely a product of the legacy of colonialism, communism, nation-state building, and settlements of two world wars—that were meant to end the wars and establish world peace. These forces acted independently to achieve different goals but have collectively promoted, consciously and unconsciously, territorial and political divisions that multiplied and deepened national and ethnic hatred. Even when the acts were meant to preserve world peace, like the formation of the United Nations and the adoption of its charter, certain provisions, particularly those intended to maintain the status quo, served indirectly to suppress and deepen conflict rather than resolve it.

Most international conflicts and civil wars that are intractable are ethnic. They are difficult to resolve because they are fought over values that are non-negotiable. The source of such conflict is "the denial of those elements required in the development of all people and societies, and whose pursuit is a compelling need in all. These are security, distinctive identity, social [and political] recognition of identity, and effective participation in the process that determines such developmental requirements."[7]

Ethnic and nationality conflicts of today are international phenomena that characterize international affairs in general. They also represent a major force affecting the political and social developments of most countries of the world, which in turn affect state politics and influence national perceptions: "The world is made up of many more nations than there are states. Few states control territories that locate a single people within those borders and nowhere else."[8] Statistics seem to indicate that probably no more than 5 percent of all states in the world have populations that could be considered homogeneous, having no substantial ethnic minorities requiring special attention. According to a declaration issued by the International Institute for Nationality Rights and Regionalism in Munich, "only nine percent of the states in the world are ethnically homogeneous."[9] This declaration, however, was made years before the collapse of communism and when Yugoslavia, the Soviet Union, Ethiopia, and Czechoslovakia were only four states, rather than over twenty.

The overwhelming majority of the states in the world have substantial ethnic, national, or religious minorities. They are "majorities and minorities that differ to a varying degree ethnically, linguistically, culturally and also religiously. Yet they must live together, thus creating a potential for conflict."[10] In fact, almost all states with substantial minorities today face serious problems for which no practical solutions have been found. Some of these problems and the violent conflicts they have fueled have claimed the lives of millions of people in Africa, Asia, and Europe. While some states have acknowledged the existence of minority problems in their countries, most other states have continued to deny having such problems that require special attention.

The Iraqi government, for example, has long acknowledged the need to address the grievances of its Kurdish minority. Nevertheless, it has failed to find the solution that could satisfy the basic needs of Iraq's Arabic and Kurdish populations. In contrast, the Turkish government, which has a larger Kurdish minority, has only recently and grudgingly acknowledged the existence of a Kurdish problem in Turkey. As Ted Gurr writes, "Until 1990, the Turkish government referred to the country's Kurdish minority as 'Mountain Turks' and banned speaking, writing and publishing in the Kurdish language."[11] However, the government of the Islamic Republic of Iran has continued to deny the existence of a Kurdish minority, which has different aspirations and grievances and needs certain political changes.

During a conference on human rights in Islam held in Hamburg, Germany in September 1992, a member of the Iranian delegation presented a paper on minorities in Iran. The paper talked about religious minorities only, acknowledging the existence of most but not all of such minorities. National and ethnic minorities were not mentioned at all. Even the discussion of religious minorities was not thorough or convincing. For example, the paper failed to list Bahaism as a religion because Islam recognizes two other religions only, Christianity and Judaism. In addition, the rights of all recognized religious groups as guaranteed by the Iranian constitution were subject to limitations and interpretations that only the Iranian religious system is entitled to make.[12]

The complexity and sensitivity of issues in ethnic conflicts make them difficult problems to resolve, sometimes even to fully understand. Despite their long, bloody history, no international consensus has emerged concerning their real causes and no acceptable political solutions were found to eliminate conflict or recognize and protect the rights of both national minorities and majorities. Political arrangements that resolved disputes involving ethnic and nationality conflicts in the Aland Islands, South Tyrol, Trieste and Northern Epirus were the exceptions.[13] These conflicts were resolved peacefully, and the solutions devised to deal with them have produced results that seem satisfactory, at least for the time being.

In these four cases, rationality and compromise characterized both the processes to devise solutions and the ways to implement them. In the case of the Aland Islands, where the population is Swedish and the territorial sovereignty is Finnish, the population was granted political autonomy, self-government and economic management, while Finland maintained political sovereignty and security control. The islands have a representative in the Finnish Parliament who acts as a liaison with the legislative body in Helsinki. Recently, the self-governing authority of the islands tried to issue its own currency, but the Helsinki government opposed the move and the attempt was thwarted.[14]

In the South Tyrol region, the Italian government granted its German-speaking minority self-determination in educational and cultural matters, linguistic rights, and some autonomy in managing its economic affairs. In the dispute over Trieste, a partition plan dividing the disputed territory between the conflicting states was implemented. But in recognition of ethnic identity, minorities that were created on both sides of the partition line were given cultural rights.[15]

The Northern Epirus dispute between Greece and Albania was resolved more by default than by design. While the Albanian government moved to acknowledge the cultural rights of its Greek minority, the Greek government stopped raising the issue. The universality of the Albanian communist ideology and its Islamic religion created a tolerant and open environment for the integration of the Greek minority into the Albanian political system.

While the above disputes involving ethnic minorities were settled peacefully, all other ethnic conflicts were either settled by force or remained unresolved, fueling hatred, war, and violence. Ethnic conflicts in Sudan, the Philippines, Sri Lanka, Myanmar, India, South Africa, and the former Yugoslavia are examples of unresolved, violent conflicts. On the other hand, Nigeria, Zaire, Zimbabwe, and Indonesia provide examples of conflicts that were settled through the use of force.

In almost all cases where ethnic conflict was settled by force, the state was able to win the contest at a high cost in human and material terms. The defeated minority was subsequently placed under strict governmental control or was pacified through a process of gradual political integration. Only in the cases of Eritrea and Bangladesh did the opposition win the battle with the central government and succeed in leading its constituency to independence. In Czechoslovakia, the dispute was resolved peacefully as the two major national groups agreed to an amicable divorce after seventy years of partnership.

Ethnic and national disputes may be divided into three general categories depending on their nature and objectives. All ethnic disputes, however, are value-related and self-centered and thus hard to resolve.

The first type of ethnic conflict involves conflicting territorial claims by two neighboring states, where the conflict is primarily due to the partition of people rather than the territory itself. In these cases, territory belongs to one state, while its predominant inhabitants belong ethnically and culturally to another state. Two historical processes are responsible for the creation of this type: conquest motivated by ideology or colonialism, and immigration motivated by persecution or economic need. A good example of this type of conflict is the dispute between Azerbaijan and Armenia over Nagorno-Karabakh, which belongs politically to Azerbaijan but is claimed by Armenia because of its Christian Armenian majority.

The second type involves disputes between different ethnic, cultural, or religious groups living together in one land and under one state authority. Conflicts of this type tend usually to be over political participation and representation, over religious rights and freedoms, or over cultural identities and the right of self-determination. Conflicts in Cyprus between its ethnic Greek and Turkish communities, in the Indian province of Punjab between Muslims and Hindus, and in Iraq between the Kurds and the Iraqi government are examples of this type of ethnonational dispute.

The third type involves a small nation living in its homeland under a rule it views as foreign, inherently discriminatory and colonialist in nature. The overriding objective of a self-conscious national community in such a situation is not limited to achieving social justice or even autonomy but to effect self-determination and political independence. Examples of this type of conflict are found in India between the Kashmiris and the Indian government, in China between the people of Tibet and the Chinese government, in Palestine between the Palestinian people and Israel, and to some extent in the Sudan between the South and the North.

Conquest and the world war settlements are largely to blame for this type of national conflict.

## LEGACY OF COLONIALISM AND THE COLD WAR

The primary causes of all types of contemporary ethnic and national conflicts are rooted in the colonial era and the post-1919 and -1945 political settlements to end the two world wars, as well as in the division of Europe into two political and ideological camps. Political maps drawn at the end of each war were tailored to reward the victors, appease the powerful, and punish the losers. The perceived strategic interests of the great powers led the victors to redraw the political map of Europe along ideological lines that eventually created two opposing political and military alliances. Competition between the two blocs served to freeze conflicts within each, perpetuate the artificially drawn political borders, and facilitate domination by the two superpowers of their allies and most of the world.

At the end of World War II, the United States entered into a Cold War with the Soviet Union that divided Europe into two spheres of influence. The Yalta arrangement enabled both states "to present their relationship as an unlimited ideological confrontation, with the important proviso that no changes in the East-West line were to occur and no actual military confrontations were to ensue, especially in Europe."[16]

But since the Cold War had to be fought and the ideological conflict had to be waged, the Third World was used as a primary battlefield. Client states were created, agents were recruited, and allies were supported and protected, regardless of their commitment to the ideals promoted by each superpower. Third World dictators were encouraged to suppress political dissent, particularly when dissidents sympathized with the ideological or political views of the opposing superpower. Most Third World conflicts and civil wars that ensued were largely fought on behalf of superpowers that never had the interests of the poor Third World masses on their minds, only their own strategic and economic interests. They were interests stipulated by two opposing ideologies and dictated by a need to contain the influence and weaken the power base of the other superpower. It was a need, the world later learned, that was more perceived than real, and more costly to all parties concerned than anyone had anticipated.

As Graham Fuller writes, "The Cold War guaranteed that no nation could remain outside the armed camps of the long ideological struggle. In one sense, the international order was corrupted [and governed] by the existence of this struggle, for it meant that no issue could be looked at in its own right; every political development invariably raised the question in all major world capitals as of whose interests were being served by such events."[17] Thus, the international dimension of the Cold War served to validate the ideological struggle around the globe, denying almost all nations the opportunity to speculate about economic integration, political and economic restructuring, and regional cooperation.

Robert Pranger says that the globalization of East-West relations, as manifest in the Cold War, meant "the replacement of the power of ideas that any nation large or small might produce, with military power that the ancient Greek dismissed as the source of strength preferred by barbarians."[18] In regions such as the Mediterranean, Pranger argues, the cultural balance that existed for some 2,000 years "was replaced in 1945 by a military balance" that changed the region "in ways that are neither positive nor of a lasting value."[19]

The post-1945 settlements neither tried to correct the mistakes made by the colonial powers nor set the new nations on a course toward economic integration and regional cooperation. Only the process of decolonization was accelerated. However, the many arrangements that facilitated the dismantling of colonialism were rarely helpful in resolving ethnic conflict. Most were instrumental in inflaming national passions, deepening ethnic hatred, and implanting seeds for future inter-state conflict. Once the Cold War ended and foreign control loosened, the old passions were awakened, the dormant ethnic rivalries and hatred resumed, and border disputes intensified, causing war and destruction.

During the colonial era, all European colonial powers sought direct political control, economic advantage, and cultural domination. To achieve these goals, the colonizers in general adopted policies to divide the people they controlled, dehumanize them, and slowly create new indigenous or mixed social classes to facilitate political control and economic exploitation. The composition of these social classes and their socio-political role were important to facilitating continued colonialism, and therefore their members were carefully selected, trained, and linked to the colonial power.

This class was not always indigenous or even mixed; at times it was imported and implanted in completely foreign environments to guarantee allegiance to the masters and lack of sympathy for the colonized. In most cases, however, this class was a mixture of local and foreign nationals who were appointed as bureaucrats and middlemen between the European masters and their indigenous subjects. To secure continued loyalty, members of this class were allowed, even encouraged by the colonial masters to participate in the process of exploitation and dehumanization to which the indigenous populations were subjected.

During their rule, all colonial powers acted to create political and socio-economic structures to facilitate continued control. These structures were meant also to secure substantial political and economic influence after the colonizers' departure. Countries and nations were divided, and new states were created, rarely in accordance with historical facts on the basis of ethnic and tribal affiliations, or even in response to economic imperatives, but often despite them. For example, many African tribes that maintained ethnic unity for centuries were divided and separated by the state structures and political borders. Other nations, like the Kurds, were robbed of the opportunity to remain united and to have a state of their own as their homeland was divided between neighboring states. Thus, states encompassing territories belonging to more than one national or ethnic group became common, giving rise to territorial disputes, ethnic conflicts and consequently to repression, violence, civil and inter-state wars.

When the colonial powers realized that they had to depart, they made every effort to transfer the helms of power to their friends and local agents. In an era dominated by a Cold War mentality, such friends and agents were generally viewed by the West as moderates who would comply with the wishes of the old and new masters of the world. The United States, which played a leadership role in the decolonization process and assumed the leadership of the "free world," sought to achieve a gradual, relatively bloodless decolonization of Asia and Africa through the so-called moderate leadership. Moderation, however, was defined as "the absence of significant ideological links of this leadership to the USSR and World Communism and, even more, the willingness of the decolonized states to participate in the existing set of international economic arrangements."[20] This means that even after the end of colonialism, the United States and its European allies continued to seek the same objectives of political control and economic advantage. The only difference was in the means used, military assistance, economic aid, security arrangements, coercion, and the creation of client states characterized relations between the great and the small nations in the post–World War II era.

Moreover, the emergence of the United States and the Soviet Union as the only superpowers meant that no major conflicts could be sustained or resolved without their active involvement. However, superpower competition meant that regional conflicts were more inflamed than contained by superpower intervention. David Newson has said that "where cases are perceived to be primarily regional, Americans are prepared to accept compromise in the interest of a solution. That is less true where regional conflict is seen as an episode in a superpower competition; the objective in such situations is generally to try to impose an American solution."[21] But because the Soviet Union always opposed the imposition of American solutions, almost all regional, inter-state, and national conflicts were intensified or contained, but not resolved.

The so-called "Third World" that emerged at the closing of the colonial era was weak, divided, poor, and very much dependent on the United States and its European allies. Many of its states were and continued to be today in search of a cultural identity, a new resource base, and a role to play in regional and international settings. Most international political and security arrangements that were established since then were either harmful or of little help to the cause of international peace and Third World development.

For example, the United Nations was established at the end of World War II as an international organization to maintain and foster world peace. At the time, the United Nations reflected the will of the United States and the wisdom of its political elite, which wanted a stable world political arena and sought the preservation of the status quo created by the old colonial powers and the post-1945 settlements. As a result, the UN Charter was written to oblige all member states to respect the political independence, sovereignty, and territorial integrity of all other states. It also called for non-interference in the internal affairs of sovereign states.

Such provisions in the UN Charter, though supportive of the so-called "nation-state" system, were unhelpful to the many divided national peoples and the numerous oppressed minorities. Divided nations seeking unity and the restoration of identity were met with rejection, denial, and at times, persecution. States opposing the unity of divided nations and lands were able to use the UN Charter to justify their positions and even their acts of violence against ethnic groups and smaller nations calling for restitution.

Because political borders have largely become inviolable and the yearning for national unity and the recovery of lost homelands cannot be wished away, a formula must be found to facilitate the restoration of legitimate rights without violating today's political facts. A formula to accomplish this seemingly unachievable goal will be articulated in Chapter 9 under the title "The Shared Homeland Model." It calls for separating political rights from all other rights, while redefining the concepts of sovereignty and self-determination to make them more modest, less threatening to neighbors, and more in tune with the spirit of our time.

## THE ROLE OF MARXISM

In Eastern and Central Europe, Marxism had for decades imposed its own socio-political system on all people under its control. It was a system to separate the people from their past and collective memories, undermine their traditional ways of life, and remold their thinking and social attitudes. Peoples living under Soviet control were encouraged, sometimes forced by a combination of political and economic circumstances, to resettle in regions other than their own, creating "minority problems" in almost every region within the Soviet Union. This situation was also aggravated by the political divisions imposed on Europe by the victorious allies of the two World Wars, and also by the Yalta agreements that divided the world into two spheres of influence.

Examples of minority problems created during the Soviet domination and annexation of neighboring countries are found everywhere, particularly in the Baltic Republics of Latvia, Lithuania, and Estonia, where Russian minorities represent 25 percent to 50 percent of the total populations. Albanian minorities in Serbia and Macedonia, Serbian minorities in Croatia and Bosnia-Herzegovina, Hungarian minorities in Romania, Slovakia, and Ukraine, and the Turkish minority in Bulgaria were all the result of the divisions imposed after the two world wars and the strategic alliances they produced and perpetuated for decades. Today, an estimated 75 million former Soviet citizens live outside their ethnic homelands, about 25 million of them Russians.[22]

History cannot be erased or altered; it can only be rewritten to justify questionable acts and legitimize largely illegitimate arrangements. Traditional loyalties and cultural and religious affiliations continued to tie peoples together and define their individual and group identities despite Marxism and Soviet control. Nationalism and other cultural and ethnic bonds, though much weakened, were neither eliminated nor effectively replaced. While the Marxist economic system had failed to create shared economic interests among its subjects, the ideology was incapable of providing a coherent political and cultural identity to replace older identities.

In fact, Marxism did not try to replace national and cultural identities of the Soviet peoples with a new one; it only tried to tie them together by creating a new ideological bond: "Socialist policies emphasized equality of political and economic opportunity, but not cultural assimilation. On the contrary, most national peoples were encouraged to maintain their own languages and cultural forms."[23]

However, the brutality of the Marxist system forced old identities and cultural loyalties into a prolonged period of hibernation lasting until the end of the Cold War. Andrei Cordescu wrote recently in *The New York Times* that "someone who went to sleep in 1938 and woke up in 1992 might think little has changed."[24]

"During the Soviet period," wrote Paul B. Henze, "all history was suppressed or forced into a rigid, dogmatic framework which left most peoples feeling cheated of their past, but deeply concerned about their identity and their roots."[25]

As Marxism collapsed, national and cultural aspirations and traditional loyalties suddenly re-emerged, giving a second birth to older nations. As those nations began to reclaim long-confiscated political rights and rebuild the much-distorted cultural identities, dormant ethnic hatred and rivalries resumed. Former Yugoslav Ambassador Cvijete Job wrote, "Our society's collapse is partly because the promises of democracy and the rule of law were betrayed. Instead of just hating the regimes oppressing them, our peoples resumed their hatreds of each other. Ancient bigotry and ethnic aggression took hold. The tolerance and rationality that had helped bind us together slowly frayed."[26]

Minorities living in the new proclaimed states reacted to the emerging threat by asserting their cultural identities and demanding that their political rights be recognized and respected. But demagogues determined to exploit popular yearning for independence and narrow-minded nationalists hungry for power began to blame their people's misfortunes not only on the defunct communist system but also on other minorities living among them. They did so despite the fact that they were minorities created and victimized by the world war settlements and a misguided Soviet policy. Members of such minorities were forced by circumstances beyond their control to live either in their historical homelands under foreign control or in foreign lands separated from the centers of their indigenous culture and identity.

The actions of the new majorities and the reactions of the new minorities created a sense of insecurity on all sides. Each ethnic group began to nourish "its own version of its origin and its past and these, more often than not, conflict with neighbors' versions."[27] This in turn is helping the radical elements within each group to take things into their own hands and plan for a future that excludes all other groups. Because each state of Eastern and Central Europe has at least one ethnic minority, ethnic conflict is spreading, and violence is claiming the freedoms and the lives of the innocent and the guilty in a cycle of violence that has increasingly become self-sustaining.

The failure to stop the bloodshed in the former Yugoslavia is causing pessimism and frustration to overshadow European thinking and action. Writing in the *International Herald Tribune,* Samuel Pisar said recently that "though fascism and bolshevism have been consigned to oblivion, our century seem suddenly in danger of ending the way it began."[28]

Ethnic diversity in Central and Eastern Europe is like a puzzle, with no one knowing how it was put together or how to approach it. It is even harder to understand because European history is full of civil wars, invasions, population mobility, and the persecution of minorities. It is also a history rich in justified national claims and counter-claims, such that no claim is totally wrong or totally right, but is right and wrong at the same time. While all claims have some validity, none has unquestioned historical backing to command moral authority and enough political legitimacy to solicit clear international support.

Ethnic conflict in Eastern and Central Europe, if left unresolved, is likely to lead either to the return of dictatorship in the name of nation-

alism, or to prolonged civil wars causing the disintegration and canton-
ization of several European countries. Both consequences are destined to
cause untold human suffering, economic dislocation, and mass migra-
tions. Certain minorities, such as the Gypsies in Romania and Muslims
in Serbia, may be subjected to denial of legitimate rights, oppression,
and persecution. Several states have tacitly adopted policies to deal with
their own minorities based on "ethnic cleansing," political exclusion, or
repression and persecution, as Serbia, Romania, and Latvia have demonstrated.

For example, the Vatra Romaneaca Association, which supposedly was
established to "clean" Romanian soil of all "non-Romanians," has committed itself publicly to expelling or liquidating members of all Hungarian, German, and Gypsy minorities. Some of the tactics it claims to have
adopted are so notorious that they could be defined as terroristic.

Clause No. 18 of its manifesto, adopted February 20, 1990, reads as
follows:

Our association specifies as its principle task the implementation of different
forms and methods of intimidation. Accordingly, we will eliminate or neutralize
the most talented leaders of our opponents. This is the most important and most
urgent step of our association. Next, making the non-Romanians aware of the
fact that they have no business here in Romania any more and that neither their
physical nor their mental safety will be guaranteed here in the future. Thus it
will be impossible not to be able to clean the holy Romanian soil from these
blemishes by the emigration of these foreign elements. In order to annihilate
those who stay we shall apply later the most effective methods.[29]

A human rights report issued in September 1992 by the Helsinki
Watch Group described the inhumane treatment of Gypsies in Romania.
It said: "Gypsies in Romania have been the target of increasingly violent
attacks since the revolution that toppled Nicolae Ceauşescu. Their homes
have been burned down and vandalized, they have been beaten by vig-
ilante mobs, and on occasion arrested by police and beaten in police
custody, and they have been chased out of one village after another."[30]
Hungarians in Romania, while not subject to such extreme tactics, are
nevertheless, being oppressed and denied their cultural rights.

In the former state of Yugoslavia, the situation concerning ethnic conflict and minorities' rights is much worse. Serbia, which views itself as
the legitimate heir of the disintegrating Yugoslav republic and the representative of the largest ethnic group, began a war of territorial conquest
as soon as it became clear that it could no longer hold the former union
together. The apparent aim of Serbia's "nationalist" leadership is to realize the dream of a Serbia free of ethnic minorities. A policy of "ethnic
cleansing" and persecution was thus implemented in all regions occu-

pied by Serbia, particularly in Croatia and Bosnia-Herzegovina. The European press reported in 1992 that when the leader of Serbia was asked about the borders of his state, he said, "Serbia is where Serbians live."

In September 1992, Estonia held its first election since gaining freedom from Soviet rule. According to the new Estonian citizenship law, 42 percent of the population was disqualified and not allowed to vote. The 42 percent represents the other ethnic minorities who have been living in Estonia for generations and did not wish to leave after independence. They are mainly Russians but also include Ukrainians, Byelorussians, and others. Under the new Estonian law, only those who were citizens of Estonia in 1940 and their direct descendents are entitled to citizenship and the right to vote. But as Russia's Foreign Minister Andrei V. Kozyrev said, excluding 42 percent of the population from voting on matters that affect their lives "does not in any way fit in the framework of international law."[31] It also does not correspond to democratic ideals.

In a speech to the UN General Assembly a day after the Estonian election in September 1992, Kozyrev appealed to the United Nations for help, suggesting that it should consider setting up international trusteeships to oversee the move to independence by former Soviet non-Slavic republics to prevent discrimination against minorities. Kozyrev said, "The victims of the old totalitarian regimes and ideologies needed protection."[32] He also expressed his government's concern "with the growing discriminatory practices against Russians, Ukrainians, Byelorussians, Jews and other nonindigenous nationalities in Latvia and Lithuania."[33]

If the disenfranchisement of Russian minorities in the former communist states of Eastern Europe and Asia continues, Russia will be forced to intervene, causing armed confrontations, renewed Russian hegemony, and possibly the fall of Russian itself under the control of radical nationalists. In October 1992, Russia intervened in Georgia to prevent the Georgian government from asserting control over Abkhazia, a region within Georgia whose population has resorted to violence to press its demands for independence. The Russian intervention on behalf of Abkhazia was in reality an intervention to protect Abkhazia's Russian community, whose members have become the overwhelming majority of that part of Georgia. In 1992, the Abkhazi were only 17 percent of the total population in their homeland of Abkhazia, and only about 2 percent of the population of Georgia.[34]

The Russian military intervention in Abkhazia came despite Russia's recognition of Georgia's sovereignty over that region. On September 3, 1992, Russian President Boris Yeltsin and Georgian President Edward Shevardnadze signed an agreement in which Russia committed itself to recognizing Abkhazia as a region within the internationally recognized borders of Georgia. The agreement was also countersigned by the Abkhaz leader, Victor Ardzinba.[35] The executive director of Helsinki Watch

Group wrote recently that "the Russian army during Yeltsin's rule has been playing a provocative role in various armed conflicts that have erupted in regions of the former Soviet Union, in secessionist struggle in Moldova, south Ossetia, Abkhazia, and Nagorno-Karabach, and in the civil war in Tajikistan." He added that "the army invariably takes the side of those who are Russian or pro-Russian in secessionist struggle."[36]

On February 26, 1993, news services reported that Yeltsin had suggested that the Russian army has a role to play in territories witnessing conflict outside the borders of the Russian Federation. The objective, he maintained, is to end armed conflicts in the former Soviet republics where security concerns threaten Russian itself.

Also in October 1992, Kuwait held its first election since its liberation from Iraqi occupation. Only men over the age of twenty-one who could trace their Kuwaiti roots back to 1921 were allowed to vote. Many others who had lived in Kuwait for generations and who were the first to die defending Kuwait in 1990 and helping to liberate it in 1991 were excluded from political participation. As a result, only 81,400 Kuwaitis out of a population of 606,000 were qualified for voting.[37]

Even in the former Cezechoslovakia, the land of the "velvet revolution," the revival of nationalism has terminated the more than 70-year-old union between the Slovak and the Czech peoples. This happened despite Czechoslovakia's relative prosperity, its peaceful transformation from the Marxist system to a Western-styled democracy, and the fact that the unity of the two peoples had preceded the imposition of Marxism by a quarter century.

The discrediting of the communist ideology and its political system and the sudden retreat of Soviet power have encouraged all states that emerged following these developments to move toward democracy. The populations of these states, meanwhile, are moving against central authority in general and toward strengthening their traditional ties and ethnic loyalties in particular. The political and ideological forces that used to bind peoples, nations, and even states together have totally disappeared, paving the way for conflict and violence. As W. Scott Thompson writes, "It is precisely because of higher loyalties to smaller units on the part of so many people that conflict does ensue, and the grand schemes fall apart."[38]

Ethnic conflict in Asian and African states provides other examples of the failure of many social and political orders that were imposed on different peoples and used to build nation-states comprising more than one nation. Iftikar Malik wrote recently that "the intermittent conflict in the Pakistani province of Sindh among certain ethnic groups testifies to the bankruptcy of existing administrative structures and states' institutions, all of which have no built-in mechanisms for the participation of the have-nots."[39] Oppressed minorities, exploited social classes, and disenfranchised cultural groups have always resorted to violence to express their frustration and press demands for change and justice when their grievances failed to attract the attention they deserved.

The French historian Pierre Behar has observed that during the totalitarian period, which Eastern and Central Europe just left, when states used every means at their command to suppress free thought and speech, a psychological deformity was produced in the people who were its victims. They were put in a position where they could only think negatively about what they hated and opposed. They had no positive thoughts because positive ideas were useless.[40] The need to change such psychological deformity and build new positive ethnic relationships is emerging as the most important challenge facing the post-Cold War era (which might better be described as the Ethnic Conflict era), and the international community at large. It is a challenge that cannot be ignored and a task that requires vision, new thinking, and, above all, a strong commitment to equality, justice, and world peace.

## NOTES

1. Raymond Cohen, *Negotiation Across Cultures* (Washington, D.C.: United States Institute of Peace, 1991), p. 24.

2. Francis Fukuyama, *The End of History and the Last Man* (New York: The Free Press, 1992), p. 271.

3. Richard Rubenstein, "Unanticipated Conflict and the Crisis of Social Theory," in John Burton and Frank Dukes, eds., *Conflict: Readings in Management and Resolution* (New York: St. Martin's Press, 1990), pp. 321–22.

4. Quncy Wright, "The Nature of Conflict," in John Burton and Frank Dukes, eds., *Conflict: Readings in Management and Resolution* (New York: St. Martin's Press, 1990), pp. 18–19.

5. Ted Gurr, *Minorities at Risk* (Washington, D.C.: United States Institute of Peace, 1993), p. 15.

6. Ibid., p. 15.

7. Edward Azar, "Protracted International Conflicts, Ten Propositions," in John Burton and Frank Dukes, eds., *Conflict: Readings in Management and Resolution* (New York: St. Martin's Press, 1990), p. 146.

8. Louis Kriesberg, *International Conflict Resolution, the U.S.-U.S.S.R. and Middle East Cases* (New York: Yale University Press, 1992), p. 18.

9. *Rights of Nationalities and Protection of Minorities*, International Institute for Nationality Rights and Regionalism, Munich, Germany, 1984, p. 12.

10. Ibid., p. 12.

11. Ted Gurr, *Minorities at Risk*, p. 5.

12. Mostafa Mohagegh Damad, "Religious Minorities in the Islamic Republic of Iran." Paper presented at a conference on Human Rights in Islam, Hamburg, Germany, September 22–24, 1992.

13. Hugh Miall, "Peaceful Settlement of Post-1945 Conflicts: A Comparative Study." Paper presented at a conference on Conflict Resolution in the Third World, sponsored by the United States Institute of Peace in Washington, D.C., October 1990.

14. Interview with Saara-Maria Paakkinen, first deputy speaker of the Finnish Parliament, Helsinki, November 1991.

15. Hugh Miall, "Peaceful Settlement," pp. 11–12.

16. Immanuel Wallerstein, *Geopolitics and Geoculture* (Cambridge, England: Cambridge University Press, 1991), p. 66.

17. Graham E. Fuller, "Soviet-American Cooperation in the Middle East." Paper presented at a conference on Conflict Management in the Middle East, Los Angeles, August 1990, p. 3.

18. Robert J. Pranger, "Cultural Conflict and Mediterranean Security," *Mediterranean Quarterly*, 2 (1990): 38–39.

19. Ibid., p. 39.

20. Immanuel Wallerstein, *Geopolitics*, p. 66.

21. David D. Newson, "Diplomacy and Negotiation," in W. Scott Thompson et al., eds, *Approaches to Peace* (Washington, D.C.: United States Institute of Peace, 1991), p. 31.

22. Stephen F. Cohen, "Can We Convert Russia?" *The Washington Post*, March 28, 1993.

23. Ted Gurr, *Minorities at Risk*, p. 62.

24. Andrei Cordescu, "A Gypsy Tragedy with a Dark Parallel," *International Herald Tribune*, September 24, 1992.

25. Paul B. Henze, "Conflict in the Caucasus." Unpublished paper, Washington, D.C., February 4, 1993, p. 1.

26. Cvijete Job, "Requiem for a Nation," *The Washington Post*, March 5, 1992.

27. Paul B. Henze, "Conflict," p. 1.

28. Samuel Pisar, "For Europe, Union or Demons," *International Herald Tribune*, September 24, 1991.

29. Excerpts from the declaration were translated and published by the Society for the Protection of the Minorities in Central and Eastern Europe, Zurich, Switzerland, 1991.

30. Andrei Cordescu, "A Gypsy Tragedy."

31. Thomas Friedman, "Russia Suggests Estonia and Latvia Be U.N. Trusts," *International Herald Tribune*, September 24, 1992.

32. Kozyrev's quote was included in the above cited article.

33. Ibid.

34. International Alert, *Georgia Report* (London: International Alert, 1993), p. 1.

35. Ibid., p. 3.

36. Jeri Labor, "Does Yeltsin Respect Democratic Limits?" *The Washington Post*, April 8, 1993.

37. "Elections in Kuwait," *Al-Quds Al-Arabi* (an Arab daily newspaper published in London), October 17, 1992.

38. W. Scott Thompson, "The Antinomies of Peace," in W. Scott Thompson et al., eds., *Approaches to Peace* (Washington, D.C.: United States Institute of Peace, 1991), p. 344.

39. Iftikar Malik, "Islam, the West and Ethnonationalism: A Comparative Analysis of Contemporary Central and South Asia," *The American Journal of Islamic Social Studies, 9*, 1 (Spring 1992): 67.

40. William Pfaff, "As the Violence Spreads Again the People Will Pay," *International Herald Tribune*, September 10, 1992.

*Chapter Nine*

# THE SHARED HOMELAND
# MODEL

The democratization process that took place in Eastern Europe, Latin America, the Middle East, and other regions of the world has demonstrated that the will of the people is stronger than the power of violence and tyranny. The Palestinian uprising against Israeli occupation, the popular revolt in Abkhazia against the Georgian authority, and the revolt of Muslims in the Philippines are signs that the time has come for smaller nations and oppressed minorities to reclaim freedom, thus making nationalism a force to be reckoned with. As a result, national aspirations have become a powerful and urgent problem to be addressed. People everywhere seem today to view nationalism as a way to liberate themselves, revive their traditional cultures, and attain freedom and economic progress. Among all of the secular ideologies of the past two centuries, nationalism has been the most widespread, the most persistent, and most influential. "It led to unification of peoples; it provoked the collapse of colonial empires," argues Stanley Hoffman.[1]

The new political and democratic leadership of Eastern and Central Europe, Asian, and African countries seems to think that democracy and civil rights can solve the nationality problem. But democracy, while essential to political dialogue and conflict resolutions, is incapable by itself of addressing problems related to conflicting territorial claims and clashing national identities. In addition, decades of Marxist policy to discredit and diminish nationalism and a Cold War balance of power that caused Third World conflicts to be either frozen or intensified have created an identity crisis in almost every country that was recently introduced to democracy and has to face a new world of uncertainty. This crisis is not only political but cultural as well as social and economic. It is this crisis that forms today the foundations of ethnic conflict, instability, and loss of direction in Eastern and Central Europe as well as in many non-European states.

Ethnic and national conflicts arise from the fact that two or more peoples who feel different from each other live together in one country and are tied to each other in formal relationships that are perceived by one or more parties as unsatisfactory or discriminatory. They usually live together on the same piece of land and are subject to the same laws and regulations that fail to satisfy the needs of certain groups. Some feel that the formal relationships are means to exploit them and give advantage to their partners, which creates grievances and fuels mutual hostility. The more groups with inconsistent ideologies and clashing cultural values are in close contact, the more tension, competition, and possible conflict will arise between them.[2]

Since continued denial of national aspirations in this age is no longer possible or acceptable, special efforts must be made to manage their peaceful realization. Such a realization should be made in light of the spirit of the time and in accordance with UN principles, which recognize the right of all nations to self-determination. However, the realization of the aspirations of one nation or an ethnic minority should not be allowed to undermine the rights of other national minorities. It should also guarantee that the new arrangements will pose no serious threats to the interests of neighboring states. Democracy should be introduced to facilitate the transformation of people's power into constitutional power, to institutionalize political and cultural pluralism, and to instill political dialogue as a mechanism to deter the extremes of nationalism while facilitating the peaceful resolution of conflict. However, it cannot and should not be introduced as the means to resolve ethno-national conflict.

In addition, as Bertrand Schneider writes, "the long established democracies, which have functioned tolerably well during the past 200 years, seem to have grown old and, in their complacent stagnation, show little evidence of real leadership and innovation. The new age demands new visions, new policies, new structures and new people."[3] The need is for new visions and structures not only to revive democracy in the West, but also to find new democratic arrangements to address the grievances and meet the group needs of ethnic, cultural and national entities in other parts of the world. The need is for a new concept that accepts groups exhibiting internal cohesion and solidarity as units of analysis and as building blocks around which new democratic structures are built and activated.

Recent history strongly indicates that political moves toward independence were usually accompanied or immediately followed by demands for economic independence. Political and economic independence have always been viewed by ethnic minorities and colonized nations as the most basic prerequisite for achieving freedom and socio-economic progress. However, recent developments, particularly in Western Europe, indicate that regional economic interdependence rather than national economic independence has come to be viewed as the safest way to achieve the desired political and economic objectives. In addition, all national movements in Africa, Latin America, the Middle East, and most of Asia that sought economic independence as a means to pursue economic progress have failed and, in the process, lost much of their political independence.

The process to end the Cold War, which the popular upheavals in Eastern and Central Europe have helped to accelerate, has created a need for a new world order. The new order, which is still in the making, seems to have accepted the post-World War II national borders as permanent while adopting economics as a major organizing principle. Consequently, existing state borders have largely become not only legitimate but inviolable, and interests rather than values have become the motivating force regulating inter-state relations.

Economic changes causing increased interdependence, political developments causing more freedom, and technological changes causing the world to shrink further are also causing state sovereignty to decrease and the need for a new world order to increase. Miriam Campanella writes, "Nowhere is interdependence so obvious as it is in international economics, and nowhere is it so sensitive and vulnerable as in world order."[4]

Global changes have also caused the world to become less stable and less centralized because power is increasingly becoming more discrete and more evenly distributed among several international actors.[5] Nevertheless, the new world order that is being promoted by the great powers does not offer more than the rules of a free market, a call for human rights, and a plea for stability. Joseph Nye Jr. argues that the need is for new arrangements "to preserve some order in the traditional terms of the balance of power among sovereign states, while also moving toward an order based on justice among peoples."[6]

The collapse of communism, the popular upheavals in Europe and elsewhere, and cooperation by the great powers to establish a new world order have created a dynamic new era. It is an era characterized by a global movement toward political freedom and democracy, greater respect for human rights, and a quest for economic development and regional cooperation. This movement characterizes our era as one of dynamic change and socio-political transformation. It seems to be leading toward the fragmentation of some larger countries into smaller political entities and the consolidation of other states into larger economic communities. Political fragmentation is being viewed by smaller nations and oppressed ethnic minorities as a tool to revive national heritage, enhance cultural particularism, and gain freedom. Economic consolidation is viewed by established and fairly stable states as a suitable framework for achieving socio-economic development and maintaining political stability and regional security.

However, the dynamism of this movement, the unpredictability of its outcome and the lack of established rules and traditions to define and guide its course are intensifying older conflicts and creating new ones. On the political side, "the main actors that shape international law, the states, consider the recognition of the rights of minorities as a potential threat to their own existence."[7] Thus the nation-state system has become an obstacle rather than an asset in the quest for freedom and justice, specifically in regard to the world's many oppressed and discriminated-against minorities. On the economic side, increased competition among the world's great economic and technological powers for markets and resources on the one hand, and a prolonged worldwide economic recession and structural unemployment on the other have made the road to economic cooperation rough and, for some nations, unsafe and hard to manage.

Therefore, to address the legitimate aspirations of smaller nations and oppressed ethnic minorities, we should proceed within a framework of political separation and economic integration. The first is needed to restore national rights and other freedoms; the second serves to consolidate fragmented economic assets and enhance prospects for socio-economic development, stability, and regional cooperation.

Based on the above, methods to deal with the nationality problem in Europe and elsewhere and to address the grievances of the many ethnic minorities should be governed by certain conditions and understandings. Notable among them are:

1. General acceptance of the inviolability of existing state borders.
2. Recognition of the need for and benefits of economic integration and regional cooperation.
3. Respect for the rights of others to choose their own political and economic systems as well as cultural identity.
4. Mutual commitments to democratic pluralism as a way to govern oneself, conduct political dialogue, and deal with the never-ending social and political conflict with others.
5. Acceptance of collective security arrangements as a means to enhance mutual independence and as political frameworks to improve prospects for regional stability.

In addition, the world community must view the resolution of the many ethnic and nationality problems as a positive development that serves the individual as well as the collective interests of its members. The recognition of the national identity of one nation must be viewed as an opportunity to enhance the national identities of all other nations, and be considered part of a process to strengthen world peace and regional stability. Volodymyr Vassilenko wrote recently that "an integrated global society has to secure close and friendly relations between different ethnic, national and cultural entities without discrimination and without destruction of the identity of each. Diversity in unity and unity in diversity must be the basic principle of public governance."[8]

The concept proposed to facilitate the fulfillment of national aspirations for many ethnic groups and oppressed nations is called the "shared homeland." The introduction of this concept is meant to manage the peaceful transformation of ethnic relationships from a state of antagonism and hostility to a new state of peaceful coexistence and partnership that serves an enlightened common interest.

## CREATING A SHARED HOMELAND

The basic assumptions of the shared homeland model call for political separation along nationality or ethnic lines, while maintaining or initiating economic and social unity across political lines. This means that national minorities aspiring to independence within existing states would be allowed to form autonomous regions or mini-states of their own and have separate homelands in which they could enjoy their freedom. However, all political entities emerging from this process would be required to share their land with other ethnic groups and national minorities living within the borders of the larger state, giving them equal access to all social and economic services provided by the mini-states. While each national minority would have a homeland of its own, the combined homelands of all political entities would form a shared homeland for members of all national groups to enjoy.

The shared homeland model, however, does not require the creation of fully autonomous political entities or independent states. It is a flexible concept designed to meet the requirements of ethnic minorities that have different political or cultural needs that cannot be met within existing orders. The model allows politicized groups to gain more control over decisions that affect their lives. As such, the model provides for either cultural independence and near-total political separation, full autonomy within existing social orders and political borders, limited self-rule, cultural autonomy, and control only of specific matters such as religious affairs. Regardless of the arrangements envisioned and implemented, the model requires that all entities share their national or group resources with other entities that emerge at the end of the process, making all groups, cultural autonomous regions, and mini-states partners in a jointly owned and managed homeland. In addition, no mini-state or autonomous region would be allowed to have an army of its own; it would be obliged to remain within restructured security arrangements that represent all entities and recognize their rights.

According to the logic and proposition of this concept, national minorities as different cultural groups would be divided. However, as individual, economic concerns, and social organizations, they would remain or become united. Ethnic politics apart, all people belonging to all nationalities would become partners in sharing a larger homeland and enjoying the economic resources and the socio-cultural and residential opportunities it has to offer.

The shared homeland model has three major components, the full implementation of which would create separate political entities, a collective security system, and a unified economic and residential framework that respects cultural diversity. They are a political component, an economic component, and a security component. A socio-cultural component also exists within the political one. In other words, it is a model to create a new socio-political order based on separation regarding political identities, functional cooperation regarding economic interests, shared ownership regarding land and natural resources, and joint arrangements regarding security.

Political separation is meant to enable ethno-national groups living in separate regions but with other similar groups in one state to gain control of decisions that affect their lives. It is also meant to enable such groups to acquire distinct political or cultural identities of their own. An act to effect political separation is thus an important step to enable ethnic and religious groups to define themselves as they wish, to manage their own cultural and certain political affairs without outside interference, and to have a socio-cultural and economic life of their own making.

Economic integration is meant to retain the unity of the land, and/or to enlarge the size of the potential shared homeland. It maximizes the economic and investment advantages usually associated with economic integration and the creation of common markets, while avoiding the economic costs and problems that normally accompany political separation. It is also an arrangement to create a dynamic economic process in which individuals, economic concerns, and political entities compete and cooperate to develop a much larger, more competitive economy.

Collective security is meant to minimize the cost of protecting the common peace and defending the shared homeland, while preventing military rivalry among ethnic groups or political entities from emerging. It is also meant to tie the fate of all ethnic groups or political entities together. Because no individual state or ethnic group sharing the same homeland will be allowed to have a separate army, chances for the outbreak of intergroup violence will be vastly diminished if not eliminated altogether. Cultural independence and group equality is intended to enable each group to revive its culture and strengthen its sense of identity which suits its traditions and strongly held values. An ethnic group that gains the right to define itself as it wishes and feels no external threats is more likely to regain self-confidence and overcome bad experiences of the past.

National security, as the experience of many countries has proven, rests not only on military power to defend against possible foreign aggression but also, and more importantly, on eliminating the principal sources of internal threat and instability. Notable among such sources are the denial of national self-determination and cultural identity to ethnic groups, group repression, poverty and economic deprivation, social injustice, and military build-ups that consume valuable resources.

National security, ethnic identity, economic progress, and cultural equality require that individuals be free, that ethnic groups have the right to choose their own identities, and that cultural communities and smaller states develop shared economic and security interests to induce them to cooperate collectively. The shared homeland model provides a realistic, yet futuristic framework to maximize the benefits that usually come with economic integration, minimize the losses that normally accompany political separation, and eliminate inherent threats of competing security arrangements. It is a comprehensive arrangement to expand the space in which people make choices that intersect and cause conflict. It is also a framework to enable people to live with conflict without being consumed by it, and it is a new way to think about the future and to view inter-group relationships more positively.

Regions claimed by national minorities and recognized as their historical homelands would be allowed to declare independence and create new mini-nations as separate political entities to be tied to the mother state in close economic and security arrangements. Yet all territories under the control of the central authority before the start of this process would be declared a shared homeland for all minorities and majorities alike. As a result, each national group would gain a distinct political and cultural identity of its own, while having a homeland to enjoy and share with other national or ethnic groups.

The acquisition of a specific political identity would give members of each national group exclusive rights to participate in the politics of their own mini-state, but no rights to participate in the national politics of other states. Political choice for each national group would be limited to the borders of its own state, while economic choice and residential preference would be extended to include all territories within the outer borders of all other states sharing the same homeland. Members of each national group, moreover, would acquire citizenship rights only in their own state but residency rights in states other than their own, residency rights being equivalent to citizenship rights with the sole exception of participating in the national politics of other states. Participation in local politics, however, is a right that all majorities and minorities would enjoy without limits because of its impact on the daily life of all residents on the one hand, and its minor relevance to national politics on the other.

Meanwhile, citizens of the new nation-states would be obligated under the shared homeland provisions to share their homeland with the citizens of other states. The provisions creating the shared homeland would therefore supersede all other laws enacted by individual states regarding political sovereignty and economic independence.

Thus, the creation of a shared homeland would permit several political entities to coexist harmoniously within one homeland, while preserving their separate national identities and cultural sovereignties. Peoples sharing a homeland would be permitted to belong to separate nation-states, while enjoying equal non-political rights and privileges in all other states. The shared homeland concept redefines the notion of national sovereignty, making it less ambitious and inclusive, and more accommodating and open.

The shared homeland would meet the need to address the legitimate rights of national minorities to freedom and self-determination, while posing no threat to neighboring states or endangering the rights of other minorities to similar entitlements. In addition, it protects the rights and properties of individuals living outside their own ethnic homelands, while allowing them to peacefully and voluntarily relocate as they may wish. As such, it facilitates cultural homogenization by choice, not "ethnic cleansing" by force.

John Burton has written that "all people, in all cultures, at all times and in all circumstances have certain needs that have to be, that will be fulfilled; not should, or ought, but will be fulfilled, regardless of consequences to self or system."[9] But the fulfillment of needs that does not respect existing systems and fails to observe moral values is likely to hurt many people, including those it was intended to help, and is less likely to endure in the long run. Edward Azar has suggested that ethnic conflicts cannot be enduringly resolved except within decentralized structures, "designed to serve the psychological, economic and relational needs of groups and individuals within nation-states."[10]

The shared homeland concept could also be used to facilitate the resolution of other types of conflicts, particularly claims concerning disputed territories by neighboring states. In such cases, disputed regions would be declared a shared homeland to be enjoyed by both peoples, while maintaining existing political affiliation at the time. Accordingly, citizens of both states who claim the disputed region to be their homeland would acquire equal rights to live and work in that region, political rights being the exception. This means that both groups belonging to conflicting states would be treated equally under existing laws, while maintaining existing nationalities according to their citizenship. Under such an arrangement, the political affiliation of the disputed region would be preserved, while the denied homeland rights of the other groups would be restored. However, the political rights of the non-citizens who gain homeland rights would continue to be expressed in the other state.

In cases where territorial disputes are caused by ethnic conflict, the disputed region in which a distinct ethno-national group lives would be granted autonomy and declared a shared homeland. Nagorno-Karabach is a good example of such a case, in which this concept could help resolve the conflict between the states of Armenia and Azerbaijan.

Nagorno-Karabach, whose population is predominately Christian and Armenian in origin, has for a long time been a part of Azerbaijan, whose population is overwhelmingly Muslim. To settle the conflict over that region, Nagorno-Karabach would be granted full autonomy and declared a shared Armenian-Azerbaijani homeland, giving all citizens of both states the right to live there. Azerbaijan would maintain sovereignty and assume political and security responsibilities, while Armenians of Nagorno-Karabach would be granted the right to establish cultural and economic ties with Armenia without outside interference. A decentralized Nagorno-Karabach government system would further allow Muslim enclaves within Nagorno-Karabach to govern themselves and maintain strong political and cultural ties to Azerbaijan's central government and cultural centers. Most members of the Conference on Security and Cooperation in Europe believe that borders should not be changed by force. The position of CSCE is that "Nagorno-Karabach should remain part of Azerbaijan, as a fully autonomous region, with guarantees for the cultural and political rights of the Armenians."[11]

Another problem of inter-state conflict caused by the political division of ethnic groups is that of Hungarians living outside Hungary. Out of an estimated 15 million Hungarians, about five million live outside the political borders of today's Hungary. These are ethnic Hungarians who, due to the two world war settlements, found themselves living in their historical homelands under foreign control. The overwhelming majority of those people live in the four neighboring states of Romania, Serbia, Slovakia and Ukraine. The shared homeland concept could be utilized to resolve those Hungarians' problem without endangering the rights of other ethnic groups or threatening the sovereignty and the security of the states in which they live.

In a recent article, Amitai Etzioni argued against the creation of smaller states and harshly criticized the right of self-determination. He said, "The world may well survive the creation of ever more toy states, but what meaning will self-determination have when minuscule countries are at the economic and military mercy, even whim, of larger states—states in whose governments they have no representation at all?"[12]

Joseph Nye has also argued that if every ethnic group is granted its own state, the prospects for a stable world order will be slim, provoking more, not less conflict.[13] This is no doubt a legitimate concern, but it is not limited to "toy states" alone. Rather, it is a concern shared by all states, large and small, whose economic welfare and security needs have become tightly linked to those of neighboring states suffering from ethnic conflict and economic collapse. In addition, states dominating the world economy or controlling vital resources, such as oil, have diminished the sovereignty and freedom of action of all other states. In this age of increased interdependence, spreading ethnic conflict, and closely connected economic and security matters, national concerns and problems cannot be adequately addressed using old concepts of political sovereignty and working through known institutions of the nation-state system alone.

Ethnic groups that feel different or discriminated against but are tied together because of political affiliations with the same state cannot satisfy their needs without changing some of the facts that govern their lives and relationships. To be successful, changes must recognize the existence of conflicting cultures and respect the rights of others to define themselves and participate in decisions that affect their lives.

In conceiving the shared homeland model, the European Union was treated as the point of departure, and the economic arrangements that led to political coordination were used to project the future of the community beyond the end of the century. The future is envisioned as forming a community of peoples, not states, who share a larger European homeland that cuts across existing political borders of all member states. The Vatican's status within the Italian state was also considered a valuable example, demonstrating the possibility of creating a homeland for a minority within the borders of a larger state without endangering its security and while enriching the cultural lives of all parties concerned. The shared Greek-Turkish responsibility in Cyprus to jointly manage most affairs of the divided city of Nicosia is another example that was incorporated in formulating and integrating the four components of the shared homeland concept.

## SHARED HOMELAND AND CONFLICT RESOLUTION

For at least a decade, the world has been moving slowly but surely toward ideological compatibility, particularly in the economic and political fields. Western ideas of a free market economy and political democracy are fast gaining worldwide acceptance, largely because they are associated with economic progress, higher standards of living, and more respect for human rights. Meanwhile, the information revolution and recent advances in the fields of communications and human rights have enabled the media to become a major player in shaping people's expectations, while increasing their awareness of themselves and others. In so doing, the media have contributed substantially to advancing the ideas of capitalism; democracy; and national, ethnic, and cultural identity.

In performing their tasks, the media have also enabled most cultures and subcultures to be revitalized and become more viable and active in influencing the national and international processes of socio-economic and political developments. As a result, societies in general are moving in two different, largely contradictory directions. The first is a movement toward the universal adoption of similar, if not identical economic and political systems rooted in capitalism and democracy. The second is a movement toward the reinforcement of ethnic identity rooted in nationalism, cultural particularism, and religious fundamentalism.

While the first movement tries to pull peoples and states together toward a unity of interests and societal organization, the second pulls them apart toward different, often clashing cultural values and political loyalties. Thus, conflict is generally heightened, and the ideas of neither capitalism nor democracy can be advanced internationally. The experiences of Algeria, Egypt, Peru, Russia, India, and several other countries demonstrate that the forces of ethno-nationalism, cultural particularism, and religious fundamentalism are determined to undermine the logic of the first movement and halt its progress.

In view of this and other important global developments, a need has emerged for a new framework to allow ethno-national groups living together in one state to develop culturally on their own, to be recognized and accepted as equal political partners, to share a belief in democratic principles, and to cooperate with other groups in developing and protecting shared homelands. The need is for new political, economic, and security arrangements that can enable oppressed minorities to regain lost rights, and strengthen a group's self-confidence that has been weakened by prolonged foreign control, while viewing the attainment of similar political and cultural goals by other groups as an opportunity for all to resolve conflict, foster peace, and prosper.

For people to be productive and imaginative, and to induce them to take initiatives needed to develop and defend a common good, they have to be free to act. They have also to feel secure to associate with others without endangering their cultural identities and group loyalties. They have to be free not only from oppression and discrimination, but also from hatred, bigotry, and intolerance. And they have to feel secure to pursue their own individual and group interests through cooperative arrangements that recognize and respect the freedoms and rights of others.

Ethno-national groups living together within existing nation-states tend to have conflicting interests and to feel victimized by the state and/or each other. This in turn tends to fuel mutual hatred, invoke strong emotions, create conflict, and encourage most ethnic groups to define themselves and their national goals in terms that negate the identity of others and reject their legitimate rights. But since no ethnic group was born from nothing or came to existence from nowhere, every group has some valid claims and legitimate rights. Mutual acceptance of such claims and rights is a necessary condition for transforming ethnic antagonism and hostility into group cooperation and peaceful coexistence. Faith in how society functions and in chosen institutions is important and can sustain community self-confidence at critical points of national development, reducing tension and the possibility of uncontrollable conflict.[14]

The shared homeland model is an integrative approach to conflict resolution that seeks the fulfillment of the basic needs of all groups and recognizes the legitimate rights of all concerned parties. Through its four components of political separation, economic integration, cultural equality, and collective security, the concept works to enrich the cultural life of all groups, while providing for the individual pursuit of enjoyment and self-fulfillment. In so doing, it also works to transform conflicting group values into competing individual interests, and it replaces ethnic antagonism and hostility with cooperation and peaceful coexistence that accepts cultural diversity.

As for the nation-state, the implications of self-determination, full autonomy, or self-rule for minorities do not pose a threat to its territorial integrity and claimed sovereignty when implemented within the shared homeland context. On the contrary, they represent an opportunity to resolve ethnic-national conflict amicably, nourish cultural diversity, and encourage the consolidation of fragmented economic bases. They also work to create a new socio-cultural and political environment more conducive to political stability, cultural vitality, individual initiative, economic progress, democracy, and dynamism. Most important, they work to transform ethnic perceptions from being grounded in the past to being oriented toward the future.

The shared homeland concept is a visionary model to build a new state system that can reconcile two values essential to human fulfillment: the free development of each individual and the meaninglessness of individual life without association with like-minded people.[15] It is a model to expand the available space for individual economic, cultural, and social fulfillment and to allow the expression of group identity and the development of cultural values, free from state coercion and outside interference. It is also a model to tie the fate of conflicting groups together, expanding shared interests and strengthening collective security arrangements that keep the peace and foster domestic and regional stability.

In general, approaches that seek the implementation of the shared homeland model to resolve conflict must meet the following criteria:

1. Provide for the cultural development of ethnic groups without outside interference.

2. Provide ethnic groups with the opportunity to control decisions that affect their daily lives and with the authority to govern themselves where they live as majorities, particularly in regions known as a part of their historical homelands.

3. Guarantee equality with others, as individuals and as cultural communities and/or political entities.

4. Ensure that group self-determination or national self-determination does not limit the individual's rights to self-determination and assimilation.

5. Guarantee the continuation or encourage the creation of economic arrangements that promote economic integration and further cooperation.

6. Ensure that security matters remain a collective responsibility of all ethnic groups or states sharing the same homeland.

The German intellectual and member of Parliament Peter Glotz asked recently, "How else are the radical conflicts of Hungarians in Slovakia, Hungarians in Transylvania, Serbs in Croatia, Kurds in Turkey, the Irish in Britain, Basques in Spain and France to be resolved if not through a combination of federalist and supernationalist structures?"[16] It is a call for the creation of shared homelands that permit political separation but dictate economic integration and collective security arrangements.

Throughout history, nation-states have tended to accept a minimum of cultural diversity in a maximum of space under their control, and to impose the maximum homogeneity in the minimum space they considered a national homeland. That is, the policy was to promote national and ideological homogeneity and oppose social and cultural diversity. This led generally to the suppression of dissent, denial of certain human and ethnic rights, and intellectual rigidity. But in an age of instant communications, the explosion of information, growing global interdependence, increased respect for human rights, and the movement toward ideological compatibility, policies are changing to accommodate maximum diversity in the minimum space.

Societies that allowed such changes to take place are undergoing new experiences that serve to enrich the lives and cultural experiences of individuals and groups, as well as the societies themselves. This has made creativity and personal initiative the norm rather than the exception, and a matter to be appreciated rather than a behavior to be admonished. For such a trend to accelerate and contribute positively to all aspects of human life, individual political freedom, recognition of minority rights, and ethno-national identities must be recognized and respected. This can only be done under new socio-economic systems and collective political and security arrangements that value social justice, political freedom, cultural diversity, and human dignity, and strive openly and diligently to achieve them.[17]

Examples of complicated ethno-national and religious conflicts that would find the shared homeland model helpful are found in most regions of the world, particularly in China, Cyprus, Ethiopia, Britain, India, Iraq, Palestine, Russia, Turkey, and Yugoslavia. The following section will provide brief descriptions of how the model might facilitate the resolution of the major ethnic conflicts facing some states. However, the complexity and unique nature of the conflict in each case require more in-depth analysis and most likely a modified version of the arrangements outlined.

## APPLYING THE MODEL

It was commonly thought that as nations developed and societies reached higher levels of urbanization and education, ethnic differences would begin to disappear and an emphasis on cultural particularism would recede. But the experience of most Third World countries, the former communist states, and some European nations seems to indicate that development processes seldom touch the collective consciousness of most ethnic groups. In fact, the fast pace of change that the world has witnessed during the last two decades has contributed to the revival of social conservatism, religious fundamentalism, and nationalism, strengthening awareness at the group level.

The difficulties that ordinary people encounter while living in foreign countries and having to adjust to strange customs and traditions are similar to those experienced by the many ethnic and religious groups that coexist in one land governed by one law. Because over 90 percent of all states in the world are made up of more than one ethnic or national group, ethnic conflict has become a socio-political force causing internal tension and contributing to regional instability. It has also become an important factor influencing the direction of international relations, certain aspects of international law, and the world order in general.

The formation of the current nation-state, with its lack of cultural and/or ethnic homogeneity, is due to conquest, colonialism, migration, or the political settlements to end the two world wars. These settlements were largely drawn to reward the winners and their allies and punish the losers and their accomplices, while diminishing the capacity of other nations to become world powers in the future.

Following the end of the Cold War, and due to a worldwide movement to adopt democracy and be more respectful of human rights, which themselves are being expanded to include cultural and political group rights, the capacity of the nation-state to rule without internal challenge began to decline. In the wake of this development, a rather narrow type of nationalism re-emerged as a socio-political force, to legitimize and defend the existing nation-state system and to weaken its grip on power and force its political restructuring.

While majorities invoke nationalism as a means to legitimize the state's borders and justify its control over other peoples, minorities invoke it to revive ethnic cultures and regain lost national and other group rights. The result undermines the powers of the current nation-state, and may dismantle it into smaller nation-states or autonomous national homelands. Radical nationalism seems to be emerging as a new force fueled by contradictory motives to strengthen the concept of the nation-state at the ethnic group level and weaken its power at the larger state level, the so-called national level.

Contradictions that contribute to the formation and vitality of many national movements are, says Andrus Pork, vertical and horizontal. "Vertical contradictions are those that have emerged from the colonial exploitation of local resources by the central government bureaucracy. Horizontal contradictions are those that have emerged from conflicting economic, political, cultural, and other interests of various nationalities."[18] Regardless of the nature of the contradictions that drive nationalism, its radical re-emergence in violent forms has created a need to deal with its manifestations without delay and create new political processes to address its causes—processes that fundamentally change existing ethnic and socio-economic relations that feed conflict.

The shared homeland model attempts to reconstruct such relations and transform ethnic hostility into mutual acknowledgment of group rights, creating shared interests and responsibilities that dictate cooperation and foster stability. Below is a brief description of how the model would facilitate the resolution of ethnic conflict, placing ethnic relations in a new context that promises more freedom, progress, and peace.

## CHINA

In China, the conflict in Tibet is one where the shared homeland model would be helpful. The Tibetans and their political and spiritual leader, the Dalai Lama, claim that their country maintained its independence until invaded by the communist Chinese forces in 1950. In contrast, the Chinese government maintains that Tibet has been a part of China since the thirteenth century. In 1959, an uprising in Tibet failed to achieve its objectives because the Chinese forces crushed the rebellion and forced its leaders to flee the country. Since then, the conflict between the Buddhists of Tibet and the communists of China has continued.

Allowing the people of Tibet to establish a state of their own within the parameters of the shared homeland concept would end this conflict to the satisfaction of both parties. While the Tibetans could exercise their right to self-determination, they would gain the freedom to revive their own culture and define themselves in terms of their choosing. The Chinese would continue to be able to live and work in Tibet, while benefiting from the cultural and economic diversity that an independent Tibet would bring. The Chinese government would also acquire a new, more progressive image, enhancing its international standing and moral authority.

As part of the arrangements, the Tibetans would agree to remain within the existing security system maintained by China. Tibet would have no army of its own, only a police force to guarantee the security of its citizens and maintain law and order at home. The new arrangements would reduce China's current security requirements, enrich its cultural life, and improve its image worldwide, with no sacrifice or loss. Tibetans and Chinese alike would have equal access to opportunities that both states offer, but would be restrained from participating in the national politics of each other.

## CYPRUS

Until 1974, Cyprus was an independent state in which two distinct ethnic and religious groups lived together without serious problems. These were a Greek community constituting about 80 percent of the island's total population, and a Turkish group constituting about 19 percent of the population. Both ethnic groups continued to maintain strong cultural identities of their own and to express allegiance to their mother cultures and nations of the neighboring states of Greece and Turkey. Because of that, and longstanding Greek-Turkish animosity, an undercurrent of mutual hostility between Cyprus' two ethnic groups was created and maintained, keeping the two communities apart.

In 1974, ethnic tension developed into open conflict and an armed intervention by Turkey on behalf of the island's Turkish minority led to the division of Cyprus into two parts between the two antagonistic ethnic groups. About 200,000 Greeks left the north part of the islands, which had fallen under Turkish control, and about 40,000 Turks left the southern part, which fell under Greek control, creating a serious refugee problem. In addition, the new partition left the Turkish minority in control of 38 percent of the island, double its size as a percentage of the total population. Consequently, the cultural lines that had divided the two ethnic groups were reinforced by the addition of political and military lines, and ethnic tension was deepened by creating new grievances that the population transfers caused.

Despite the political and human separation, the international community condemned Turkish military intervention, opposed partition, and rejected the Turkish claim of independence. As it continued to recognize the central authority controlled by the Greek majority, it called for mediation to settle the conflict in a manner that restores the unity of the island. The United Nations was asked to launch a diplomatic effort to resolve the conflict, which divided the island since 1974, and reestablish unity. But despite twenty years of mediation, no solutions have been found and the aspirations and rights of the uprooted Greek and Turkish people have remained unmet.

Using the shared homeland model to settle the conflict in Cyprus may be the only way to end ethnic hostility and reunite the land, creating a new, mutually beneficial relationship between the two communities. The formula that could achieve this goal calls for the creation of two political entities, or mini-states, along lines that facilitate a higher degree of ethnic homogeneity, while restoring Cyprus to its previous status as a shared homeland to be enjoyed by all its Greek and Turkish citizens. Greeks living in the Turkish mini-state would be entitled to participate only in the national politics of the Greek entity; similarly, Turks living in the Greek mini-state would participate in the national politics of only the Turkish entity. However, all citizens of both states, regardless of their place of residence, would be entitled to participate in local elections. It is further suggested that citizens of both ethnic states be granted the same identity card or passport, identifying them as citizens of Cyprus.

Both states would be allowed to open economic, cultural, and information offices in foreign countries, but would not be permitted to establish political representation abroad. However, each state would be granted observer status at the UN political body but full membership status in all other UN agencies and non-political international organizations. A confederate state would be formed to join the two mini-states together, issue passports, and assume responsibilities related to foreign political affairs and security matters. The confederate state would have two legislative bodies, a lower house elected directly by the people, and a higher house appointed by the authorities of the mini-states. This latter house would be divided equally between the two communities and would have veto power regarding issues of common concern.

## YUGOSLAVIA

The situation in the former Yugoslavia is much more complicated than in most other countries suffering from ethnic and national conflict. Yugoslavia was made up of six republics, four of which have declared independence. No republic has escaped the problem of having a substantial minority or minorities of other nationalities on its soil. In addition, there are at least three major minorities that identify themselves with foreign nations, with no acknowledged homelands of their own within the borders of former Yugoslavia. While borders between the Yugoslav republics are not beyond dispute, neighboring states, particularly Albania, Bulgaria, Greece, and Italy, have claims on Yugoslav territory. Such claims, though not serious at the present, could become so if civil war were to engulf the entire country, leading to chaos and political disintegration.

Dusan Janjic of the Institute of Social Sciences in Belgrade has said, "Europe is divided in such a way that any violation of borders in the present circumstances, no matter where it begins, would end up in a dangerous war game with a null score."[19] Therefore, he maintained, "we should search for solutions on the other side, i.e., in further promotion of the current integration trends in Europe, and its regionalization, disregarding the importance of the state borders."[20] Central and Eastern European states have so far chosen to ignore the proposition.

The shared homeland model is probably the only way to reduce ethnic tension and resolve the very complicated nationality problem in the long run. At the same time, the model embodies the democratic principles of freedom, equality between individual and nations, and a recognition of the right of others to be free.

According to the plan, each Yugoslav citizen would be given the right to choose the nationality with which he identifies. The six republics would be allowed to declare independence and have their own nation-states within existing borders. However, the entire territory of Yugoslavia as it existed before 1991 would be declared a shared homeland for all the citizens of the six nation-states. Thus, members of all ethnic groups, business entities, and socio-economic and cultural organizations within the borders of former Yugoslavia would have the right to reside, work, and operate in every state.

Individuals identifying with the nationality of each state would acquire citizenship rights in their own state. Others identifying with other nationalities would acquire residency rights only. This means that each individual, regardless of national identification and place of residence, would acquire citizenship rights in one state only, but residency rights in every other state. Citizenship rights entitle people to participate in the national politics of that state, while residency rights limit such participation to local politics.

In addition, each nation-state would be free to choose its own political and economic systems and organize its socio-cultural institutions as it sees fit. However, all states would be required to join in a confederation to provide for the security needs of all member states and to create a framework for coordinating political, financial, and other matters of shared concern. States' economic policies would continue to function within one economic community that provides for state initiative, individual creativity, and continued economic integration.

## CZECH REPUBLIC

The situation in the Czech Republic today is probably the best suited to adopt the shared homeland model to resolve conflicts over disputed territories between two neighboring states or national groups.

A year after the collapse of communism and the introduction of democracy, nationalism emerged in the former Czechoslovakia as a strong socio-political movement that led in 1992 to the separation of Czechoslovakia into two republics, the Czech and the Slovak. The adoption of the shared homeland model would help absorb the lingering tension between the peoples of the two republics, facilitate the resolution of the problem of ethnic Hungarians in Slovakia, and reintegrate the economies of the two republics. In addition, it would facilitate the resolution of the German-Czech dispute regarding the rights and grievances of the former Sudetenland Germans.

According to the principles of the shared homeland concept, the Czech and Slovak republics would continue to form separate political entities, or nation-states. The entire territory of the two states would be declared a shared homeland for the enjoyment of all citizens of both states. Slovaks living in Slovakia would acquire citizenship rights, while those living in the Czech Republic would acquire residency rights only. The same would apply to the Czechs living in both states. The two states would form a confederation to construct and manage a collective security system and regulate inter-state relations as well as coordinate political and monetary policies and other matters of mutual concern.

For disputed regions between neighboring states, the Sudetenland provides a good example of how the shared homeland model would work. While the Sudetenland is no longer a territory disputed by Germany and the Czech Republic, it still evokes strong emotions among Germans who were driven out of their homes at the end of World War II and against whom an "ethnic cleansing" policy was implemented. Declaring this region a shared German-Czech homeland would remove the bitterness still felt by many Germans and thus create a more positive atmosphere for cooperation between the two neighboring states of Germany and the Czech Republic.

According to the proposed arrangements, former Sudetenland Germans would acquire the right to go back and live in what they consider their historical homeland, while the Sudetenland region would continue to be a part of the Czech Republic. However, returning Germans would enjoy equal rights with other Czech citizens, with the exception of political rights. Politically and legally, Germans living in Sudetenland would continue to be German citizens despite being Czech residents. As such, their political choice would be limited to Germany, while their economic choice and residential preference would be extended to include the Sudetenland.

A shared homeland between Germany and the Czech Republic would be mutually beneficial in other ways. Having Germans go back to Sudetenland to live with their government's blessing would help to transform the economy of that region. For domestic political considerations, the Bonn government might be inclined to compensate returning Germans for property lost at the end of the war and thus provide the funds needed to develop and industrialize the Sudetenland region, using German money and expertise. Open borders and continual interaction between the peoples of the two neighboring states would establish a cooperation that is mutually beneficial and self-perpetuating and would hasten the integration of the Czech people into the European Union.

## THE KURDS IN IRAQ, IRAN, AND TURKEY

The Kurds are an old nation whose land was divided among five neighboring states, most of which are in Iraq, Iran, and Turkey. Despite being in their homeland, Kurds in each of these three states have lived as minorities, denied many, if not most of their rights for decades. Over the years Kurds have mounted several attempts to regain lost rights, particularly cultural independence and statehood and unity of the divided homeland. Kurdish challenges to the sovereignty of all states, and a fear that a Kurdish success in one state might set an example forcing other states to recognize Kurdish demands on their soil on the other, have led the three neighboring states to suppress the Kurds, at times in a coordinated manner that increased Kurdish suffering immensely. Meanwhile, animosity among the three neighboring states and foreign powers' intervention to weaken one state or the other have led to manipulating the Kurds repeatedly, using them as tools to settle disputes and contain the ambitions of the three regional powers.

Iraq was the first state to recognize the existence of a Kurdish minority, and it moved to resolve the Kurdish problem with an offer of autonomy. But despite decades of negotiations and several agreements, no satisfactory solution has been found. Following the Gulf war of 1991, the Western allies decided to protect the Kurds in northern Iraq and thus enabled them to set up a regional government without Baghdad's consent.

Iran, meanwhile, has continued to suppress the Kurds, refusing to negotiate with them or recognize their existence as an ethnic minority. In fact, the Islamic government of Iran, in accordance with Islamic ideology, does not recognize ethnic minorities. It believes that all Muslims are one nation and thus it recognizes only non-Muslims as minorities who belong to the two other religions recognized by Islam as godly religions, Christianity and Judaism.

Similarly, Turkey has continued to suppress its Kurdish population, denying them not only their cultural and group rights but also the rights of ethnic identity. In 1992, however, the government of Turkey decided that it could no longer deny the existence of a large non-Turkish minority on its soil that refuses to be assimilated. Consequently, it began to consider granting the Kurds cultural rights. This move came in response to increased international criticism and intensified clashes between the armed forces of the state and the fighters of the Kurdish nationalist movement. After the Kurds of Iraq gained a de facto self-government following the Gulf war of 1991, both the clashes in Turkey and international criticism increased, particularly by human rights organizations. Nevertheless, the president of Turkey continued to refer to his Kurdish constituents as "those people" and to deny having done anything wrong to them.

International efforts to resolve the many conflicts plaguing the Middle East and to restore hope and political stability must also try to resolve the Kurdish problem in Iran, Iraq, and Turkey. A solution to end conflict with the Kurdish minority in each of the three states would also ease tension among them, denying each state the Kurdish card to wage war against one another by proxy, while paving the way for regional cooperation and the restoration of stability. The proposal suggested to resolve this problem is the shared homeland model, to create in each state a Kurdish region enjoying autonomy and self-government.

The Kurds of Iraq would continue to be citizens of the Iraqi state, enjoying the right to live anywhere in Iraq and to have access to all government services as do all other citizens of the state, who would also be entitled to live in the Kurdish region and have access to all its resources. Iraq's Kurds would acquire the right to participate fully in the national politics of their region, but only in the local politics of the regions where they reside outside their political entity. Other citizens of the Iraqi state would acquire similar rights regarding residency in the Kurdish region. Security matters and foreign political affairs would continue to be handled by the central government in Baghdad, which would have to give the Kurds a voice regarding such matters commensurate with their proportion of the country's total population.

The Kurds of Iran and Turkey would also be granted similar rights, and the Iraqi-Kurdish arrangements would be duplicated to create three adjacent Kurdish regions. The three Kurdish regions would then be declared a shared Kurdish homeland, allowing all Kurds to move freely, interact with each other, and work together to fully develop their culture and ethnic identity.

This arrangement would meet all basic needs of the Kurds, resolve their conflict with Iraq, Iran, and Turkey, and compel the three neighboring states to coordinate political, security, and economic matters. They would be forced to cooperate in matters related to migration, security, and regional politics and coordinate policies related to investment, tariffs, labor, trade, and other issues. This cooperation could lead to regional stability, economic integration, and peaceful coexistence.

Because all political solutions to the conflict call for compromises, none would satisfy the demands of all parties concerned. To prevent dissatisfied minorities from renewing conflict and gaining control by force or intimidation, democracy must be introduced as a political system through which people's participation in politics would be ensured. It should also be adopted as a socio-political value to encourage dialogue and tolerance and to facilitate the resolution of conflict by peaceful means.

## NOTES

1. Stanley Hoffman, "The Passion of Modernity," *The Atlantic* (August 1993): 101–106.

2. Quincy Wright, "The Nature of Conflict," in John Burton and Frank Dukes, eds., *Conflict: Readings in Management and Resolution* (New York: St. Martin's Press, 1990), pp. 18–20.

3. Bertrand Schneider, "A New Approach to the World Global Problematique," in Suheil Bushrui, Iraj Ayman, and Ervin Laszlo, eds., *Transition to Global Society* (Oxford, England: Oneworld Publications, 1993), p. 96.

4. Miriam L. Campanella, "Global Society, Global Problems and New Formats of Global Decision-Making," in Suheil Bushrui, Iraj Ayman, and Ervin Laszlo, eds., *Transition to Global Society* (Oxford, England: Oneworld Publications, 1993), p. 59.

5. Ibid., pp. 54–58.

6. Joseph N. Nye Jr., "The Self-Determination Trap," *The Washington Post*, December 15, 1992.

7. Theo van Boven, "The Rights of Minorities in International Law," Birn newsletter, Lelio Basso International Foundation for the Rights and Liberation of Peoples (Rome, Italy: 1991), p. 121.

8. Volodymyr Vassilenko, "Peaceful Disintegration of the Soviet Totalitarian Empire as a Necessary Precondition for the Transition to Global Society," in Suheil Bushrui, Iraj Ayman, and Ervin Laszlo, eds., *Transition to Global Society* (Oxford, England: Oneworld Publications, 1993), p. 69.

9. John Burton, "International Conflict Resolution and Problem Solving," in Dennis J. D. Sandole and Ingrid Sandole-Staroste, eds., *Conflict Management and*

*Problem Solving: Interpersonal to International* (New York: New York University Press, 1987), p. 255.

10. Edward Azar, "Protracted International Conflicts," in John Burton and Frank Dukes, eds., *Conflict: Readings in Management and Resolution* (New York: St. Martin's Press, 1990), pp. 150–151.

11. Raymond Bonner, "Nagorno-Karabach," *The New York Times*, Aug. 2, 1993.

12. Amitai Etzioni, "The Evils of Self-determination," *Foreign Policy* (Winter 1992–93): 28.

13. Joseph Nye Jr., "The Self-Determination Trap," *The Washington Post*, December 15, 1992.

14. Robert Artigiani, "Building a Global Society, Progress and Procedures," in Suheil Bushrui, Iraj Ayman, and Ervin Laszlo, eds., *Transition to Global Society* (Oxford, England: Oneworld Publications, 1993), pp. 38–39.

15. Michael N. Nagler, "Ideas of World Order and the Map of Peace," in W. Scott Thompson et al., eds., *Approaches to Peace* (Washington, D.C.: United States Institute of Peace, 1990), p. 380.

16. Peter Glotz, "Internationalization of Politics and Economics and the Challenge of Nationalism, Immigration, Ethnic and Minority Conflict." Paper presented at a conference, "Toward a Civil Society," in Washington, D.C., Sept. 12–15, 1991.

17. Mohamed Rabie, *The New World Order* (New York: Vantage Press, 1992), pp. 167–68.

18. Andrus Pork, "Global Security and Soviet Nationalities," *The Washington Quarterly* (Spring 1990): 39.

19. Dusan Janjic, "Ways and Means of Overcoming the Heritage of Central European Nationalism, the Case of Yugoslavia." Paper presented at a conference in Prague in October 1991.

20. Ibid.

## Chapter Ten

# CONFLICT AND CHANGE

The global developments that ended the Cold War and marginalized its ideological conflict were also instrumental in exposing the shortcomings of the major socio-economic systems, capitalism, communism, and Third World socialism. In the process, the balance of military power that the Cold War had fostered, at a very high cost in material, human and political terms, also ended. As a result, popular beliefs in the efficacy of the old socio-political systems were either weakened or destroyed, undermining the forces that bled many nations and states for decades. This in turn is creating new attitudes regarding political change, economic cooperation, socio-cultural transformation, the environment, and national and state security.

The unexpected collapse of Marxism and the end of the Cold War created a chaotic situation, causing a loss of direction and the spread of conflict. An urgent need was created for the articulation of a new theory of socio-political change to explain current developments and identify the forces of change—a theory to guide change and help develop a strategy to maximize the benefits of change and minimize the losses of conflict.

Richard Rubenstein argues that existing social theories have failed to develop an adequate concept of the individual in society. He believes there is a need for a new theory to help us understand the world in which we live.[1] This theory is needed to explain the change taking place around us, identifying its causes, forces, direction, and possible outcomes and implications.

Most events and developments that seem disconnected or unrelated are tied to each other in causal relationships that never stop changing.

Economic recessions, for example, affect politics and politicians, compelling them to respond to educational, training, job creation, equity and other issues, which in turn affect economics as well as politics. The theory we need is one that can help us see and understand the nature of inter-system relationships so that we may develop a sense of where we are going and how to manage processes of social change—a theory to tie the present to the future, not the past, so that we may predict the future and participate in shaping it.

Robert Artigiani argued recently that "history teaches us to analyze the processes facilitating social evolution instead of trying to identify a vision of a feasible and desirable future."[2] He added, "If we cannot know the future, we are inescapably part of a present allowing no moral alternative to action."[3] While it is important to know history, we must realize that we cannot and should not be prisoners of history. Changes may be provoked by history, but progress cannot be made without an eye on the future.

Today, the leading nations of the world are re-examining the old notions of economic management, political organization, and international relations to find answers to the pressing questions raised by new global developments and to bring conflict under control. However, official policies and popular measures that were initiated as a result seem to have failed to achieve their objective. This is primarily due to the inability of the leadership of these nations to develop a new vision for a feasible and desirable future and to understand the futility of relying on the past and protecting the status quo.

For example, all forces of social and political change in Russia have expressed strong desire for change, yet they have failed to articulate a new vision to guide change, contain and redirect conflict, and rationalize the processes of socio-political transformation. In the United States, change was limited to moderating the socio-political orientation of the ruling elite, as expressed by the transfer of power in 1992 from the conservative Republican Party to the Democratic Party. In France, change occurred in the opposite direction as the more conservative forces won an unprecedented majority in Parliament, handing the socialist forces their worst defeat ever. In Italy, all forces of the traditional right and left were defeated in the 1994 elections.

In Germany, neither the conservatives nor the socialists have convinced an increasingly cynical public to move and effect political change. The general mood in Germany seems to be pointing toward political paralysis, although the Socialist forces seem to be gaining more strength. While the public recognizes the need for profound change, it lacks confidence in the ability of both major political parties to effect the desired change. No political force in Germany seems capable of conceiving a vision for a new social system that could restore social cohesion and reverse declining economic security. If the Social Democratic party wins in the October 1994 elections, its victory will be due more to its rivals' shortsightedness than to its own foresightedness.

In the Third World, the need for drastic change advocated by the most active segments of society is still not shared by most governments. Because political processes of succession and popular legitimacy are either weak or nonexistent, change seems to be leading to increased conflict and gradual political disintegration. This conflict manifests itself today in power struggles and/or ethnic conflict, often making anarchy the new order of the day and the major force shaping future change. The world has entered a new, much-changed era that no one anticipated or was prepared to deal with. As Miriam Campanella writes, "The global society in which we live is a highly complex and dynamic state of the world, in which regressive, self-destructive trends and unpredictable events occur, and in which all parts evolve irreversibly."[4]

The former communist nations of Europe began to talk about post-Marxism, the Western nations about the aftermath of the Cold War, and Third World nations about post-socialism and non-alliance. But no nation seems to be talking about the future in clear terms and concrete visions, making the word "post" a metaphor for change without much meaning or content. Using the word "post" when talking about change implies recognition of passing from something to almost nothing, from a historical phase we knew but were compelled to leave behind, to a new, uncharted phase. It is a phase that promises something new, but is vague and indefinable. We still define our present and future by reference to our past, which is increasingly losing its relevance to the new reality. In fact, we are yet to recognize the new reality.

Using the word "post" to describe the new phase that we just entered can only define that phase in terms that differ, supercede, contradict, or even negate the old phase we just left. Because we know what we have either chosen or been forced to abandon, while lacking the ability to know what we have entered, we seem to know with certainty what we stand against but lack the knowledge, sometimes the courage, to define with confidence what we stand for. As a result, confusion seems to have assumed the leadership role, while disorder is moving to dominate states of economic and socio-political affairs.

"The surest sign of our confusion," wrote E. J. Dionne Jr. recently, "is the omnipresence of the word post. We talk about post-modernism, post-communism, even post-history. We do not know what we are. We only know that we are post."[5] Even what we are "post" is hard to define because of the continued change and the predominance of the old political and intellectual mentality. It is largely a mentality rooted in the Cold War and unable to define the new reality except by reference to the past. In addition, change that has begun to dominate most aspects of life is neither universal nor uniform, proceeding neither at a regular pace nor in one direction. Most difficult of all is the task to explain how we got where we are and what caused the status quo, which appeared stable and entrenched just a few years ago, to suddenly become a part of our discarded and discredited past. Even the past, in view of the uncovering of many secrets and increased freedom and openness, is changing both as facts and fading memories in front of our eyes.

It is a past that some people eulogize with tears and sorrow, while others celebrate with fanfare and enthusiasm. The majority, however, appear bewildered, confused, and largely limited to asking questions about what has happened, what to expect, and how to manage change. Despite the legitimacy and importance of these questions, no one knows how to answer them with certainty. Only Western conservatives, diehard communists, religious fundamentalists and extreme nationalists claim to have the answers, as they maintain that only history, culture and religion have the answers. But because all the sources for the much-sought answers are part of a discredited past that has been overtaken by events, the real answers are still beyond our reach. This creates a need for a new theory to define the current states of socio-economic and political affairs and explain the nature and direction of the change that dominates our life. Updating old theories and reinterpreting old concepts do not and cannot suffice.

Chaos theory says that chaotic developments tend to produce patterns of change that create new balances, leading to the establishment of new systems and relationships. It claims that nature has a capacity to organize and reorganize complexity, implying that we are not prisoners of our past, and that genuine change is possible. It is a theory that gives us hope but does no help us find our way to a better life and a more secure future, for it has no real answers to our problems. While this theory may explain the nature of change and its probable outcome regarding systemic relationships, it does not explain the pace of change or identifying its major forces. Several questions, therefore, remain unanswered:

1. What causes chaos in the first place? What causes stability and balance to degenerate into instability, disorder, or chaos?

2. Do all chaotic situations produce self-organizing systems that lead to renewed balance and stability?

3. What are the major forces whose relationships are to blame for chaos, and how do they interact and affect one another?

4. How can we manage chaos or influence its course, and thus predict its outcome or possible outcomes?

Since confusion is universal, each socio-economic system has entered a crisis of its own, losing much of its ability to inspire confidence, restore stability or help counterweigh the impact of other systems. A lack of clear vision regarding the future and dissatisfaction with the immediate past have rendered all systems either deficient or unworthy of further support. The traditional tools and rules of political behavior, social organization, and economic management have become either partially or totally irrelevant.

In their search for safer, more certain answers, people have begun to dig deeper into their past, rediscovering their history and reinterpreting their collective memory. In the process, ethnicity, nationalism, culture, and religion are revived, revitalized, and reorganized to provide social and psychological frameworks to define individual identity, channel group action, and redirect change.

Throughout history, change and conflict have maintained a mutually reinforcing relationship, causing people to experience both without interruptions. At times, change precipitated conflict; at others, conflict paved the way for change. Because of this intertwined relationship, the extent of both change and conflict has largely become a function of each other and often a consequence of how each is managed. People can avoid neither change nor conflict, neither can they escape the implications of either one on their individual lives and collective consciousness.

Change is usually caused by the introduction of new ideas that have socio-political implications, or new technologies that have organizational and economic applications. Change may occur first at the intellectual level, creating a new state of mind, which in turn labors to change the actual states of economic and political affairs. Change may also start by the introduction of new technology in either the economic or the political arena and work slowly to change the prevailing state of mind. Such a change starts normally as an integral part of the existing order, not as a challenge to it, and usually emerges as a byproduct of continued efforts to develop and become more efficient.

Changes that technological developments precipitate do not tend to be revolutionary, profound, or contrary to the basic interests of the prevailing social order. Adjustments, rather than conflict, will be the path through which technological change travels into the larger society to effect societal and institutional change. In the process, it changes those social forces and institutions that perceive change in their own interest, and leaves behind other forces and institutions that detest change or perceive it as contrary to their own interest. This in turn creates new balances of power and social gaps that reflect the establishment of new states of economic and political affairs.

In contrast, change that starts with the state of mind presents a challenge to existing systems and institutions because of its capacity to transform social perceptions and political perspectives. Established systems and institutions are normally resistant to change, particularly change dictated by a new state of mind that places all major institutions and systems in a much different philosophical context. Because of this, change that begins at the state of mind is likely to be revolutionary rather than evolutionary, causing conflict and probably violence before effecting the desired change in the states of economic and political affairs.

Change may still occur at both levels without lag, leading to reform that does not amount to profound change in either the prevailing state of mind or the existing states of economic and political affairs. In situations of the past, such change was almost always the product of indigenous forces that perceived the need for change. It was a need to make the states of political and economic affairs correspond more to a new state of mind, or to make the state of mind more in tune with the new states of economic and political affairs. Modifying one state to correspond to changes in others causes conflict that usually is resolved in favor of the stronger forces, which may represent those defending the status quo or others promoting change and transformation.

Conflict that is resolved at the expense of the more enlightened forces of change is likely to delay social transformation, but it is unlikely to eliminate the need for it. As a result, solutions will be temporary rather than permanent, creating transitional stages in which conflict festers, its roots deepen, and its direction takes a more radical and profound path. In contrast, conflict that is resolved at the expense of the forces of continuity is likely to lead to new balances that create different states of political and economic affairs, but not necessarily progress, equity, or long-term stability.

The change introduced by Marxism in Russia started as a change in the state of mind and therefore did not come in response to technological or other developments in the existing economic and political spheres. It was a change led by a much-transformed state of mind that acted on the basis of specific predictions and in anticipation of perceived socio-cultural developments under capitalism. But in so doing, Marxist leaders unwittingly precipitated three separate yet related developments having great impact on the future of both communism and capitalism:

1. They aborted the processes of socio-economic transformation in Russia itself, which might have led to the kind of conflict necessary to undermine capitalism and give a natural birth to socialism.

2. They alerted all capitalist nations to the dangers of communism, which led them to introduce social programs to tout the benefits of capitalism throughout society and weaken the logic of communism.

3. They caused the creation of a new social order that was radically different from all existing orders at the time, an order that was supposed to build the future model for peace, stability, equality, and progress but in fact lacked the flexibility to adapt to changing circumstances and failed to see its mission as an evolving task.

The errors of the communist model, wrote Volodymyr Vassilenko, "were not due to its basic aims of social justice, solidarity, altruism and friendship but rather to the attempts to put the model into practice by ignoring fundamental and universal principles. The stubborn refusal of the communist regimes to comply with these principles led to the denial of human freedom and to enforced uniformity of all spheres of life."[6]

Regardless of their ideological nature and social objectives, systems are creatures of societal processes that are themselves both products and forces of change. Thus, all social systems have a life of their own that can be short, long, stagnant, dynamic, dull, or interesting, but not perpetual. All systems reach their limits and will need restructuring or replacement; alterations may be sufficient to adapt to moderate changes but total restructuring or replacement is inevitable in the long run. Even universal principles cannot maintain their universal applicability and utility and will have to undergo changes to make them more relevant to changed circumstances and transformed needs.

Ideologies in general, including religion and nationalism, tend to reduce the individual to a mere number to be manipulated and used by the ideology and its leadership. While having an ideology makes people feel more equal and committed to a higher cause, ideologies tend to make adherents less independent and to limit and channel their contributions to promoting one cause and serving its institutions. In addition, the introduction of new ideologies and the revival of old ones usually create radical movements to effect change and permit individuals to dominate such movements. This in turn creates superleaders, national heroes, or holy men and consequently widens the gap between those at the top of the political and religious ladder and the rest of the population. In the process, new relationships are created that reduce the humanity of everyone involved. Those at the top of the ideological and political ladder tend to develop a sense of superiority that denigrates the value of the lives of those at the bottom of the ladder, and those at the bottom tend to feel that their life is only worth what they can do in the service of their leaders at the top.

Centuries ago, changes in states of mind represented great motivational forces that united people and moved nations and leaders to act decisively. Religion and nationalism were probably the most effective of all ideologies that grew as transformations in the state of mind of peoples and drastically changed the states of economic and political affairs. But by uniting individuals and tribes to create nations and by strengthening the ties that bind them, nationalism and religion widened the gaps that separated nations and accentuated real and perceived differences that cause ethnic, religious, and inter-state conflict.

Social collectives built around ideology are not viewed by each other or by themselves as individuals in plural. They are viewed as "entities with personalities independent from the individuals who constitute them."[7] They also behave as collectives led by a strong, often aloof leadership committed to an ideological zeal that has no place for the individual, except to serve the zeal blindly and worship the leadership: "When ideology prevails as a national identity, people tend to think in purely political terms and symbolic language as signs of leadership commitment and achievement, not in economic, welfare, wages, freedom terms."[8] Thus, the major strength of all ideologies is their major weakness.

For example, religious ideologies in general, and the monotheistic ones in particular, are dedicated to life after death more than to life before death. They promise heaven to true believers and are committed to helping the largest number of believers get to heaven. Because of that, religious institutions tend to be preoccupied with the task of explaining the road to heaven. Believers are usually asked to obey God, follow the teachings of their religious leadership, and perform noble tasks that have little to do with enhancing the material, social, or intellectual quality of their lives. But to care less about life on earth than about a life beyond it is to ignore life's complexity, which is a major ideological weakness and a prescription for socio-economic failure. Promising everything later and little or nothing today may be a source of individual satisfaction and social peace, absolving religious ideologies of their responsibilities on earth and glorifying religious institutions and leaders, but it condemns individuals to a life unworthy of their potential and humanity.

Ideologies in general, though successful in controlling and motivating the individual in the short run, are destined to fail in the long run. Their success and failure create violence and conflict, structural injustice to protect the privileges of those in control in the short run, and open conflict to reclaim lost rights and the humanity of the masses in the long run.

The process of change that started in the former communist countries has created a chaotic situation dominated by conflicting ideas and social forces and influenced more by propaganda and perception than by reality. To effect change, which they can hardly define, some forces are resorting to violence, regardless of its moral and political implications.

In the Third World, developments since the end of the Cold War are moving in three different and rather contradictory directions. The first is a process to maintain the status quo and strengthen the major forces of continuity led by regimes in power. These forces comprise the army, the secret police, the bureaucracy, and the media, all of which are controlled by governments and serve as tools to seize, control, and maintain power. This goal requires the suppression of dissent and individual initiative, and the manipulation of the masses to be more submissive.

The second is a movement backward to strengthen group identity, led by nationalist, religious, and ethnic forces whose goal is to revive and preserve cultural particularism. It is a goal that seems to justify using history, religion, collective memories, and minority status to claim legitimacy and gain support. It also uses the right of self-determination under international law to justify policies based on denial, discrimination, and even genocide. Because of its tactics and objectives, weakening social cohesion, aborting progress, and turning cultural diversity into ethnic exclusivity.

The third is a movement to imitate the West, borrowing heavily from its economic and political experiences. This movement is led by an intellectual and business elite, most of whom were educated in the West or have maintained strong business connections with it. Despite its enlightened ideas and good intentions, it is a movement that largely ignores both history and reality and shows more interest in preserving the privileges of those in control and gaining popular legitimacy. Therefore, it can neither protect nor perceive a common good.

While all processes try to deal with change, each has its own way of doing it. The first process, led by regimes in power, rejects change and tries to freeze rather than recognize reality as a means to resolve problems. The second tries to build a future in the image of a fading, largely fictitious past whose values, systems, concerns, and institutional relationships have little to do with reality. The third tries to reshape the present according to a foreign model to which the majority of the masses cannot relate, and in which they perceive a threat to their cultural identity and traditional values.

In the West, developments since the end of the Cold War have been moving toward the maintenance of national interests at the expense of social change and international involvement. As a result, change is largely limited to rotating factions of the political elite without altering either the state of mind or the states of economic and political affairs in a meaningful way. In France, for example, the major conservative forces badly defeated the socialists in the March 1993 parliamentary elections. But despite Europe's strong political and ideological traditions, conservatives who won in France did not offer the voters new programs or make hopeful and concrete promises. Voters seem to have concluded that the socialists had ruled for a long time and had failed to protect the national interest, therefore, it was time for a change. The March elections were more a vote against the socialists than a vote for the conservatives. The outcome is not expected to solve problems, causing France to join Britain, Germany, and Italy on the road to nowhere. These nations and leaders are moving in place without making progress; they think of the future in the past tense.

## CHANGE AND CONFLICT

Change, particularly profound change, is a major source of conflict and cannot perform its task without causing conflict. Conflict often occurs when efforts to introduce change, specifically social change induced by a transformed state of mind, encounter opposition and significant political obstacles. Change and conflict are two sides of a single process whose objective is to restructure societal and organizational relationships that have been invalidated, outdated, or undermined by socio-political forces and economic and technological developments.

Every relationship, it must be noted, has components that are interlinked and mutually reinforcing. One represents cooperation between the parties concerned; the other represents competition among them. Relationships that lack either component are unhealthy, lack dynamism, reflect dependency rather than partnership, and consequently will fail. For a relationship to be viable and dynamic, the level of cooperation must be perceived by the concerned parties as good or at least satisfactory and the level of competition healthy or at least tolerable.

Relationships that fail over time and become invalidated do not transform themselves into more relevant ones without conflict. The more partners there are in a relationship, the more problems will be created and obstacles encountered before a new, healthier relationship emerges. Complex relationships that involve numerous partners may go through chaotic transitions and break up into several very different relationships before stability is restored and a new set of functioning systems and institutions evolves.

Systems and organizations are made up of subsystems, goals, individuals and rules that determine the structure, and operational objectives of each system or organization. However, systemic and institutional behavior is not a function of structures, rules, and goals only, but also of relationships to other systems and organizations and procedures to implement goals. Goals, be they individual, organizational, or societal, cannot be attained without procedures. Procedures, meanwhile, are selected with certain goals in mind and therefore cannot be separated from intended goals: "A procedure is chosen because it can accomplish a goal, and successful societies pursue goals within methodological reach."[9] Thus, systemic and organizational goals, structures, procedures, and relationships are more important than individuals and individual components in shaping both reality and change.

The increasing dynamism and complexity of our world make the break-up of older systemic relationships easier to effect, while making the rearrangement of older structures more difficult to initiate and sustain. The first is easier because it tends to be governed by interests that never stop changing, while the latter is usually governed by values and procedures that seldom change. That is, relationships are more likely to experience drastic changes as interests and circumstances change, while structural arrangements of organizations and systems tend to be stable for extended periods of time due to the rigidity of values. Thus, institutional changes usually lag behind changes in relationships, leading to frustrating efforts to build new, more responsive institutions to exploit the many opportunities that emerge. When the time lag is long and the need for change is perceived as urgent, conflict arises to settle differences, causing the suppression of interests or the undermining of values.

In Iran, for example, the drastic changes introduced by the Shah's regime in the 1970s and the emergence of a consumer society pursuing new interests and undermining old values led to a conflict that ended with the traditional value system as the victor. Those espousing value changes were either suppressed, driven out of the country, or forced to go underground. The new order that emerged is value-based and ideologically oriented, making it rigid and largely immune to most changes induced by economic developments and socio-political needs.

In the former communist countries, change has occurred in response to the failure of forces espousing both values and interests. Peoples in those nations were awakened a few years ago to the news that all they believed in was not only bad but also immoral. Meanwhile, nearly all economic and political institutions, which represented both interests and values, collapsed, leaving a great vacuum. It is a vacuum that neither the interest-based nor the value-oriented forces can fill, although certain radical forces could partially exploit it. Consequently, no balance between values and interests can be established or perceived.

Societies dominated by value-oriented social orders tend to emphasize ethics, justice, equity, and solidarity with the poor and weak. Disparity among social classes is usually small, encouraging social peace rather than alienation. Such societies, moreover, place little value on interests and often discourage aggressive activities that seek the fulfillment of material needs. Individuals lack the incentive to pursue certain economic activities and tend to nurture attitudes that inhibit engagement in purely material endeavors. Laws in such societies are rooted in values, not needs, and therefore play a generally minor role in organizing and managing economic, social, and political activities.

To compensate for the lack of individual motivation to pursue personal interests and material gains, value-oriented social orders instill in people non-material incentives to encourage hard work. Such incentives are usually centered on the promotion of ideology, defense of the state, community involvement, and service to both the ideological zeal and the spiritual or national leadership. But because all social orders are destined to become less responsive to changed circumstances and individual needs, the exposure of their limits is certain to make people less ideologically or spiritually committed and more inclined to pursue individual interests. If the order is too rigid to facilitate individual initiative and accommodate non-ideological and spiritual needs, particularly material needs, it will be undermined and eventually collapse.

In their decline, and in order to survive, most such orders are likely to overlook activities that are not socially accepted and ideologically sanctioned. But in so doing, they unwittingly weaken their own logic and rationale, strengthen the forces of change, and cause widespread corruption. The result is the bankruptcy of the order and the undermining of the underlying value system of the society as a whole.

In contrast, societies dominated by interest-oriented social orders tend to emphasize interests and de-emphasize values, encouraging individual initiative and personal gains. The disparity among social classes is usually wide, causing alienation and nurturing class conflict. Laws and regulations replace ethics, causing social responsibility in general to become a function of compliance with the law rather than personal commitment. To most people, however, social responsibility is a function of their inability to cheat the law. Although such societies do not discourage values, they do not place limits on interest-seeking activities, which causes values to decline and degenerate.

Decline in social responsibility, increased dependence on the law to organize and regulate relations and activities, and emphasis on interests and personal gains cause societies to become individualistic, individuals less honest, and the socio-political environment less humane. Consequently, community involvement becomes an act of altruism, helping the poor is a sacrifice of doubtful value, and commitment to national, spiritual, ideological or environmental goals is the expressions of frustration, desperation, or idealism. The law is developed to protect and expand individual rights as if such rights have no limits, further weakening social responsibility and community rights.

Roger Conner writes, "Any serious quest for a just society, or a good life, starts with a recognition that the values represented by rights and responsibilities are morally equal, yet always in tension. Finding the right balance involves a never-ending sequence of adjustments."[10] Societies dominated by value-oriented philosophies tend to emphasize individual responsibilities and de-emphasize individual rights. Societies dominated by interest-based philosophies tend to emphasize individual rights and de-emphasize individual responsibilities. Both philosophies and the societies they shape cannot maintain a healthy balance between values and interests, between rights and responsibilities, which is a precondition for social justice, political stability, and economic progress.

Systemic and organizational relationships cover all aspects of societal life and all fields of endeavors, leaving nothing untouched and no possible combination of arrangements unexplored. Because of that, and the continued change induced by internal and external forces, conflict always erupts, breaking up older relationships, building new institutions, and transforming existing states of mind and political and economic affairs. But before new structures emerge and new functioning systems are put in place, societies experience a loss of direction, generally characterized by either political disorientation, economic decline, and social regression or a combination of the above.

The major forces that determine the course of societal life, cause the break-up of older systemic relationships, and compel organizational re-structuring are the political, economic, and socio-cultural processes, and the media. They are societal forces that transcend international borders, function across cultures, and affect the local, national, and global levels of human, organizational and state interaction.

## PROCESSES OF CHANGE

The four societal processes of change and management have specific tasks and goals that are shaped by independent decisions and greatly influenced by process interaction.

### The Political Process

The political process includes the forces, decisions, and activities that manage all political affairs of nations. It usually performs its task by responding to political needs at the local level, shaping politics at the national level, and influencing change or adapting to changed circum-stances at the international level. Political decisions and activities that may be initiated by this process are usually taken by the political elite and influenced by special interest groups and are often determined by the nation's overall philosophy and perceived need to protect its national interest.

As a result, the political process of nations has become more of a col-lection of several largely competing local, national, and international sub-processes, each responding to its constituency and perceived interests. Meanwhile, global developments precipitated by the communications and information revolutions, particularly after the decline of ideology, have intensified competition among the many components of the polit-ical process. This in turn has weakened the process in general and dif-fused its focus in particular, causing governments to have difficulty coordinating the functions of the political process at the different levels. Because of that, it usually lacks coherence and seldom develops a clear and comprehensive set of objectives or a well-defined course of action. The door is opened for external forces and non-political considerations to greatly influence its course of action.

In the past, the local political process was limited to narrowly defined local issues that were more administrative than political in nature. The national process, meanwhile, was independent of the local one and largely geared to issues shaping the political direction of the nation and managing its political system as well as competition among the major national political forces. The international process was closely tied to the national one and more interested in inter-state relations and international conflict. This process has become subject to control by the "national interest," which kept changing, and fell under the influence of an international law that lacked clarity and effectiveness.

Global developments during the last two decades have caused the local and international political processes to become more active, largely at the expense of the national process. This is partly due to the reoccurrence of economic recessions, to increased emphasis on individual human and minority rights, to cultural diversity, to a more open trading system, and to the emergence of an investment environment that caused the internationalization of certain local economic activities. Other developments that the economic and the socio-cultural processes have precipitated have forced the national political process to turn inward and give more attention to local politics.

Consequently, the political process lost focus and was forced to respond to constituents with varied, sometimes contradictory interests, vastly weakening its ability to shape and manage national and international politics. Today, most nations, great powers included, are no longer able to form and sustain clear national and international policies projecting definite images and pursuing well-defined goals while gaining popular support. All nations, with a few exceptions, have lost the organizing principle of their national and international politics, allowing the local political processes, with their competing groups and contradictory objectives, to influence policy at all levels.

### The Economic Process

The economic process includes the forces, activities, and business concerns that shape economic policy and manage the economic affairs of nations. It usually performs its task by responding to market forces that reflect consumer preferences as well as to profit incentives that motivate people to engage in business activities. It also includes opportunities created by new technologies and changed domestic and international investment climates, which are subject to competition and cooperation. Because money and profits are usually made by producing and selling goods and services where and when favorable conditions prevail, the economic process functions at all levels. Exceptions that might limit the ability of this process to work at a certain level are usually imposed by the political process and tend to be resisted by the economic one.

It was previously thought that "need was the mother of invention," but the involvement of the media in the economic process and the institutionalization of research and development as an integral part of that process have reversed the trend. New technologies are being developed

as byproducts of continued scientific investigation and increased intellectual curiosity. They have become important factors in creating new
human and industrial needs, motivating people to demand more, produce more, and create more needs. The media, in conjunction with the
economic process, are creating new needs in anticipation of new products, making manipulation of people's fears, desires and emotions a legitimate business activity.

For example, the emphasis on crime in the United States has created
a need for personal and property protection by heightening people's fear,
leading to the development of a multi-billion dollar industry in a short
period of time. This need evolves, due to a sustained emphasis on law-
lessness, increased crime, the continued development of technologies related to security systems, and the promotion of advanced equipment to
update or replace older systems.

Since products, unlike political decisions, can be marketed for profit
wherever and whenever demand exists, the economic process could not
be limited to one level alone. Attention is paid to all potential markets
without much distinction. Because profits are the major organizing principle of business decisions in general, economic considerations, rather
than political and ideological ones, are able to dominate the economic
process and greatly influence its relationships to other societal processes.
Meanwhile, the globalization of markets, the internationalization of financial policy, the mobility of investment capital and human talent, and
the commercialization of the media and other aspects of cultural life are
leading the economic process to become global in concept, outreach, and
application.

Consequently, attention traditionally devoted to local markets and associated community issues began to shift to a focus on global markets
and associated international considerations. Global considerations related to maximizing economic returns are claiming priority over local
needs, the national interest, and environmental considerations, as a result. Local and national issues, such as the need to create more employment opportunities, to upgrade employee training, and to develop
surrounding communities, are receding in importance, if not visibility.
This in turn is motivating the political process at the local level to become
more active to pressure the national political process to give more attention to local issues, which it could not do without devoting less attention
to national and international ones.

The retreat of the economic process from its responsibilities regarding
the needs of local communities, the activation of the local political process, and the increased involvement of the national political process in
local political and economic issues are:

1. Straining the relationship between the political process and the economic process, particularly at the local level.

2. Weakening the ability of the national political process to focus on national and international issues.

3. Giving the economic process more freedom to pursue its own interests at all levels without much fear from the political process and in marked indifference to the "national interest."

4. Enabling the economic process to exert greater influence over the political process in general.

5. Causing the emergence of a world culture centered around consumerism and the values shared and interests pursued by the world's rich.

### The Socio-Cultural Process

The socio-cultural process includes the forces, institutions, and activities that shape and manage the social and cultural affairs of nations. It performs its task by preserving and promoting the cultural heritage, by emphasizing traditional values and belief systems, and by responding and adapting to external challenges and changed political and economic environments. Because the major organizing principles of this process are values that seldom change, it has traditionally been more inclined to respect rather than challenge social forces of continuity, enabling it to maintain balance for longer periods of time without substantial transformation.

But recent developments related to internal technological change and strained ethnic and racial relations on the one hand, and external developments related to heightened economic competition and instant communications on the other have placed the socio-cultural process on a new plane of perpetual imbalance. Individuals, social classes, and institutions connected to the emerging global culture of consumerism are pressuring the national socio-cultural process to change and move away from traditions and associated social values. In contrast, cultural and religious minorities and social classes whose lives and interests are rooted in local communities and tied to traditional institutions, feeling the threat, are reacting strongly in defense of traditions and religious values. In so doing, older cultures are being revived, ethnic ties strengthened, and a new wave of conservatism, religious fundamentalism, and nationalism is fast emerging in most parts of the world.

The socio-cultural process is being transformed into two major forces, pulling almost all societies in two different, at times, opposing directions. The first calls for change and welcomes all that is new; the second calls for continuity, or revival of tradition, and opposes all that is perceived as a threat to the established value system. Due to this, almost all societies are witnessing the crystallization of two contradictory intellectual trends competing for socio-cultural and political dominance.

Social forces for change that are able to follow global change and understand the importance of new technologies and exploit the opportunities created by them are advocating fast change and promoting modernization. Because they see change as serving their own interests, they claim that the economic and technological imperatives of the time demand a positive response to almost everything that is modern. In contrast, social forces that are unable or unwilling to accommodate technological change and reconcile themselves to most ideas and attitudes precipitated by it are calling for preserving or reviving almost all that is old. As a result, no balance between the old and the new is advocated and no serious efforts are being made to reconcile differences and resolve growing conflict.

The ruling elites in most Third World countries are probably the only parties trying to reconcile the differences between the two forces. The process through which this reconciliation is accomplished includes the adoption of a few technologies without adaptation, changing certain political behavior without adequate institutional restructuring, and defending social conservatism without popular debate. This gives rise to a new phenomenon in which a dual society is created in every state and in every large city in the Third World. Affluence and consumerism are creating deep, socio-cultural divides among people who might not live more than a mile apart. People who belong and claim allegiance to the same country, culture, and nation are living two different lives socially, economically, and intellectually.

### The Media

The media include the activities, organizations, groups, and policies that manage the collection and dissemination of information, particularly the news. They perform their task by responding to events and crises, analyzing official policy, and identifying and following trends of change in other processes. The Western media have an identity of their own and are governed by standards of behavior not subject to regulation by the state. They reflect a certain worldview that, though close to that of the national political process, is seldom shared with the other societal processes.

In the West, the mass media have been generally devoting more time to the collection and dissemination of information, particularly the news, than to creating it. But despite the substantial power and the near-absolute freedom the media have in carrying out their duties and pursuing their interests around the globe, they have increasingly been subjected to manipulation by inside and outside groups. These groups include the governments, the media elite of program directors and news analysts, and the owners and business managers of news organizations. Freedom of expression, which most Western societies observe religiously, "glosses over the tremendous influence of the media, which is not controlled by any democratic participation," and thus allows small, like-minded groups to control and manipulate the news and other entertainment and educational programs.[11]

Governments have traditionally shown more interest in getting their viewpoints across than in presenting and explaining facts to the public. Thus, the information and news that governments put out tend to either exaggerate the truth, belittle its importance, or avoid dealing with it altogether. At times, governments also resort to disinformation to prepare a suspicious public to accept certain sacrifices or to mislead an enemy and confuse its leadership.

The media elite, with its professional background and institutional association, has developed certain class and ethnic biases and a unique worldview not necessarily shared by the general public. It is a view that is generally supportive of liberal causes, biased against cultural minorities and non-Western nations, and supportive of government policies regardless of philosophy.

Furthermore, the media tend, both consciously and unconsciously, to propogate their own worldview by giving unequal attention to issues and events of public concern, and by promoting the views of only a select group of news analysts and "experts." The media entrepreneurs, meanwhile, have traditionally been more interested in making money than educating the public and consequently have favored profitable programs, even when such programs were socially harmful and morally corrupt.

In most non-Western countries, the media have generally been owned and controlled by governments, which in turn have used them as a tool to manipulate public opinion to enhance the regimes' image and legitimacy. Due to this, the media are forced to spend more time publicizing governments' viewpoints and less on collecting relevant information, and almost no time on analyzing official policy and governmental performance. Lack of freedom and government ownership of the media led the media elite in these countries to become an integral part of the government bureaucracy and to see its principal role as advocating official policy and promoting government viewpoints without critical analysis.

Manipulation of the news, however, is not a policy that only Third World governments practice. The U.S. government, for example, resorted to this practice during its campaign against Iraq in 1990–1991 to sustain and foster Western public support for its goals and war activities. The Iraqi leader was portrayed as evil, Arabs and Muslims in general were dehumanized, Iraqi victims of war were rarely seen on television, the mass killing of soldiers using deadly weapons was called "surgical," civilian casualties were called "collateral damage," and the effectiveness of U.S. military technology was exaggerated.

Jordan's Crown Prince El-Hassan Bin Talal, commenting on the media dehumanization of Arabs and Muslims in the United States, wrote recently that "reductive stereotypes are insulting and ill-informed; in an ever-shrinking world, they are also dangerous."[12] He added: "At a time when the global community is becoming increasingly interdependent, effective cultural communication, mutual tolerance and understanding based on a sound grasp of traditions are of utmost importance."[13] It is a call that has little chance of being heard because we live in an age where news and entertainment imperialism has become a matter of fact. It is a part of a new global reality that supports Western economic hegemony, legitimizes American political and cultural dominance, and imposes alien socio-cultural values on a largely impoverished Third World, encouraging consumerism, wasting meager resources, spreading corruption and destroying traditional cultural balances and sustainable socioeconomic systems.

The most important contribution of modern communications, particularly instant communications, is in creating a more alert world consciousness. It is making most people on all sides of the economic, political, ideological, and cultural divides more aware of what exists on the opposite side. It provides the opportunity for people everywhere to link together, causing, on the one hand, the emergence of a world culture, and on the other, the rebirth of numerous viable subcultures. The world culture is built around the values and way of life of the Western consumer society, making the Western cultural model the organizing principle of the fast-emerging global culture. In contrast, subcultures are being revived in part because of minorities' ability to communicate on a regular basis and to link instantly with the origins of their cultures, regardless of distance, time of day, and ideology.

## CHAOS AND ORDER

Socioeconomic activities at all levels of individual and institutional interaction involve all four processes of socio-political change and economic management. Productive activities and stable societies reflect usually a largely harmonious relationship between the interactive roles of the four societal processes. Such a relationship is characterized by a satisfactory level of cooperation that is perceived as mutually beneficial and a tolerable level of competition that provides for mutual accommodation.

Looking globally at an increasingly chaotic situation, it is easy to conclude that the relationships that tie the four processes together are badly strained, antagonistic, or rapidly breaking up. At the same time, and probably for the first time in recent history, no one seems to know with confidence how to restructure the failing relationships and which principles, if any, are to be observed to build news ones and restore balance.

This is largely the result of the many recent global developments that have been shaking the foundations of the states of political and economic affairs everywhere. These developments caused the collapse of communism, exposed the failure of Third World socialism and nationalism, and underlined the shortcomings of Western capitalism, leading to the decline of ideology, the rise of economics, and the revival of narrow ethnonationalism and cultural particularism. In addition, they have also startled intellectuals everywhere, causing them to become largely demoralized and ineffective.

For example, while there is an explosion of empirical knowledge about problems related to social and business behavior in the West, there is no "similar explosion in theory, explanation, predictive power and policy insights," wrote John Burton recently. "We have a mass, a tremendous mass of empirical knowledge, most of which is not very valuable," he added.[14] In Europe, both the Right and the Left were taken by surprise when the Soviet Union collapsed and are today unable to formulate a policy to deal with the challenges that face them. Such challenges include social and economic problems related to a prolonged recession and higher unemployment, to immigration and renewed racism, and to the revival of narrow nationalism and ethnic conflict, in addition to a complex problem related to the declining popular appeal of and faith in traditional politics and political parties.

In the United States in particular, intellectual thinking has become largely totalitarian, dominated by one exclusive group. This group combines a small political elite, a growing and powerful media elite, and an established business elite, all of which are connected in a web of individual, group, and class interests. Social discrimination, the dominant form of discrimination decades ago, has effectively been replaced by economic and intellectual discrimination, vastly limiting the ability of outsiders, particularly members of America's several ethnic minorities, to penetrate the ranks of either the economic or the intellectual elite. Minority intellectuals espousing different viewpoints can hardly publish; if they do publish, their viewpoint is rarely recognized and noted.

In the former communist countries and Third World nations, the discrediting of Marxism, socialism, and Third World nationalism has greatly undermined the power and social status of intellectuals in those nations. Two new groups of claimed intellectuals have taken their place. The first is a liberal group whose goal is to imitate the Western, mainly American political and economic model, while remaining largely unaware of the shortcomings and cultural biases of that model. The latter is a conservative elite whose goal is to build a future that either mirrors an image of a glorious, mostly fictitious past, or an ethnically exclusive one that excludes and discriminates against the other.

Restructuring the failing relationships among the four societal processes at the local, national, and international levels is a formidable task.

It requires the articulation of a new visionary worldview of where things ought to be and practical guidelines for creating strategies that show how to move things from here to there.

At the same time, global developments and local issues are creating a need for more sensitivity by the economic process to local needs and more attention by the political process to international issues. Increased unemployment, poverty, and environmental damage expand the need for the economic process to give more attention to local issues. The spread of ethno-national conflict and a global economic recession call for more involvement of the political process at the international level. Insensitivity to such issues has caused the relationship between the two processes to become less cooperative, more competitive, and generally characterized by tension and hostility.

The socio-cultural process has been moving in two directions at once to accommodate the needs of both the political and economic processes. While the development of a global culture based on the values of Western consumerism accommodates the economic process, the revival of subcultures supports a revitalized local political process. Subcultures are also meant to preserve identity at the local level, assert group rights at the national level, and fill the gap created by the globalization of the economic process at both levels.

The media serve as the main vehicle to facilitate the movement of the other three processes. They expose the failings of the political process to properly attend to local issues, identify new global opportunities and open new areas for the economic process to explore and exploit, and enable the socio-cultural process to develop a global culture at the international level and numerous viable subcultures at the local and national levels.

Chaos and order exist together in one world. They are two sides of one process, for neither can survive long or be of much help by itself. Order without some chaos or uncertainty characterizes systems that lack dynamism, are rigid and unable to adapt to changed conditions, and thus are incapable of surviving in the long run. Uncontrolled chaos characterizes systems that are confused, unproductive, and ruled by the law of the jungle, and thus headed toward disintegration.

Interaction among the four societal processes constantly changes the balance of relationship forces, making them either more orderly and less chaotic, or more chaotic and less orderly. While the current interaction motivated by new global developments has made systemic and state relationships more chaotic, governmental and organizational rules and regulations are making such relationships more orderly. It is always easier to explain emerging situations than to control them and predict their outcomes. Thus, an explanation of the dynamics of the interaction among the four processes does not by itself answer the major questions regarding chaos and order posed at the beginning of this chapter. The questions of why chaos erupts, why uncertainty persists, how to manage disorder, and how to predict the outcome of such situations are important ones that require satisfactory answers.

A general theory of conflict management is useful, but it represents only one component of what is needed to manage chaos, constantly vitalize order, and maintain a healthy balance between the two. Another component that is badly needed is a strategy of international peace to envision new, more promising relationships among states, ethnic and cultural minorities, and business and political elites.

A new theory of social change to explain chaos and order and provide insights into the dynamics of the four societal processes is the third component that is needed to bridge the gap between the reality of politics and the imperatives of economics in this age. Such a theory makes it possible to use the certainty or order to regulate chaos, use the dynamics of chaos to transform order, and employ the propensities of both to resolve conflict. It can also help continually restructure the relationships among the four societal processes, facilitating cooperation without eliminating competition and making progress without accentuating conflict. They are questions that will form the core of our forthcoming book, "Conflict and Change."

## NOTES

1. Richard Rubenstein, "Unanticipated Conflict and the Crisis of Social Theory," in John Burton and Frank Dukes, eds., *Conflict: Readings in Management and Resolution* (New York: St. Martin's Press, 1990), pp. 316–21.

2. Robert Artigiani, "Building a Global Society: Progress and Procedures," in Suheil Bushrui, Iraj Ayman, and Ervin Laszlo, eds., *Transition to Global Society* (Oxford, England: Oneworld Publications, 1993), p. 30.

3. Ibid., p. 31.

4. Miriam Campanella, "Global Society, Global Problems and New Formats of Global Decision-Making," in Suheil Bushrui, Iraj Ayman, and Ervin Laszlo, eds., *Transition to Global Society* (Oxford, England: Oneworld Publications, 1993), p. 54.

5. E. J. Dionne Jr., "In the Post-Everything Age, Where Are We?" *The Washington Post*, Jan. 10, 1993.

6. Volodymyr Vassilenko, "Peaceful Disintegration of the Soviet Totalitarian Empire as a Necessary Precondition for the Transition to Global Society," in Suheil Bushrui, Iraj Ayman, and Ervin Laszlo, eds., *Transition to Global Society* (Oxford, England: Oneworld Publications, 1993), pp. 71–72.

7. Basheer Meibar, *Political Culture, Foreign Policy and Conflict* (Westport, Conn.: Greenwood Press, 1982), p. 144.

8. Ibid., p. 143.

9. Robert Artigiani, "Building a Global Society," pp. 30–31.

10. Roger I. Conner, "Total Quality Debate, *The New Republic*, Aug. 23, 1993, p. 4.

11. Quincy Wright, "The Nature of Conflict," in John Burton and Frank Dukes, eds., *Conflict: Readings in Management and Resolution* (New York: St. Martin's Press, 1990), p. 10.

12. El-Hassan Bin Talal, "Perception of a Monolithic Creed," *The Washington Post*, Aug. 4, 1993.

13. Ibid.

14. John Burton, "Introduction to Conflict Resolution and Problem Solving," in Dennis J. D. Sandole and Ingrid Sandole-Staroste, eds., *Conflict Management and Problem Solving: Interpersonal to International* (New York: University of New York Press, 1987), pp. 252–53.

# SELECTED BIBLIOGRAPHY

Axelrod, Robert M. *The Evolution of Cooperation*. New York: Basic Books, 1984.

Bok, Sisela. *A Strategy for Peace: Human Values and the Threat of War*. New York: Vintage Books, 1990.

Bondurant, Joan V. *Conquest of Violence: The Gandhian Philosophy of Conflict*. Princeton, N.J.: Princeton University Press, 1988.

Boulding, Kenneth Ewart. *Conflict and Defense: A General Theory*. Lanham, Md.: University Press of America, 1988.

Boutros-Ghali, Boutros. *An Agenda for Peace: Preventive Diplomacy, Peacemaking and Peace-keeping: Report of the Secretary-General Pursuant to the Statement Adopted by the Summit Meeting of the Security Council on 31 January 1992*. New York: United Nations, 1992.

Brocke-Utne, Birgit. *Feminist Perspectives on Peace and Peace Education*. New York: Pergamon Press, 1989.

Burton, John W. *Conflict: Resolution and Prevention*. New York: St. Martin's Press, 1990.

Carter, Jimmy. *Negotiation: The Alternative to Hostility*. Macon, Ga.: Mercer University Press, 1984.

Cassese, Antonio. *Human Rights in a Changing World*. Cambridge, England: Polity, 1990.

Choucri, Nazli and Robert C. North. *Nations in Conflict: National Growth and International Violence*. San Francisco: W. H. Freeman & Co., 1975.

Cohen, Raymond. *Negotiating Across Cultures: Communication Obstacles in International Diplomacy*. Washington, D.C.: United States Institute of Peace, 1991.

Deutsch, Morton. *The Resolution of Conflict: Constructive and Destructive Processes*. New Haven, Conn.: Yale University Press, 1973.

Fisher, Roger. *Getting to Yes: Negotiating Agreement Without Giving In*. Boston: Houghton Mifflin, 1981.

Forsythe, David P. *The Internationalization of Human Rights*. Lexington, Mass.: Lexington Books, 1991.

Friesen, Duane K. *Christian Peacemaking and International Conflict*. Scottsdale, Pa.: Herald Press, 1986.

Fukuyama, Francis. *The End of History and the Last Man*. New York: Free Press, 1992.

Galtung, Johan. *The True World: A Transnational Perspective*. New York: Free Press, 1980.

———. *Solving Conflicts: A Peace Research Perspective*. Honolulu: University of Hawaii Press, 1989.

George, Alexander L. *Forceful Persuasion: Coercive Diplomacy as an Alternative to War*. Washington, D.C.: United States Institute of Peace Press, 1991.

Goertz, Gary. *Territorial Changes and International Conflict*. London: Routledge, 1992.

Halperin, Morton H. *Self-Determination in the New World Order*. Washington, D.C.: Carnegie Endowment for International Peace, 1992.

Hannum, Hurst. *Autonomy, Sovereignty, and Self-Determination: The Accommodation of Conflicting Rights*. Philadelphia: University of Pennsylvania Press, 1990.

Horowitz, Donald L. *Ethnic Groups in Conflict*. Berkeley: University of California Press, 1985.

Ikle, Fred Charles. *How Nations Negotiate*. Millwood, N.Y.: Kraus Reprint, 1985.

Johnson, James Turner. *The Quest for Peace: Three Moral Traditions in Western Cultural History*. Princeton, N.J.: Princeton University Press, 1987.

Kelsay, John. *Islam and War: A Study in Comparative Ethics*. Louisville, Ky.: Westminister/John Knox Press, 1993.

Keohane, Robert O. and Joseph S. Nye. *Power and Interdependence: World Politics in Transition*. Boston: Little, Brown and Co., 1977.

Kremenyuk, Victor, ed. *International Negotiation: Analysis, Approaches, Issues*. San Francisco: Jossey-Bass Publishers, 1991.

Kriesberg, Louis, Terrell A. Northrup and Stuart J. Thorson, ed. *Intractable Conflicts and Their Transformation*. Syracuse, N.Y.: Syracuse University Press, 1989.

Lall, Arthur S., ed., *Multilateral Negotiation and Mediation: Instruments and Methods*. New York: Pergamon, 1985.

Lasswell, Harold. *Power and Personality*. New York: Harper and Row, 1978.

Lebow, Richard Ned. *Between Peace and War: The Nature of International Crisis*. Baltimore: Johns Hopkins University Press, 1981.

Luard, Evan. *Conflict and Peace in the Modern International System: A Study of the Principles of International Order*. Albany, N.Y.: State University of New York Press, 1988.

Mitchell, Christopher R. *The Structure of International Conflict*. London: Macmillan, 1981.

Montville, Joseph, ed. *Conflict and Peacemaking in Multiethnic Societies*. Lexington, Mass.: Lexington Books, 1990.

Moore, Christopher. *The Mediation Process: Practical Strategies for Resolving Conflict*. San Francisco: Jossey-Bass, 1986.

Newsom, David. *Diplomacy and the American Democracy*. Bloomington, Ind.: Indiana University Press, 1988.

Nicolson, Harold George. *Diplomacy*. Washington, D.C.: Institute for the Study of Diplomacy, Georgetown University, 1988.

Nye, Joseph and Robert Keohane, eds., *Transnational Relations and World Politics*. Cambridge, Mass.: Harvard University Press, 1972.

Patche, Martin. *Resolving Disputes Between Nations: Coercion or Conciliation?* Durham, N.C.: Duke University Press, 1988.

Quandt, William B. *Camp David: Peacemaking and Politics*. Washington, D.C.: Brookings Insitution, 1986.

Raiffa, Howard. *The Art and Science of Negotiation*. Cambridge, Mass.: Harvard University Press, 1982.

Rapoport, Anatol. *Peace: An Idea Whose Time Has Come*. Ann Arbor, Mich.: University of Michigan Press, 1992.

Said, Abdul Aziz. *Human Rights and World Order*. New Brunswick, N.J.: Transaction Books, 1978.

Saunders, Harold. *Other Walls: The Politics of the Arab-Israeli Peace Process*. Washington, D.C.: American Enterprise Institute, 1985.

Sharp, Gene. *The Politics of Nonviolent Action*. Boston: Sargent Publisher, 1973.

Smoke, Richard. *Paths to Peace: Exploring the Feasibility of Sustainable Peace*. Boulder, Col.: Westview Press, 1987.

Thompson, W. Scott, and Kenneth M. Jensen, eds. *Approaches to Peace: An Intellectual Map*. Washington, D.C.: United States Institute of Peace, 1991.

Touval, Saadia, and I. William Zartman, eds., *International Mediation in Theory and Practice*. Boulder, Col.: Westview Press, 1985.

Walzer, Michael. *Just and Unjust Wars: A Moral Argument with Historical Illustrations*. New York: Basic Books, 1992.

Wright, Quincy. *A Study of War*. Chicago: University of Chicago Press, 1983.

Zartman, I. William, ed. *The 50% Solution: How to Bargain Successfully with Hijackers, Strikers, Bosses, Oil Magnates, Arabs, Russians, and Other Worthy Opponents in This Modern World*. New Haven, Conn.: Yale University Press, 1976.

Zartman, I. William and Maureen R. Berman. *The Practical Negotiator*. New Haven, Conn.: Yale University Press, 1982.

# INDEX

Abbas, Mahmoud, 100
Agreements and mediation, 140
Aland Island, 160
Albania, 160
Algeria, 28
American-Israeli Public Affairs Committee (AIPAC), 141
Americans, 33
Appeasement, 27–28
Arab-Israeli conflict, 53, 56, 63, 69, 92–93, 118, 122–25, 132. *See also* Middle East; Palestinian-Israeli conflict
Arabs, 10
Armenia, 161
Artigiani, Robert, 198
Associations, forming, 1–2
Atherton, Alfred Leroy, 92
Azar, Edward, 21, 27, 48, 75, 80, 180

Bandow, Doug, 47
Banks, Michael, 11, 18
Behar, Pierre, 171
Bilder, Richard, 120, 123
Bildt, Carl, 79
Bosnia, 31, 72, 79
Boulding, Kenneth, 18, 32
Burton, John, 3, 60, 95, 116, 180, 216

Campanella, Miriam, 199
Carter, Jimmy, 141
Change and conflict, 197–223, 205–9
Chaos and order, 215–18
Chaos theory, 200
China, 161; shared homeland model, 187–88
Choucri, Nazli, 57
Civilized societies, 7
Clinton, Bill, 142
Cohen, Raymond, 35, 114, 155
Cold War, 45, 46, 56; end of, 29, 47; ethnicity in, 162–65; and Middle East, 141; peace process in, 78
Collective security, shared homeland model, 178–79
Colonialism, U.S., 45; and ethnicity, 162–65
Competitive interaction, 1–2, 50–51
Comprehensive approach, conflict resolution, 71
Conference on Security and Cooperation in Europe (CSCE), 31, 52, 181
Confidence-building measures, political dialogue, 97–100
Conflict: causes of, 21–44; and change, 197–223; definition of, 4–5; and ethnicity, 155–72; international, 15–18;

and peace, 1–19; relevance of rationality, 39–42; and role of culture, 32–39; and state structure, 25–32

Conflict management, 45–65; and conflict resolution, 57–60; and control and containment, 55–57; and crisis avoidance, 51–53; and crisis management, 53–55; managing ethnic conflict, 60–63; strategies of, 50–60

Conflict resolution: comprehensive approach to, 71; and conflict management, 57–60; constructive process of, 68; control approach to, 71, 72; democratic approach to, 72, 76; destructive process of, 68; distributive approach to, 74; integrative approach to, 71–72, 75; shared homeland approach to, 72, 76, 182–86; step-by-step approach to, 71, 74; techniques for, 7; and United States, 70

Conner, Roger, 208

Consociational model, ethnic conflict management, 61

Constructive process, conflict resolution, 68

Containment, conflict management, 55–57

Control approach: and conflict management, 55–57; and conflict resolution, 71, 72; and ethnic conflict management, 61–62

Cooperative interaction, 1–2, 50–51

Cordescu, Andrei, 166

Crisis avoidance, conflict management, 51–53

Crisis management, conflict management, 53–55

Croatia, 30–31

Cuban Missile Crisis, 53

Culture, role of, 32–39

Cyprus, shared homeland model, 188–89

Czech Republic, shared homeland model, 191–92

Czechoslovakia, 161, 170

de Reuck, Anthony, 88

De-escalation, 86

Democracy, 27–28

Democratic approach, conflict resolution, 72, 76

Destructive process, conflict resolution, 68

Deutsch, Morton, 21, 50, 68, 133

Dialogue groups and meetings, 42, 95–97, 148

Dionne, E. J., Jr., 199

Diplomats, 34

Distributive approach, conflict resolution, 74

Djerejian, Edward, 93

Domination, 74

Economic process of change, 210–12

Economic sanctions, negotiation, 126–27

El-Hassan Bin Talal, 214–15

Estonia, 169

Ethnic conflict management, 60–63; consociational model of, 61; control model of, 61–62; shared homeland model of, 63

Ethnic loyalty, 156

Ethnicity: and Cold War, 162–65; and colonialism, 162–65; and conflict, 155–72; Marxism role in, 165–71

Etzioni, Amitai, 181

Eygpt, 115

Finland, 160

Foundation for Global Community, 88

France, 205

Fukuyama, Francis, 156

Fuller, Graham, 162

Galtung, Johan, 2, 13

Georgia, Russian republic, 169

Germany, 30, 73; intolerance to non-Germans, 9; nationalism in, 32

Glotz, Peter, 185

Goble, Paul, 143

Golan Heights, Syria, 98

Gorbachev, M., 122

Greece, 160, 188–89

Groom, A.J.R., 24–25, 45, 51

Groups, 1–2
Guarantees, mediation and negotiation model, 153
Gurr, Ted, 157, 159
Gypsies, 9

Harvard University Institute for Social and Economic Policy in Middle East, 104, 105–6
Helsinki Watch Group, 168, 169
Henze, Paul B., 166
Hilf, Rudolf, 103
Hoagland, Jim, 80
Hoffman, David, 93, 118
Hoffman, Stanley, 173
Hungary, 181

Idealists, 17
Idealpolitik, 119
Ideologies, 203–4
Implementation phase, peace process, 77
Individual mediators, 131
Indyk, Martin, 142
Institute for Social and Economic Policy in Middle East, Harvard, 104, 105–6
Institute of Global Conflict and Cooperation, 104
Integrative approach, conflict resolution, 71–72, 75
Integrative model of mediation and negotiation, 144–53
Interest-related conflicts, 8, 22, 24
International conflicts, 15–18, 23; and mediation, 139
International Institute for Nationality Rights and Regionalism, 159
Iran, 207; Kurds in, 192–94
Iran-Iraq War, 59
Iraq, 59, 115, 159; Kurds in, 192–94
Islam, 35
Israel, 61
Israeli-Egyptian dispute, 24
Israeli-Palestinian conflict, 37, 88, 96, 145–51; political dialogue in, 100–107
Issue priority, negotiation, 124–25

Janjic, Dusan, 190
Japan, 73
Jews in U.S., 9–10
Job, Cvijete, 167

Kashmiris, 161
Kelman, Herbert, 100, 102
Kennedy, John F., 13
Kissinger, Henry, 69, 85, 116
Kozyrev, Andrei V., 169
Krauthammer, Charles, 48
Kriesberg, Louis, 15, 24, 25, 31, 85, 138
Kurds, 164; in shared homeland model, 192–94
Kuwait, 170

Laue, James, 6, 14, 139
Lijphart, Arend, 61
Luck, Edward, 32
Lustick, Ian, 61

Malik, Iftikar, 170
Managed negotiation, 115, 118–19
Manipulation of news, 214
Marxism, 202
Marxism role, in ethnicity, 165–71
Mazin, Abu, 100
McNamara, Robert S., 97
Media, societal process of change, 213–15
Mediation, 131–54; and agreements, 140; integrative model of, 144–53; and international conflicts, 139; and peace process, 78; role of, 134–40; of U.S. in Middle East, 141–43; and value-related conflicts, 134–35
Mediation and negotiation model: guarantees in, 153; process of, 152; strategy of, 152; team of communicators in, 152
Mediators, 131
Meibar, Basheer, 33, 50
Mexico, 28
Miall, Hugh, 8, 10, 139
Middle East, 51; and Cold War, 141; and mediation, 141–43; and peace process, 70

Milic, Goran, 36
Montville, Joseph, 95
Morris, Roger, 80
Muslims, 10

Nagorno-Karabach, 181
Nambia, 115
National conflict, 23
National security, shared homeland
    model, 179
Nationalism, 29–30; and Germany, 32
NATO, 79
Negative peace, 14, 54
Negotiation, 111–30; approaches to,
    113–15; definition of, 115–21; eco-
    nomic sanctions in, 126–27; issue
    priority of, 124–25; managed, 115,
    118–19; open, 115, 118–19; party
    preference in, 124; peace process
    phases of, 77; power of, 120; proce-
    dure of, 121–29; strategy for, 121–
    29; third-party intervention in, 125–
    29; timing of, 122–23
Netherlands, 61
Newson, David, 38, 78, 95, 100, 137,
    164
Nicholson, Michael, 40
Nigeria civil war, 73
Northern Epirus, 160
Nye, Joseph, 175, 182

Objectives, political dialogue, 89–95
Oman, 118
Open negotiation, 115, 118–19
Order and chaos, 215–18

Palestinian-Israeli conflict, 37, 145–51
Party preference, negotiation, 124
Passive peace, 14
Peace: and conflict, 1–19
Peace camps, 13
Peace process, 67–83; Cold War, 78;
    implementation phase of, 77; initia-
    tion phase of, 77; mediation phase
    of, 78; negotiation phase of, 77
Peretz, Martin, 142, 143
Pickus, Robert, 32
Pisar, Samuel, 167

Political dialogue, 85–109; confidence-
    building measures, 97–100; dia-
    logue groups, 95–97; functions of,
    90–95; Israeli-Palestinian dialogue,
    100–107; objectives, 89–95; peace
    process phases, 77; and pre-
    negotiation, 87–90; third-party inter-
    vention, 90–91; timing of peace
    process, 94; track-two diplomacy,
    95–97
Political process of change, 209–10
Pork, Andrus, 187
Positive peace, 14
Power, negotiation, 120
Pranger, Robert, 163
Pre-negotiation, 85–86; and political
    dialogue, 87–90
Procedures, 41
Process, mediation and negotiation
    model, 152

Quandt, William, 141, 145–50

Rabie, Mohamed, 63, 145–50
Rabin, Yitzhak, 93
Rationality relevance of, 39–42
Realists, 17
Realpolitik, 119
Regimes, 26
Rosenfeld, Stephen S., 72
Ross, Dennis, 142
Rothman, Jay, 87
Rubenstein, Richard, 17, 60, 136, 156,
    197
Rules, 41
Rummel, R. J., 28, 49
Russia, 198, 202

Sadat, Anwar, 116, 141
Sandole, Dennis, 54, 119
Saunders, Harold, 58, 69, 87, 88, 99,
    101–2
Schlesinger, Arthur, 29
Schneider, Bertrand, 174
Schwartz, Richard D., 97, 103
Scimecca, Joseph A., 91
Search for Common Ground (SCG),
    38–39, 104

Self-determination, 30
Serbia, 31
Shared homeland approach, 72, 76;
   applying, 186–87; China, 187–88;
   collective security in, 178–79; and
   conflict resolution, 182–86; creating,
   177–82; Cyprus, 188–89; Czech Republic, 191–92; ethnic conflict man-
   agement, 63; Kurds, 192–94; model,
   173–95; national security, 179;
   Yugoslavia, 189–91
Sherman, Edward, 7
Societal processes of change, 209–15;
   economic, 210–12; media, 213–15;
   political, 209–10; socio-cultural,
   212–13
Societies, 7
Socio-cultural process of change, 212–
   13
Socio-economic groups, 2
Somalia, 79, 143
South Tyrol, 160
Soviet Union, 46; ethnicity problems
   in, 166
Stanford Center on Conflict and Ne-
   gotiation, 88
State structure and conflict, 25–32
Step-by-step approach, conflict resolu-
   tion, 71, 74
Stoneman, Mark, 9
Strategy: mediation and negotiation
   model, 152; for peace, 121
Structural violence, 2–3
Suppression, 27–28
Susser, Asher, 119
Sweden, 160

Team of communicators, mediation
   and negotiation model, 152
Thatcher, Margaret, 79

Third party intervention: and negotia-
   tion, 125–29; and political dialogue,
   90–91
Third World, 47, 164, 199, 204
Thompson, W. Scott, 50, 123
Thorson, Stuart J., 51
Tibet, 187–88
Timing: and negotiation, 122–23; of
   peace process, 94
Track-two diplomacy, political dia-
   logue, 95–97
Turkey, 188–89; Kurds in, 192–94

U.N. Security Resolutions, 114, 141
Uninvited third party intervention,
   132
United Nations, 52
United States, 46, 123–24; and conflict
   resolution, 70; Israeli-Palestinian
   conflict, 145–51; in Middle East,
   141–43
USSR, 69

Value-related conflicts, 8, 22, 23–24;
   and mediation, 134–35
Vassilenko, Volodymyr, 177, 203
Vatra Romaneaca Association, 168

Washington Institute for Near East
   Policy, 142
Weeks, Dudley, 22, 136
Wright, Quincy, 4, 5, 23

Yalta, 162
Yemen, 118
Yugoslavia, 8, 30, 52, 168–69; shared
   homeland model of, 189–91

Zarycky, George, 8

**About the Author**

MOHAMED RABIE is an author and a former Professor of Economics. He has taught at several Arab and American universities, including Kuwait University and Georgetown University. He has published twelve books in English and Arabic and over forty papers, and he has participated in over sixty worldwide seminars and conferences dealing with economic, political, and security issues as well as the Arab-Israeli conflict. Dr. Rabie has also been a frequent participant in political dialogue groups and conflict resolution workshops.

ISBN 0-275-94598-7

HARDCOVER BAR CODE